# Critical Thinking

D1314126

Hurley

CENGAGE
Learning™

Australia • Brazil • Japan • Korea • Mexico • Singapore • Spain • United Kingdom • United States

# CENGAGE
## Learning™

**Critical Thinking**

Hurley

Executive Editors:
Michele Baird

Maureen Staudt

Michael Stranz

Project Development Manager:
Linda deStefano

Senior Marketing Coordinators:
Sara Mercurio

Lindsay Shapiro

Production/Manufacturing Manager:
Donna M. Brown

PreMedia Services Supervisor:
Rebecca A. Walker

Rights & Permissions Specialist:
Kalina Hintz

Cover Image:
Getty Images*

* Unless otherwise noted, all cover images used by Custom Solutions, a part of Cengage Learning, have been supplied courtesy of Getty Images with the exception of the Earthview cover image, which has been supplied by the National Aeronautics and Space Administration (NASA).

For product information and technology assistance, contact us at
**Cengage Learning Customer & Sales Support, 1-800-354-9706**

For permission to use material from this text or product, submit all requests online at **cengage.com/permissions**
Further permissions questions can be emailed to
**permissionrequest@cengage.com**

ISBN-13:  978-0-495-49347-1

ISBN-10:  0-495-49347-3

**Cengage Learning**
5191 Natorp Boulevard
Mason, Ohio 45040
USA

Cengage Learning is a leading provider of customized learning solutions with office locations around the globe, including Singapore, the United Kingdom, Australia, Mexico, Brazil, and Japan. Locate your local office at:
**international.cengage.com/region**

Cengage Learning products are represented in Canada by Nelson Education, Ltd.

For your lifelong learning solutions, visit **custom.cengage.com**

Visit our corporate website at **cengage.com**

Printed in the United States of America
1 2 3 4 5 6 7 12 11 10 09 08

# Acknowledgements

---

The content of this text has been adapted from the following product(s):

A Concise Introduction to Logic (with ThomsonNOW™ Printed Access Card)
Hurley ISBN-10: (0-495-50383-5)
ISBN-13: (978-0-495-50383-5)

# Table Of Contents

# 1

# Basic Concepts

## 1.1 Arguments, Premises, and Conclusions

**Logic** may be defined as the organized body of knowledge, or science, that evaluates arguments. All of us encounter arguments in our day-to-day experience. We read them in books and newspapers, hear them on television, and formulate them when communicating with friends and associates. The aim of logic is to develop a system of methods and principles that we may use as criteria for evaluating the arguments of others and as guides in constructing arguments of our own. Among the benefits to be expected from the study of logic is an increase in confidence that we are making sense when we criticize the arguments of others and when we advance arguments of our own.

An **argument,** in its most basic form, is a group of statements, one or more of which (the premises) are claimed to provide support for, or reasons to believe, one of the others (the conclusion). All arguments may be placed in one of two basic groups: those in which the premises really do support the conclusion and those in which they do not, even though they are claimed to. The former are said to be good arguments (at least to that extent), the latter bad arguments. The purpose of logic, as the science that evaluates arguments, is thus to develop methods and techniques that allow us to distinguish good arguments from bad.

As is apparent from the given definition, the term *argument* has a very specific meaning in logic. It does not mean, for example, a mere verbal fight, as one might have with one's parent, spouse, or friend. Let us examine the features of this definition in greater detail. First of all, an argument is a group of statements. A **statement** is a sentence that is either true or false—in other words, typically a declarative sentence or a sentence component that could stand as a declarative sentence. The following sentences are statements:

> Chocolate truffles are loaded with calories.
> Melatonin helps relieve jet lag.
> Political candidates always tell the complete truth.
> No wives ever cheat on their husbands.
> Tiger Woods plays golf and Maria Sharapova plays tennis.

The first two statements are true, the second two false. The last one expresses two statements, both of which are true. Truth and falsity are called the two possible **truth values** of a statement. Thus, the truth value of the first two statements is true, the truth value of the second two is false, and the truth value of the last statement, as well as that of its components, is true.

Unlike statements, many sentences cannot be said to be either true or false. Questions, proposals, suggestions, commands, and exclamations usually cannot, and so are not usually classified as statements. The following sentences are not statements:

| | |
|---|---|
| Where is Khartoum? | (question) |
| Let's go to a movie tonight. | (proposal) |
| I suggest you get contact lenses. | (suggestion) |
| Turn off the TV right now. | (command) |
| Fantastic! | (exclamation) |

The statements that make up an argument are divided into one or more premises and one and only one conclusion. The **premises** are the statements that set forth the reasons or evidence, and the **conclusion** is the statement that the evidence is claimed to support or imply. In other words, the conclusion is the statement that is claimed to follow from the premises. Here is an example of an argument:

All film stars are celebrities.
Halle Berry is a film star.
Therefore, Halle Berry is a celebrity.

The first two statements are the premises; the third is the conclusion. (The claim that the premises support or imply the conclusion is indicated by the word "therefore.") In this argument the premises really do support the conclusion, and so the argument is a good one. But consider this argument:

Some film stars are men.
Cameron Diaz is a film star.
Therefore, Cameron Diaz is a man.

In this argument the premises do not support the conclusion, even though they are claimed to, and so the argument is not a good one.

One of the most important tasks in the analysis of arguments is being able to distinguish premises from conclusions. If what is thought to be a conclusion is really a premise, and vice versa, the subsequent analysis cannot possibly be correct. Many arguments contain indicator words that provide clues in identifying premises and conclusion. Some typical **conclusion indicators** are

| | | |
|---|---|---|
| therefore | accordingly | entails that |
| wherefore | we may conclude | hence |
| thus | it must be that | it follows that |
| consequently | for this reason | implies that |
| we may infer | so | as a result |

Whenever a statement follows one of these indicators, it can usually be identified as the conclusion. By process of elimination the other statements in the argument are the premises. Example:

Tortured prisoners will say anything just to relieve the pain. Consequently, torture is not a reliable method of interrogation.

The conclusion of this argument is "Torture is not a reliable method of interrogation," and the premise is "Tortured prisoners will say anything just to relieve the pain."

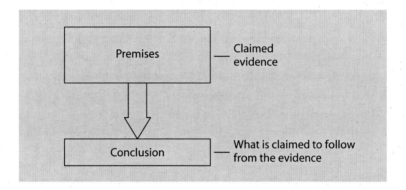

If an argument does not contain a conclusion indicator, it may contain a premise indicator. Some typical **premise indicators** are

| since | in that | seeing that |
|---|---|---|
| as indicated by | may be inferred from | for the reason that |
| because | as | inasmuch as |
| for | given that | owing to |

Any statement following one of these indicators can usually be identified as a premise. Example:

Expectant mothers should never use recreational drugs, since the use of these drugs can jeopardize the development of the fetus.

The premise of this argument is "The use of these drugs can jeopardize the development of the fetus," and the conclusion is "Expectant mothers should never use recreational drugs."

In reviewing the list of indicators, note that "for this reason" is a conclusion indicator, whereas "for the reason that" is a premise indicator. "For this reason" (except when followed by a colon) means for the reason (premise) that was just given, so what follows is the conclusion. On the other hand, "for the reason that" announces that a premise is about to be stated.

Sometimes a single indicator can be used to identify more than one premise. Consider the following argument:

It is vitally important that wilderness areas be preserved, for wilderness provides essential habitat for wildlife, including endangered species, and it is a natural retreat from the stress of daily life.

The premise indicator "for" goes with both "Wilderness provides essential habitat for wildlife, including endangered species," and "It is a natural retreat from the stress of daily life." These are the premises. By method of elimination, "It is vitally important that wilderness areas be preserved" is the conclusion.

Some arguments contain no indicators. With these, the reader/listener must ask such questions as: What single statement is claimed (implicitly) to follow from the others? What is the arguer trying to prove? What is the main point in the passage? The answers to these questions should point to the conclusion. Example:

> The space program deserves increased expenditures in the years ahead. Not only does the national defense depend on it, but the program will more than pay for itself in terms of technological spinoffs. Furthermore, at current funding levels the program cannot fulfill its anticipated potential.

The conclusion of this argument is the first statement, and all of the other statements are premises. The argument illustrates the pattern found in most arguments that lack indicator words: the intended conclusion is stated first, and the remaining statements are then offered in support of this first statement. When the argument is restructured according to logical principles, however, the conclusion is always listed *after* the premises:

> $P_1$: The national defense is dependent on the space program.
> $P_2$: The space program will more than pay for itself in terms of technological spinoffs.
> $P_3$: At current funding levels the space program cannot fulfill its anticipated potential.
> C: The space program deserves increased expenditures in the years ahead.

When restructuring arguments such as this, one should remain as close as possible to the original version, while at the same time attending to the requirement that premises and conclusion be complete sentences that are meaningful in the order in which they are listed.

Note that the first two premises are included within the scope of a single sentence in the original argument. For the purposes of this chapter, compound arrangements of statements in which the various components are all claimed to be true will be considered as separate statements.

Passages that contain arguments sometimes contain statements that are neither premises nor conclusions. Only statements that are actually intended to support the conclusion should be included in the list of premises. If, for example, a statement serves merely to introduce the general topic, or merely makes a passing comment, it should not be taken as part of the argument. Examples:

> The claim is often made that malpractice lawsuits drive up the cost of health care. But if such suits were outlawed or severely restricted, then patients would have no means of recovery for injuries caused by negligent doctors. Hence, the availability of malpractice litigation should be maintained intact.

> Currently 47 million Americans are without health insurance. When these people go to a hospital, they are routinely charged two to three times the normal cost for treatment. This practice, which covers the cost of treating indigent patients, is clearly unfair. For these reasons, a national health insurance program should be adopted. Politicians who oppose this change should be ashamed of themselves.

In the first argument, the opening statement serves merely to introduce the topic, so it is not part of the argument. The premise is the second statement, and the conclusion is the last statement. In the second argument, the final statement merely makes a passing comment, so it is not part of the argument. The premises are the first three statements, and the statement following "for these reasons" is the conclusion.

Closely related to the concepts of argument and statement are those of inference and proposition. An **inference,** in the narrow sense of the term, is the reasoning process expressed by an argument. In the broad sense of the term, "inference" is used interchangeably with "argument." Analogously, a **proposition,** in the narrow sense, is the meaning or information content of a statement. For the purposes of this book, however, "proposition" and "statement" are used interchangeably.

## Note on the History of Logic

The person who is generally credited as the father of logic is the ancient Greek philosopher Aristotle (384–322 B.C.). Aristotle's predecessors had been interested in the art of constructing persuasive arguments and in techniques for refuting the arguments of others, but it was Aristotle who first devised systematic criteria for analyzing and evaluating arguments.

Aristotle's chief accomplishment is called **syllogistic logic,** a kind of logic in which the fundamental elements are *terms,* and arguments are evaluated as good or bad depending on how the terms are arranged in the argument. Chapters 4 and 5 of this textbook are devoted mainly to syllogistic logic. But Aristotle also deserves credit for originating **modal logic,** a kind of logic that involves such concepts as possibility, necessity, belief, and doubt. In addition, Aristotle catalogued several informal fallacies, a topic treated in Chapter 3 of this book.

After Aristotle's death, another Greek philosopher, Chrysippus (280–206 B.C.), one of the founders of the Stoic school, developed a logic in which the fundamental elements were *whole propositions.* Chrysippus treated every proposition as either true or false and developed rules for determining the truth or falsity of compound propositions from the truth or falsity of their components. In the course of doing so, he laid the foundation for the truth functional interpretation of the logical connectives presented in Chapter 6 of this book and introduced the notion of natural deduction, treated in Chapter 7.

For thirteen hundred years after the death of Chrysippus, relatively little creative work was done in logic. The physician Galen (A.D. 129–ca. 199) developed the theory of the compound categorical syllogism, but for the most part philosophers confined themselves to writing commentaries on the works of Aristotle and Chrysippus. Boethius (ca. 480–524) is a noteworthy example.

The first major logician of the Middle Ages was Peter Abelard (1079–1142). Abelard reconstructed and refined the logic of Aristotle and Chrysippus as communicated by Boethius, and he originated a theory of universals that traced the universal character of general terms to concepts in the mind rather than to "natures" existing outside the mind, as Aristotle had held. In addition, Abelard distinguished arguments that are valid because of their form from those that are valid because of their content, but he

## ■ EMINENT LOGICIANS

### *Aristotle* 384–322 B.C.

© Mansell/Time Life Pictures/Getty Images

Aristotle was born in Stagira, a small Greek town situated on the northern coast of the Aegean sea. His father was a physician in the court of King Amyntas II of Macedonia, and the young Aristotle was a friend of the King's son Philip, who was later to become king himself and the father of Alexander the Great. When he was about seventeen, Aristotle was sent to Athens to further his education in Plato's Academy, the finest institution of higher learning in the Greek world. After Plato's death Aristotle left for Assos, a small town on the coast of Asia Minor, where he married the niece of the local ruler.

Six years later Aristotle accepted an invitation to return to Macedonia to serve as tutor of the young Alexander. When Alexander ascended the throne following his father's assassination, Aristotle's tutorial job was finished, and he departed for Athens where he set up a school near the temple of Apollo Lyceus. The school came to be known as the Lyceum, and Alexander supported it with contributions of money and specimens of flora and fauna derived from his far-flung conquests. After Alexander's death, an anti-Macedonian rebellion forced Aristotle to leave Athens for Chalcis, about thirty miles to the north, where he died one year later at the age of sixty-two.

Aristotle is universally recognized as the originator of logic. He defined *logic* as the study of the process by which a statement follows by necessity from one or more other statements. The most fundamental kind of statement, he thought, is the categorical proposition, and he classified the four kinds of categorical propositions in terms of their being universal, particular, affirmative, and negative. He also developed the square of opposition, which shows how one such proposition implies the truth or falsity of another, and he identified the relations of conversion, obversion, and contraposition, which provide the basis for various immediate inferences.

His crowning achievement is the theory of the categorical syllogism, a kind of argument consisting of three categorical propositions. He showed how categorical syllogisms can be catalogued in terms of mood and figure, and he developed a set of rules for determining the validity of categorical syllogisms. Also, he showed how the modal concepts of possibility and necessity apply to categorical propositions. In addition to the theory of the syllogism, Aristotle advanced the theory of definition by genus and difference, and he showed how arguments could be defective in terms of thirteen forms of informal fallacy.

Aristotle made profound contributions to many areas of human learning including biology, physics, metaphysics, epistemology, psychology, aesthetics, ethics, and politics. However, his accomplishments in logic were so extensive and enduring that two thousand years after his death, the great philosopher Immanuel Kant said that Aristotle had discovered everything that could be known about logic. His logic was not superseded until the end of the nineteenth century when Frege, Whitehead, and Russell developed modern mathematical logic.

held that only formal validity is the "perfect" or conclusive variety. The present text follows Abelard on this point.

After Abelard, the study of logic during the Middle Ages flourished through the work of numerous philosophers. A logical treatise by William of Sherwood (ca. 1200–1271) contains the first expression of the "Barbara, Celarent . . ." poem quoted in Section 5.1 of this book, and the *Summulae Logicales* of Peter of Spain (ca. 1205–1277) became the standard textbook in logic for three hundred years. However, the most original contributions from this period were made by William of Ockham (ca. 1285–1347). Ockham extended the theory of modal logic, conducted an exhaustive study of the forms of valid and invalid syllogisms, and further developed the idea of a metalanguage, a higher-level language used to discuss linguistic entities such as words, terms, and propositions.

Toward the middle of the fifteenth century, a reaction set in against the logic of the Middle Ages. Rhetoric largely displaced logic as the primary focus of attention; the logic of Chrysippus, which had already begun to lose its unique identity in the Middle Ages, was ignored altogether, and the logic of Aristotle was studied only in highly simplistic presentations. A reawakening did not occur until two hundred years later through the work of Gottfried Wilhelm Leibniz (1646–1716).

Leibniz, a genius in numerous fields, attempted to develop a symbolic language or "calculus" that could be used to settle all forms of disputes, whether in theology, philosophy, or international relations. As a result of this work, Leibniz is sometimes credited with being the father of symbolic logic. Leibniz's efforts to symbolize logic were carried into the nineteenth century by Bernard Bolzano (1781–1848).

In the middle of the nineteenth century, logic commenced an extremely rapid period of development that has continued to this day. Work in symbolic logic was done by many philosophers and mathematicians, including Augustus De Morgan (1806–1871), George Boole (1815–1864), William Stanley Jevons (1835–1882), and John Venn (1834–1923). The rule bearing De Morgan's name is used in Chapter 7 of this book. Boole's interpretation of categorical propositions and Venn's method for diagramming them are covered in Chapters 4 and 5. At the same time a revival in inductive logic was initiated by the British philosopher John Stuart Mill (1806–1873), whose methods of induction are presented in Chapter 10.

Across the Atlantic, the American philosopher Charles Sanders Peirce (1839–1914) developed a logic of relations, invented symbolic quantifiers, and suggested the truth-table method for formulas in propositional logic. These topics are covered in Chapters 6 and 8 of this book. The truth-table method was completed independently by Emile Post (1897–1954) and Ludwig Wittgenstein (1889–1951).

Toward the end of the nineteenth century, the foundations of modern mathematical logic were laid by Gottlob Frege (1848–1925). His *Begriffsschrift* sets forth the theory of quantification presented in Chapter 8 of this text. Frege's work was continued into the twentieth century by Alfred North Whitehead (1861–1947) and Bertrand Russell (1872–1970), whose monumental *Principia Mathematica* attempted to reduce the whole of pure mathematics to logic. The *Principia* is the source of much of the symbolism that appears in Chapters 6, 7, and 8 of this text.

During the twentieth century, much of the work in logic has focused on the formalization of logical systems and on questions dealing with the completeness and consistency of such systems. A now-famous theorem proved by Kurt Gödel (1906–1978) states that in any formal system adequate for number theory there exists an undecidable formula—that is, a formula such that neither it nor its negation is derivable from the axioms of the system. Other developments include multivalued logics and the formalization of modal logic. Most recently, logic has made a major contribution to technology by providing the conceptual foundation for the electronic circuitry of digital computers.

## EXERCISE 1.1

I. Each of the following passages contains a single argument. Using the letters "P" and "C," identify the premises and conclusion of each argument, writing premises first and conclusion last. List the premises in the order in which they make the most sense (usually the order in which they occur), and write both premises and conclusion in the form of separate declarative sentences. Indicator words may be eliminated once premises and conclusion have been appropriately labeled. The exercises marked with a star are answered in the back of the book.

★1. Titanium combines readily with oxygen, nitrogen, and hydrogen, all of which have an adverse effect on its mechanical properties. As a result, titanium must be processed in their absence.

*(Illustrated World of Science Encyclopedia)*

2. Since the good, according to Plato, is that which furthers a person's real interests, it follows that in any given case when the good is known, men will seek it.

(Avrum Stroll and Richard Popkin, *Philosophy and the Human Spirit*)

3. As the denial or perversion of justice by the sentences of courts, as well as in any other manner, is with reason classed among the just causes of war, it will follow that the federal judiciary ought to have cognizance of all causes in which the citizens of other countries are concerned.

(Alexander Hamilton, *Federalist Papers,* No. 80)

★4. When individuals voluntarily abandon property, they forfeit any expectation of privacy in it that they might have had. Therefore, a warrantless search or seizure of abandoned property is not unreasonable under the Fourth Amendment.

(Judge Stephanie Kulp Seymour, *United States v. Jones*)

5. Artists and poets look at the world and seek relationships and order. But they translate their ideas to canvas, or to marble, or into poetic images. Scientists try to find relationships between different objects and events. To express the order they find, they create hypotheses and theories. Thus the great scientific theories are easily compared to great art and great literature.

(Douglas C. Giancoli, *The Ideas of Physics,* 3rd ed.)

6. The fact that there was never a land bridge between Australia and mainland Asia is evidenced by the fact that the animal species in the two areas are very different. Asian placental mammals and Australian marsupial mammals have not been in contact in the last several million years.

(T. Douglas Price and Gary M. Feinman, *Images of the Past*)

★7. Cuba's record on disaster prevention is impressive. After October 1963, when Hurricane Flora devastated the island and killed more than a thousand people, the Cuban government overhauled its civil defense system. It was so successful that when six powerful hurricanes thumped Cuba between 1996 and 2002 only 16 people died. And when Hurricane Ivan struck Cuba in 2004 there was not a single casualty, but the same storm killed at least 70 people in other Caribbean countries.

(Newspaper clipping)

8. The classroom teacher is crucial to the development and academic success of the average student, and administrators simply are ancillary to this effort. For this reason, classroom teachers ought to be paid at least the equivalent of administrators at all levels, including the superintendent.

(Peter F. Falstrup, letter to the editor)

9. An agreement cannot bind unless both parties to the agreement know what they are doing and freely choose to do it. This implies that the seller who intends to enter a contract with a customer has a duty to disclose exactly what the customer is buying and what the terms of the sale are.

(Manuel G. Velasquez, "The Ethics of Consumer Production")

★10. Punishment, when speedy and specific, may suppress undesirable behavior, but it cannot teach or encourage desirable alternatives. Therefore, it is crucial to use positive techniques to model and reinforce appropriate behavior that the person can use in place of the unacceptable response that has to be suppressed.

(Walter Mischel and Harriet Mischel, *Essentials of Psychology*)

11. Profit serves a very crucial function in a free enterprise economy, such as our own. High profits are the signal that consumers want more of the output of the industry. High profits provide the incentive for firms to expand output and for more firms to enter the industry in the long run. For a firm of above-average efficiency, profits represent the reward for greater efficiency.

(Dominic Salvatore, *Managerial Economics*, 3rd ed.)

12. Cats can think circles around dogs! My cat regularly used to close and lock the door to my neighbor's doghouse, trapping their sleeping Doberman inside. Try telling a cat what to do, or putting a leash on him—he'll glare at you and say, "I don't think so. You should have gotten a dog."

(Kevin Purkiser, letter to the editor)

★13. Since private property helps people define themselves, since it frees people from mundane cares of daily subsistence, and since it is finite, no individual should accumulate so much property that others are prevented from accumulating the necessities of life.

(Leon P. Baradat, *Political Ideologies, Their Origins and Impact*)

14. To every existing thing God wills some good. Hence, since to love any thing is nothing else than to will good to that thing, it is manifest that God loves everything that exists.

(Thomas Aquinas, *Summa Theologica*)

15. Women of the working class, especially wage workers, should not have more than two children at most. The average working man can support no more and the average working woman can take care of no more in decent fashion.

(Margaret Sanger, *Family Limitations*)

★16. Radioactive fallout isn't the only concern in the aftermath of nuclear explosions. The nations of planet Earth have acquired nuclear weapons with an explosive power equal to more than a million Hiroshima bombs. Studies suggest that explosion of only half these weapons would produce enough soot, smoke, and dust to blanket the Earth, block out the sun, and bring on a nuclear winter that would threaten the survival of the human race.

(John W. Hill and Doris K. Kolb, *Chemistry for Changing Times,* 7th ed.)

17. An ant releases a chemical when it dies, and its fellows then carry it away to the compost heap. Apparently the communication is highly effective; a healthy ant painted with the death chemical will be dragged to the funeral heap again and again.

(Carol R. Ember and Melvin Ember, *Cultural Anthropology,* 7th ed.)

18. Every art and every inquiry, and similarly every action and pursuit, is thought to aim at some good; and for this reason the good has rightly been declared to be that at which all things aim.

(Aristotle, *Nicomachean Ethics*)

★19. Poverty offers numerous benefits to the nonpoor. Antipoverty programs provide jobs for middle-class professionals in social work, penology, and public health. Such workers' future advancement is tied to the continued growth of bureaucracies dependent on the existence of poverty.

(J. John Palen, *Social Problems*)

20. Corn is an annual crop. Butcher's meat, a crop which requires four or five years to grow. As an acre of land, therefore, will produce a much smaller quantity of the one species of food than the other, the inferiority of the quantity must be compensated by the superiority of the price.

(Adam Smith, *The Wealth of Nations*)

21. Neither a borrower nor lender be
For loan oft loses both itself and friend,
And borrowing dulls the edge of husbandry.

(William Shakespeare, *Hamlet* I, 3)

★22. The stakes in whistleblowing are high. Take the nurse who alleges that physicians enrich themselves in her hospital through unnecessary surgery; the engineer who discloses safety defects in the braking systems of a fleet of new rapid-transit vehicles; the Defense Department official who alerts Congress to military graft and overspending: all know that they pose a threat to those whom they denounce and that their own careers may be at risk.

(Sissela Bok, "Whistleblowing and Professional Responsibility")

23. If a piece of information is not "job relevant," then the employer is not entitled qua employer to know it. Consequently, since sexual practices, political beliefs, associational activities, etc., are not part of the description of most jobs, that is, since they do not directly affect one's job performance, they are not legitimate information for an employer to know in the determination of the hiring of a job applicant.

(George G. Brenkert," Privacy, Polygraphs, and Work")

24. Many people believe that a dark tan is attractive and a sign of good health, but mounting evidence indicates that too much sun can lead to health problems. One of the most noticeable effects is premature aging of the skin. The sun also contributes to certain types of cataracts, and, what is most worrisome, it plays a role in skin cancer.

(Joseph M. Moran and Michael D. Morgan, *Meteorology*, 4th ed.)

★25. Contrary to the tales of some scuba divers, the toothy, gaping grin on the mouth of an approaching shark is not necessarily anticipatory. It is generally accepted that by constantly swimming with its mouth open, the shark is simply avoiding suffocation. This assures a continuous flow of oxygen-laden water into their mouths, over their gills, and out through the gill slits.

(Robert A. Wallace et al., *Biology: The Science of Life*)

26. Not only is the sky blue [as a result of scattering], but light coming from it is also partially polarized. You can readily observe this by placing a piece of Polaroid (for example, one lens of a pair of Polaroid sunglasses) in front of your eye and rotating it as you look at the sky on a clear day. You will notice a change in light intensity with the orientation of the Polaroid.

(Frank J. Blatt, *Principles of Physics,* 2nd ed.)

27. Since the secondary light [from the moon] does not inherently belong to the moon and is not received from any star or from the sun, and since in the whole universe there is no other body left but the earth, what must we conclude? What is to be proposed? Surely we must assert that the lunar body (or any other dark and sunless orb) is illuminated by the earth.

(Galileo Galilei, *The Starry Messenger*)

★28. Anyone familiar with our prison system knows that there are some inmates who behave little better than brute beasts. But the very fact that these prisoners exist is a telling argument against the efficacy of capital punishment as a deterrent. If the death penalty had been truly effective as a deterrent, such prisoners would long ago have vanished.

("The Injustice of the Death Penalty," *America*)

29. Though it is possible that REM sleep and dreaming are not necessary in the adult, REM deprivation studies seem to suggest otherwise. Why would REM pressure increase with deprivation if the system is unimportant in the adult?

(Herbert L. Petri, *Motivation: Theory and Research,* 2nd ed.)

30. World government and the balance of power are in many ways opposites. World government means one central authority, a permanent standing world police force, and clearly defined conditions under which this force will go into action. A balance of power system has many sovereign authorities, each controlling its own army, combining only when they feel like it to control aggression. To most people world government now seems unattainable.

(David W. Ziegler, *War, Peace, and International Politics,* 4th ed.)

II. The following arguments were taken from magazine and newspaper editorials and letters to the editor. In most instances the main conclusion must be rephrased to capture the full intent of the author. Write out what you interpret the main conclusion to be.

★1. University administrators know well the benefits that follow notable success in college sports: increased applications for admissions, increased income from licensed logo merchandise, more lucrative television deals, post-season game revenue and more successful alumni fund drives. The idea that there is something ideal and pure about the amateur athlete is self-serving bunk.

(Michael McDonnell, letter to the editor)

2. In a nation of immigrants, people of diverse ethnic backgrounds must have a common bond through which to exchange ideas. How can this bond be accomplished if there is no common language? It is those who shelter the immigrant from learning English by encouraging the development of a multilingual society who are creating a xenophobic atmosphere. They allow the immigrant to surround himself with a cocoon of language from which he cannot escape and which others cannot penetrate.

(Rita Toften, letter to the editor)

3. The health and fitness of our children has become a problem partly because of our attitude toward athletics. The purpose of sports, especially for children, should be to make healthy people healthier. The concept of team sports has failed to do this. Rather than learning to interact and cooperate with others, youngsters are taught to compete. Team sports have only reinforced the notion that the team on top is the winner, and all others are losers. This approach does not make sports appealing to many children, and some, especially among the less fit, burn out by the time they are twelve.

(Mark I. Pitman, "Young Jocks")

★4. College is the time in which a young mind is supposed to mature and acquire wisdom, and one can only do this by experiencing as much diverse intellectual stimuli as possible. A business student may be a whiz at accounting, but has he or she ever experienced the beauty of a Shakespearean sonnet or the boundless events composing Hebrew history? Most likely not. While many of these neoconservatives will probably go on to be financially successful, they are robbing themselves of the true purpose of collegiate academics, a sacrifice that outweighs the future salary checks.

(Robert S. Griffith, "Conservative College Press")

5. History has shown repeatedly that you cannot legislate morality, nor does anyone have a right to. The real problem is the people who have a vested interest in sustaining the multibillion-dollar drug industry created by the laws against drugs. The legalization of drugs would remove the thrill of breaking the law; it would end the suffering caused by unmetered doses, impurities, and substandard paraphernalia. A huge segment of the underground and extralegal economy would move into a legitimate economy, taking money away from criminals, eliminating crime and violence, and restoring many talented people to useful endeavor.

(Thomas L. Wayburn, letter to the editor)

6. Infectious disease is no longer the leading cause of death in this country, thanks to antibiotics, but there are new strains of bacteria that are resistant to—and others that grow only in the presence of—antibiotics. Yet Congress wants to cut the National Institutes of Health budget. Further cuts would leave us woefully unprepared to cope with the new microbes Mother Nature has cooking in her kitchen.

(Valina L. Dawson, letter to the editor)

★7. At a time when our religious impulses might help heal the pains and strains in our society, today's television pulpiteers preach intolerance, censure, and discrimination. They package a "believer life-style," and rail against everyone who doesn't fit it—homosexuals, communists, Jews and other non-Christians, sex educators, and so on. Such intolerance threatens to undermine the pluralism that marks our heritage. The packaging of that intolerance in slick Hollywood programming or under the guise of patriotic fervor is skillfully accomplished on many fronts. That, however, does not make it right.

(Peter G. Kreitler, "TV Preachers' Religious Intolerance")

8. Ideally, decisions about health care should be based on the doctor's clinical judgment, patient preference, and scientific evidence. Patients should always be presented with options in their care. Elective cesarean section, however, is not used to treat a problem but to avoid a natural process. An elective surgery like this puts the patient at unnecessary risk, increases the risk for complications in future deliveries, and increases health care costs.

(Anne Foster-Rosales, M.D., letter to the editor)

9. Parents who feel guilty for the little time they can (or choose to) spend with their children "pick up" after them—so the children don't learn to face the consequences of their own choices and actions. Parents who allow their children to fail are showing them greater love and respect.

(Susan J. Peters, letter to the editor)

★10. Most of the environmental problems facing us stem, at least in part, from the sheer number of Americans. The average American produces three quarters of a ton of garbage every year, consumes hundreds of gallons of gasoline, and uses large amounts of electricity (often from a nuclear power plant, coal burning, or a dam). The least painful way to protect the environment is to limit population growth.

(Craig M. Bradley, letter to the editor)

III. Define the following terms:

| | | |
|---|---|---|
| logic | conclusion | inference |
| argument | conclusion indicator | proposition |
| statement | premise indicator | truth value |
| premise | | |

IV. Answer "true" or "false" to the following statements:

1. The purpose of the premise or premises is to set forth the reasons or evidence given in support of the conclusion.
2. Some arguments have more than one conclusion.
3. All arguments must have more than one premise.
4. The words "therefore," "hence," "so," "since," and "thus" are all conclusion indicators.
5. The words "for," "because," "as," and "for the reason that" are all premise indicators.
6. In the strict sense of the terms, *inference* and *argument* have exactly the same meaning.
7. In most (but not all) arguments that lack indicator words, the conclusion is the first statement.
8. Any sentence that is either true or false is a statement.
9. Every statement has a truth value.
10. The person usually credited with being the father of logic is Aristotle.

---

## 1.2     Recognizing Arguments

Not all passages contain arguments. Because logic deals with arguments, it is important to be able to distinguish passages that contain arguments from those that do not. In general, a passage contains an argument if it purports to prove something; if it does not do so, it does not contain an argument. Two conditions must be fulfilled for a passage to purport to prove something:

1. At least one of the statements must claim to present evidence or reasons.
2. There must be a claim that the alleged evidence supports or implies something— that is, a claim that something follows from the alleged evidence or reasons.

As we have seen, the statements that claim to present the evidence or reasons are the premises, and the statement that the evidence is claimed to support or imply is the conclusion. It is not necessary that the premises present actual evidence or true reasons nor that the premises actually support the conclusion. But at least the premises must *claim* to present evidence or reasons, and there must be a *claim* that the evidence or reasons support or imply something.

The first condition expresses a **factual claim,** and deciding whether it is fulfilled often falls outside the domain of logic. Thus, most of our attention will be concentrated on whether the second condition is fulfilled. This second condition expresses what is called an **inferential claim.** The inferential claim is simply the claim that the passage expresses a certain kind of reasoning process—that something supports or implies something or that something follows from something. Also, you should recognize that this claim is not equatable with the intentions of the arguer. Intentions are subjective and, as such, are usually not accessible to the evaluator. Rather, the inferential claim is an objective feature of an argument grounded in its language or structure.

An inferential claim can be either explicit or implicit. An *explicit* inferential claim is usually asserted by premise or conclusion indicator words ("thus," "since," "because," "hence," "therefore," and so on). Example:

> Mad cow disease is spread by feeding parts of infected animals to cows, and this practice has yet to be completely eradicated. Thus, mad cow disease continues to pose a threat to people who eat beef.

The word "thus" expresses the claim that something is being inferred, so the passage is an argument.

An *implicit* inferential claim exists if there is an inferential relationship between the statements in a passage, but the passage contains no indicator words. Example:

> The genetic modification of food is risky business. Genetic engineering can introduce unintended changes into the DNA of the food-producing organism, and these changes can be toxic to the consumer.

The inferential relationship between the first statement and the other two constitutes an implicit claim that evidence supports something, so we are justified in calling the passage an argument. The first statement is the conclusion, and the other two are the premises.

In deciding whether there is a claim that evidence supports or implies something, keep an eye out for (1) indicator words and (2) the presence of an inferential relationship between the statements. In connection with these points, however, a word of caution is in order. First, the mere occurrence of an indicator word by no means guarantees the presence of an argument. For example, consider the following passages:

> Since Edison invented the phonograph, there have been many technological developments.

> Since Edison invented the phonograph, he deserves credit for a major technological development.

In the first passage the word "since" is used in a *temporal* sense. It means "from the time that." Thus, the first passage is not an argument. In the second passage "since" is used in a *logical* sense, and so the passage *is* an argument.

The second cautionary point is that it is not always easy to detect the occurrence of an inferential relationship between the statements in a passage, and one may have to review a passage several times before making a decision. In reaching such a decision, one may find it helpful to mentally insert the word "therefore" before the various statements to see whether it makes sense to interpret one of them as following from the others. Even with this mental aid, however, the decision whether a passage contains an inferential relationship (as well as the decision about indicator words) often involves a heavy dose of interpretation. As a result, not everyone will agree about every passage. Sometimes the only answer possible is a conditional one: "*If* this passage contains an argument, then these are the premises and that is the conclusion."

To assist in distinguishing passages that contain arguments from those that do not, let us now investigate some typical kinds of nonarguments. These include simple noninferential passages, expository passages, illustrations, explanations, and conditional statements.

## Simple Noninferential Passages

Simple noninferential passages are unproblematic passages that lack a claim that anything is being proved. Such passages contain statements that could be premises or conclusions (or both), but what is missing is a claim that any potential premise supports a conclusion or that any potential conclusion is supported by premises. Passages of this sort include warnings, pieces of advice, statements of belief or opinion, loosely associated statements, and reports.

A **warning** is a form of expression that is intended to put someone on guard against a dangerous or detrimental situation. Examples:

> Watch out that you don't slip on the ice.
> Whatever you do, never confide personal secrets to Blabbermouth Bob.

If no evidence is given to prove that such statements are true, then there is no argument.

A **piece of advice** is a form of expression that makes a recommendation about some future decision or course of conduct. Examples:

> You should keep a few things in mind before buying a used car. Test drive the car at varying speeds and conditions, examine the oil in the crankcase, ask to see service records, and, if possible, have the engine and power train checked by a mechanic.

> Before accepting a job after class hours, I would suggest that you give careful consideration to your course load. Will you have sufficient time to prepare for classes and tests, and will the job produce an excessive drain on your energies?

As with warnings, if there is no evidence that is intended to prove anything, then there is no argument.

A **statement of belief** or **opinion** is an expression about what someone happens to believe or think about something. Examples:

> We believe that our company must develop and produce outstanding products that will perform a great service or fulfill a need for our customers. We believe that our

business must be run at an adequate profit and that the services and products we offer must be better than those offered by competitors.

> (Robert D. Hay and Edmund R. Gray, "Introduction to Social Responsibility")

> When I can read the latte menu through the hole in my server's earlobe, something is seriously out of whack. What happened to an earring, maybe two, in each lobe? Now any surface is game. Brow, lip, tongue, cheek, nose. I've adjusted to untied shoelaces and pants that make mooning irrelevant. But when it comes to piercings, I just can't budge.

> (Debra Darvick, "Service with a Smile, and Plenty of Metal")

Because neither of these authors makes any claim that his or her belief or opinion is supported by evidence, or that it supports some conclusion, there is no argument.

**Loosely associated statements** may be about the same general subject, but they lack a claim that one of them is proved by the others. Example:

> Not to honor men of worth will keep the people from contention; not to value goods that are hard to come by will keep them from theft; not to display what is desirable will keep them from being unsettled of mind.

> (Lao-Tzu, *Thoughts from the Tao Te Ching*)

Because there is no claim that any of these statements provides evidence or reasons for believing another, there is no argument.

A **report** consists of a group of statements that convey information about some topic or event. Example:

> Even though more of the world is immunized than ever before, many old diseases have proven quite resilient in the face of changing population and environmental conditions, especially in the developing world. New diseases, such as AIDS, have taken their toll in both the North and the South.

> (Steven L. Spiegel, *World Politics in a New Era*)

These statements could serve as the premises of an argument, but because the author makes no claim that they support or imply anything, there is no argument. Another type of report is the news report:

> Witnesses said they heard a loud crack before a balcony gave way at a popular nightspot, dropping dozens of screaming people fourteen feet. At least eighty people were injured at the Diamond Horseshoe casino when they fell onto broken glass and splintered wood. Investigators are waiting for an engineer's report on the deck's occupancy load.

> (Newspaper clipping)

Again, because the reporter makes no claim that these statements imply anything, there is no argument.

One must be careful, though, with reports *about* arguments:

"The Air Force faces a serious shortage of experienced pilots in the years ahead, because repeated overseas tours and the allure of high paying jobs with commercial
airlines are winning out over lucrative bonuses to stay in the service," says a
prominent Air Force official.

(Newspaper clipping)

Properly speaking, this passage is not an argument, because the author of the passage
does not claim that anything is supported by evidence. Rather, the author reports the
claim by the Air Force official that something is supported by evidence. If such passages
are interpreted as "containing" arguments, it must be made clear that the argument is
not the author's but one made by someone about whom the author is reporting.

## Expository Passages

An **expository passage** is a kind of discourse that begins with a topic sentence followed by one or more sentences that develop the topic sentence. If the objective is not
to prove the topic sentence but only to expand it or elaborate it, then there is no argument. Examples:

There are three familiar states of matter: solid, liquid, and gas. Solid objects ordinarily
maintain their shape and volume regardless of their location. A liquid occupies a
definite volume, but assumes the shape of the occupied portion of its container.
A gas maintains neither shape nor volume. It expands to fill completely whatever
container it is in.

(John W. Hill and Doris K. Kolb, *Chemistry for Changing Times,* 7th ed.)

There is a stylized relation of artist to mass audience in the sports, especially in baseball. Each player develops a style of his own—the swagger as he steps to the plate,
the unique windup a pitcher has, the clean-swinging and hard-driving hits, the
precision quickness and grace of infield and outfield, the sense of surplus power
behind whatever is done.

(Max Lerner, *America as a Civilization*)

In each passage the topic sentence is stated first, and the remaining sentences merely develop and flesh out this topic sentence. These passages are not arguments, because they
lack an inferential claim. However, expository passages differ from simple noninferential
passages (such as warnings and pieces of advice) in that many of them can also be taken
as arguments. If the purpose of the subsequent sentences in the passage is not only to
flesh out the topic sentence but also to prove it, then the passage is an argument. Example:

Skin and the mucous membrane lining the respiratory and digestive tracts serve as
mechanical barriers to entry by microbes. Oil gland secretions contain chemicals
that weaken or kill bacteria on skin. The respiratory tract is lined by cells that sweep
mucus and trapped particles up into the throat, where they can be swallowed. The
stomach has an acidic pH, which inhibits the growth of many types of bacteria.

(Sylvia S. Mader, *Human Biology,* 4th ed.)

In this passage the topic sentence is stated first, and the purpose of the remaining
sentences is not only to *show how* the skin and mucous membranes serve as barriers to

microbes but also to *prove* that they do this. Thus, the passage can be taken as both an expository passage and an argument.

In deciding whether an expository passage should be interpreted as an argument, try to determine whether the purpose of the subsequent sentences in the passage is merely to develop the topic sentence or also to prove that it is true. In borderline cases, ask yourself whether the topic sentence makes a claim that everyone accepts or agrees with. If it does, the passage is probably not an argument. In real-life situations authors rarely try to prove something is true when everyone already accepts it. However, if the topic sentence makes a claim that many people do not accept or have never thought about, then the purpose of the remaining sentences may be both to prove the topic sentence is true as well as to develop it. If this be so, the passage is an argument.

Finally, if even this procedure yields no definite answer, the only alternative may be to say that *if* the passage is taken as an argument, then the first statement is the conclusion and the others are the premises.

## Illustrations

An **illustration** is an expression involving one or more examples that is intended to show what something means or how it is done. Illustrations are often confused with arguments because many illustrations contain indicator words such as "thus." Examples:

> Chemical elements, as well as compounds, can be represented by molecular formulas. Thus, oxygen is represented by "$O_2$," water by "$H_2O$," and sodium chloride by "NaCl."

> A deciduous tree is any tree that loses its leaves during the winter. For example, maples are deciduous. And so are elms, poplars, hawthorns, and alders.

These selections are not arguments, because they make no claim that anything is being proved. In the first selection, the word "thus" indicates how something is done—namely, how chemical elements and compounds can be represented by formulas. In the second, the examples cited are intended to illustrate the meaning of the word "deciduous." It pins down the meaning by providing concrete instances.

However, as with expository passages, many illustrations can be taken as arguments. Such arguments are often called **arguments from example.** Here is an instance of one:

> Although most forms of cancer, if untreated, can cause death, not all cancers are life-threatening. For example, basal cell carcinoma, the most common of all skin cancers, can produce disfigurement, but it almost never results in death.

In this passage the example given is intended to prove the truth of "Not all cancers are life-threatening." Thus, the passage is best interpreted as an argument.

In deciding whether an illustration should be interpreted as an argument, determine whether the passage merely shows how something is done or what something means, or whether it also purports to prove something. In borderline cases it helps to note whether the claim being illustrated is one that practically everyone accepts or agrees with. If it is, the passage is probably not an argument. As already noted, in real-life situations authors rarely attempt to prove what everyone already accepts. But if the claim being illustrated is one that many people do not accept or have never thought about, then the passage may be interpreted as an argument.

Thus, in reference to the first two examples we considered, most people are aware that elements and compounds can be expressed by formulas—practically everyone knows that water is $H_2O$—and most people have at least a vague idea of what a deciduous tree is. But they may not have ever considered whether some forms of cancer are not life-threatening. This is one of the reasons for evaluating the first two examples as mere illustrations and the last one as an argument.

## Explanations

One of the most important kinds of nonargument is the explanation. An **explanation** is an expression that purports to shed light on some event or phenomenon. The event or phenomenon in question is usually accepted as a matter of fact. Examples:

> The sky appears blue from the earth's surface because light rays from the sun are scattered by particles in the atmosphere.

> The AIDS virus causes sickness and death because it infects certain white blood cells called T cells, and these cells are essential to the body's immune system.

> Naval oranges are called by that name because they have a growth that resembles a human naval on the end opposite the stem.

Every explanation is composed of two distinct components: the explanandum and explanans. The **explanandum** is the statement that describes the event or phenomenon to be explained, and the **explanans** is the statement or group of statements that purports to do the explaining. In the first example above, the explanandum is the statement "The sky appears blue from the earth's surface" and the explanans is "Light rays from the sun are scattered by particles in the atmosphere."

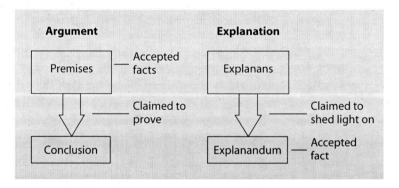

Explanations are sometimes mistaken for arguments because they often contain the indicator word "because." Yet explanations are not arguments, because in an explanation the purpose of the explanans is to shed light on, or to make sense of, the explanandum event—not to prove that it occurred. In other words, the purpose of the explanans is to show *why* something is the case, whereas in an argument, the purpose of the premises is to prove *that* something is the case.

In the first example given, the fact that the sky is blue is readily apparent to everyone. The statement that light rays from the sun are scattered by particles in the atmosphere is not intended to prove *that* the sky is blue, but rather to show *why* it is blue. In the second example, practically everyone knows that the AIDS virus causes sickness and death. The purpose of the passage is to explain *why* this happens—not to prove *that* it happens. Similarly, in the third example, it is obvious that naval oranges are called naval oranges. The purpose of the passage is to shed light on why they have this name.

Thus, to distinguish explanations from arguments, identify the statement that is either the explanandum or the conclusion (usually this is the statement that precedes the word "because"). If this statement describes an accepted matter of fact, and if the remaining statements purport to shed light on this statement, then the passage is an explanation.

This method usually works to distinguish arguments from explanations. However, some passages can be interpreted as both explanations and arguments. Example:

> Women become intoxicated by drinking a smaller amount of alcohol than men because men metabolize part of the alcohol before it reaches the bloodstream, whereas women do not.

The purpose of this passage could be to prove the first statement to those people who do not accept it as fact, and to shed light on that fact to those people who do accept it. Alternately, the passage could be intended to prove the first statement to a single person who accepts its truth on blind faith or incomplete experience, and simultaneously to shed light on this truth. Thus, the passage can be correctly interpreted as both an explanation and an argument.

Perhaps the greatest problem confronting the effort to distinguish explanations from arguments lies in determining whether something is an accepted matter of fact. Obviously, what is accepted by one person may not be accepted by another. Thus, the effort often involves determining which person or group of people the passage is directed to—the intended audience. Sometimes the source of the passage (textbook, newspaper, technical journal, etc.) will decide the issue. But when the passage is taken totally out of context, ascertaining the source may prove impossible. In those circumstances the only possible answer may be to say that *if* the passage is an argument, then such-and-such is the conclusion and such-and-such are the premises.

## Conditional Statements

A **conditional statement** is an "if . . . then . . ." statement; for example:

> If professional football games incite violence in the home, then the widespread approval given to this sport should be reconsidered.

> If Lance Armstrong has won the Tour de France seven consecutive times, then he ranks as king of the hill in the world's most famous bicycle race.

Every conditional statement is made up of two component statements. The component statement immediately following the "if" is called the **antecedent,** and the one following the "then" is called the **consequent.** (Occasionally, the word "then" is left out, and occasionally the order of antecedent and consequent is reversed.) In the first example, the antecedent is "Professional football games incite violence in the home," and the consequent is "The widespread approval given to this sport should be reconsidered." In both of these examples, there is a meaningful relationship between antecedent and consequent. However, such a relationship need not exist for a statement to count as conditional. The statement "If Janet Jackson is a singer, then Denver is in Colorado" is just as much a conditional statement as those about professional football and Lance Armstrong.

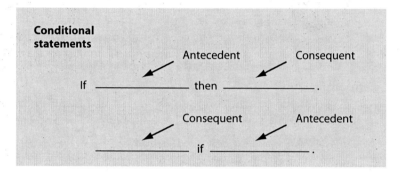

Conditional statements are not arguments, because they fail to meet the criteria given earlier. In an argument, at least one statement must claim to present evidence, and there must be a claim that this evidence implies something. In a conditional statement, there is no claim that either the antecedent or the consequent presents evidence. In other words, there is no assertion that either the antecedent or the consequent is true. Rather, there is only the assertion that *if* the antecedent is true, then so is the consequent. Of course, a conditional statement as a whole may present evidence because it asserts a relationship between statements. Yet when conditional statements are taken in this sense, there is still no argument, because there is then no separate claim that this evidence implies anything.

Some conditional statements are similar to arguments, however, in that they express the outcome of a reasoning process. As such, they may be said to have a certain inferential content. Consider the following:

> If Arnold Schwarzenegger was born a citizen of Austria, then he cannot be elected president of the United States.

> If Jennifer Lopez is Marc Anthony's wife, then Marc Anthony is Jennifer Lopez's husband.

The link between the antecedent and consequent of these conditional statements resembles the inferential link between the premises and conclusion of an argument. Yet there is a difference because the premises of an argument are claimed to be true, whereas no such claim is made for the antecedent of a conditional statement. Accordingly, these conditional statements are not arguments.* Yet their inferential content may be reexpressed to form arguments:

---

*In saying this we are temporarily ignoring the possibility of these statements being enthymemes. As we shall see in Chapter 5, an *enthymeme* is an argument in which a premise or conclusion (or both) is implied but not stated. If, to the second example, we add the premise "Jennifer Lopez is Marc Anthony's wife" and the conclusion "Therefore, Marc Anthony is Jennifer Lopez's husband," we have a complete argument. To decide whether a conditional statement is an enthymeme, we must be familiar with the context in which it occurs.

> Arnold Schwarzenegger was born a citizen of Austria.
> Therefore, he cannot be elected president of the United States.

> Jennifer Lopez is Marc Anthony's wife.
> Therefore, Marc Anthony is Jennifer Lopez's husband.

Finally, while no single conditional statement is an argument, a conditional statement may serve as either the premise or the conclusion (or both) of an argument, as the following examples illustrate:

> If Iran is developing nuclear weapons, then Iran is a threat to world peace.
> Iran is developing nuclear weapons.
> Therefore, Iran is a threat to world peace.

> If borders are secure, then terrorists cannot enter the country.
> If terrorists cannot enter the country, then acts of terrorism will be reduced.
> Therefore, if borders are secure, then acts of terrorism will be reduced.

The relation between conditional statements and arguments may now be summarized as follows:

1. A single conditional statement is not an argument.
2. A conditional statement may serve as either the premise or the conclusion (or both) of an argument.
3. The inferential content of a conditional statement may be reexpressed to form an argument.

The first two rules are especially pertinent to the recognition of arguments. According to the first rule, if a passage consists of a single conditional statement, it is not an argument. But if it consists of a conditional statement together with some other statement, then, by the second rule, it *may* be an argument, depending on such factors as the presence of indicator words and an inferential relationship between the statements.

Conditional statements are especially important in logic because they express the relationship between necessary and sufficient conditions. *A* is said to be a **sufficient condition** for *B* whenever the occurrence of *A* is all that is needed for the occurrence of *B*. For example, being a dog is a sufficient condition for being an animal. On the other hand, *B* is said to be a **necessary condition** for *A* whenever *A* cannot occur without the occurrence of *B*. Thus, being an animal is a necessary condition for being a dog. These relationships are expressed in the following conditional statements:

> If *X* is a dog, then *X* is an animal.
> If *X* is not an animal, then *X* is not a dog.

The first statement says that being a dog is a sufficient condition for being an animal, and the second that being an animal is a necessary condition for being a dog. However, a little reflection reveals that these two statements say exactly the same thing. Thus, each expresses in one way a necessary condition and in another way a sufficient condition. The terminology of sufficient and necessary conditions will be used in later chapters to express definitions and causal connections.

## Summary

In deciding whether a passage contains an argument, you should look for three things: (1) indicator words such as "therefore," "since," "because," and so on; (2) an inferential relationship between the statements; and (3) typical kinds of nonarguments. But remember that the mere occurrence of an indicator word does not guarantee the presence of an argument. You must check to see that the statement identified as the conclusion is claimed to be supported by one or more of the other statements. Also keep in mind that in many arguments that lack indicator words, the conclusion is the first statement. Furthermore, it helps to mentally insert the word "therefore" before the various statements before deciding that a statement should be interpreted as a conclusion. The typical kinds of nonarguments that we have surveyed are as follows:

| | |
|---|---|
| warnings | reports |
| pieces of advice | expository passages |
| statements of belief | illustrations |
| statements of opinion | explanations |
| loosely associated statements | conditional statements |

Keep in mind that these kinds of nonargument are not mutually exclusive, and that, for example, one and the same passage can sometimes be interpreted as both a report and a statement of opinion, or as both an expository passage and an illustration. The precise kind of nonargument a passage might be is nowhere near as important as correctly deciding whether or not it is an argument.

After working the exercises in this section, you may, if you wish, proceed directly to Section 1.6 ("Extended Arguments").

### EXERCISE 1.2

I. Determine which of the following passages are arguments. For those that are, identify the conclusion. For those that are not, determine the kind of nonargument.

★1. The turkey vulture is called by that name because its red featherless head resembles the head of a wild turkey.

2. If public education fails to improve the quality of instruction in both primary and secondary schools, then it is likely that it will lose additional students to the private sector in the years ahead.

3. Freedom of the press is the most important of our constitutionally guaranteed freedoms. Without it, our other freedoms would be immediately threatened. Furthermore, it provides the fulcrum for the advancement of new freedoms.

★4. A mammal is a vertebrate animal that nurses its offspring. Thus, cats and dogs are mammals, as are sheep, monkeys, rabbits, and bears.

5. It is strongly recommended that you have your house inspected for termite damage at the earliest possible opportunity.

6. Mosquito bites are not always the harmless little irritations most of us take them to be. For example, some mosquitoes carry West Nile virus, and people who are infected can become very sick or even die.

★7. If stem-cell research is restricted, then future cures will not materialize. If future cures do not materialize, then people will die prematurely. Therefore, if stem-cell research is restricted, then people will die prematurely.

8. Fictional characters behave according to the same psychological probabilities as real people. But the characters of fiction are found in exotic dilemmas that real people hardly encounter. Consequently, fiction provides us with the opportunity to ponder how people react in uncommon situations, and to deduce moral lessons, psychological principles, and philosophical insights from their behavior.

(J. R. McCuen and A. C. Winkler, *Readings for Writers,* 4th ed.)

9. I believe that it must be the policy of the United States to support free peoples who are resisting attempted subjugation by armed minorities or by outside pressures. I believe that we must assist free peoples to work out their own destinies in their own way. I believe that our help should be primarily through economic and financial aid, which is essential to economic stability and orderly political processes.

(President Truman, Address to Congress, 1947)

★10. Five college students who were accused of sneaking into the Cincinnati Zoo and trying to ride the camels pleaded no contest to criminal trespass yesterday. The students scaled a fence to get into the zoo and then climbed another fence to get into the camel pit before security officials caught them, zoo officials said.

(Newspaper clipping)

11. Mortality rates for women undergoing early abortions, where the procedure is legal, appear to be as low as or lower than the rates for normal childbirth. Consequently, any interest of the state in protecting the woman from an inherently hazardous procedure, except when it would be equally dangerous for her to forgo it, has largely disappeared.

(Justice Blackmun, *Roe v. Wade*)

12. The pace of reading, clearly, depends entirely upon the reader. He may read as slowly or as rapidly as he can or wishes to read. If he does not understand something, he may stop and reread it, or go in search of elucidation before continuing. The reader can accelerate his pace when the material is easy or less than interesting, and can slow down when it is difficult or enthralling. If what he reads is moving he can put down the book for a few moments and cope with his emotions without fear of losing anything.

(Marie Winn, *The Plug-In Drug*)

★13. I'm sick and tired of living in fear. I'm tired of plastic bags and duct tape. I'm tired of alerts telling me whether or not I can walk outside. America should be a bastion of hope. Jobs, affordable health care and respect from the world. These will bring hope, and hope is what prevents terrorism.

(Steve Mavros, letter to the editor)

14. Lions at Kruger National Park in South Africa are dying of tuberculosis. "All of the lions in the park may be dead within ten years because the disease is incurable, and the lions have no natural resistance," said the deputy director of the Department of Agriculture.

(Newspaper clipping)

15. Economics is of practical value in business. An understanding of the overall operation of the economic system puts the business executive in a better position to formulate policies. The executive who understands the causes and consequences of inflation is better equipped during inflationary periods to make more intelligent decisions than otherwise.

(Campbell R. McConnell, *Economics,* 8th ed.)

★16. Bear one thing in mind before you begin to write your paper: Famous literary works, especially works regarded as classics, have been thoroughly studied to the point where prevailing opinion on them has assumed the character of orthodoxy.

(J. R. McCuen and A. C. Winkler, *Readings for Writers,* 4th ed.)

17. Young people at universities study to achieve knowledge and not to learn a trade. We must all learn how to support ourselves, but we must also learn how to live. We need a lot of engineers in the modern world, but we do not want a world of modern engineers.

(Winston Churchill, *A Churchill Reader,* ed. Colin R. Coote)

18. No business concern wants to sell on credit to a customer who will prove unable or unwilling to pay his or her account. Consequently, most business organizations include a credit department which must reach a decision on the credit worthiness of each prospective customer.

(Walter B. Meigs and Robert F. Meigs, *Accounting*)

★19. For organisms at the sea surface, sinking into deep water usually means death. Plant cells cannot photosynthesize in the dark depths. Fishes and other animals that descend lose contact with the main surface food supply and themselves become food for strange deep-living predators.

(David H. Milne, *Marine Life and the Sea*)

20. Since the 1950s a malady called whirling disease has invaded U.S. fishing streams, frequently attacking rainbow trout. A parasite deforms young fish, which often chase their tails before dying, hence the name.

("Trout Disease—A Turn for the Worse," *National Geographic*)

21. Dachshunds are ideal dogs for small children, as they are already stretched and pulled to such a length that the child cannot do much harm one way or the other.

(Robert Benchley, quoted in *Cold Noses and Warm Hearts*)

★22. Atoms are the basic building blocks of all matter. They can combine to form molecules, whose properties are generally very different from those of the constituent atoms. Table salt, for example, a simple chemical compound formed from chlorine and sodium, resembles neither the poisonous gas nor the highly reactive metal.

(Frank J. Blatt, *Principles of Physics,* 2nd ed.)

23. The coarsest type of humor is the *practical joke:* pulling away the chair from the dignitary's lowered bottom. The victim is perceived first as a person of consequence, then suddenly as an inert body subject to the laws of physics: authority is debunked by gravity, mind by matter; man is degraded to a mechanism.

(Arthur Koestler, *Janus: A Summing Up*)

24. If a man holding a belief which he was taught in childhood or persuaded of afterwards keeps down and pushes away any doubts which arise about it in his mind, purposely avoids the reading of books and the company of men that call in question or discuss it, and regards as impious those questions which cannot easily be asked without disturbing it—the life of that man is one long sin against mankind.

(W. K. Clifford, "The Ethics of Belief")

★25. It is usually easy to decide whether or not something is alive. This is because living things share many common attributes, such as the capacity to extract energy from nutrients to drive their various functions, the power to actively respond to changes in their environment, and the ability to grow, to differentiate, and to reproduce.

(Donald Voet and Judith G. Voet, *Biochemistry,* 2nd ed.)

26. Words are slippery customers. The full meaning of a word does not appear until it is placed in its context. . . . And even then the meaning will depend upon the listener, upon the speaker, upon their entire experience of the language, upon their knowledge of one another, and upon the whole situation.

(C. Cherry, *On Human Communication*)

27. Haydn developed the string quartet from the eighteenth century *divertimento,* giving more substance to the light, popular form and scoring it for two violins, a viola, and a cello. His eighty-three quartets, written over the course of his creative lifetime, evolved slowly into a sophisticated form. Together they constitute one of the most important bodies of chamber music literature.

(Robert Hickok, *Exploring Music*)

★28. A person never becomes truly self-reliant. Even though he deals effectively with things, he is necessarily dependent upon those who have taught him to do so. They have selected the things he is dependent upon and determined the kinds and degrees of dependencies.

(B. F. Skinner, *Beyond Freedom and Dignity*)

29. There is no doubt that some businessmen conspire to shorten the useful life of their products in order to guarantee replacement sales. There is, similarly, no

doubt that many of the annual model changes with which American (and other) consumers are increasingly familiar are not technologically substantive.

(Alvin Toffler, *Future Shock*)

30. Water is a good solvent for many different substances, and it picks them up as it moves through the environment. For example, rain water flowing over and under the ground dissolves minerals such as limestone.

(Gilbert Castellan et al., *The World of Chemistry*)

★31. In areas where rats are a problem, it is very difficult to exterminate them with bait poison. That's because some rats eat enough poison to die but others eat only enough to become sick and then learn to avoid that particular poison taste in the future.

(Rod Plotnik, *Introduction to Psychology*, 4th ed.)

32. Men are less likely to develop osteoporosis until later in life than women and seldom suffer as severely because they have 30 percent more bone mass on the average and don't undergo the sudden drop in estrogen that occurs with menopause.

(Matt Clark, "The Calcium Craze," *Newsweek*)

33. Newspapers, radio, and television are essential for a democracy. They are the critical link between the people and their government. They provide information and analysis about policy issues, and they also sensitize policymakers to public opinion—which enables them to respond to the needs and desires of the population. Finally, the media play a critical role in reporting and evaluating the decisions of government.

(Stephen J. Wayne et al., *The Politics of American Government*)

★34. Nations are made in two ways, by the slow working of history or the galvanic force of ideas. Most nations are made the former way, emerging slowly from the mist of the past, gradually coalescing within concentric circles of shared sympathies, with an accretion of consensual institutions. But a few nations are formed and defined by the citizens' assent to a shared philosophy.

(George Will, "Lithuania and South Carolina")

35. Although the plane mirror is perhaps the oldest optical instrument known to man, it remains an important element in the modern arsenal of sophisticated optical devices. For example, the earth-moon laser-ranging experiments, initiated in 1969, rely on high-quality reflectors.

(Frank J. Blatt, *Principles of Physics*, 2nd ed.)

II. The following selections were originally submitted as letters to the editor of newspapers and magazines. Determine which of them can, with good reason, be considered arguments. In those that can, identify the conclusion.

★1. What this country needs is a return to the concept of swift and certain justice. If we need more courts, judges and prisons, then so be it. And as for capital punishment, I say let the punishment fit the crime. When criminals behave more like humans, then we can start to treat them more humanely. In the meantime, I would like to see the Night Stalkers of our society swiftly executed rather than coddled by our courts and prisons.

(John Pearson)

2. The big problem with computers in elementary schools isn't their minimal educational value but the fact that they often replace science in the budget and curriculum. Our local Parent Teachers Association is throwing away science equipment as fervently as it raises money for more computers. I use computers extensively in the college physics classes I teach, so I appreciate their value in communications and advanced computation. But in elementary schools, too much is being sacrificed so that children can have all those pricey beige boxes.

(Roger G. Tobin)

3. Is there any country in the world that worries more about its kids having fun in school, making lessons exciting and relevant, and then is more disappointed with the result than the United States? We think learning is like buying a car or smoking a cigarette. Just get into the thing or draw a breath and you will be effortlessly transported to lands of pleasure and excitement.

(Charles M. Breinin)

★4. After reading your cover story, I find that cable TV has simply flooded our airwaves with more sex, violence, and teen-age punk junk. Now our children can spend even less time studying and we can spend more time in blank-space stares at the idiot box. Cable would be fine with more educational channels—and fewer cheap thrills aimed at narrow-minded bubble brains.

(Jacqueline Murray)

5. In opposing obligatory prayer in the public schools, I am not deserting my god (and I would like to think of myself as a Christian). On the contrary, it is perfectly possible that I am thus serving my god, who I believe wants his children to pray to him of their own free will and not because some legislator, who may or may not be motivated by truly religious considerations, forces them to.

(Philip D. Walker)

6. My own son returned from his public elementary school with a book on dinosaurs loaned to him by his first-grade "science" teacher. It depicted the beasts as fire-breathing dragons and said the Bible informs us they were this way. God help us to achieve an educated and scientifically literate society, because these narrow-minded cretins won't.

(Bruce Strathdee)

★7. The poor quality of parenting and the lack in continuity of adult care provided to many U.S. children contribute to a passivity and a sense of helplessness that hobbles individuals for the remainder of their lives. Their subsequent unemployment, lack of education, and inability to make necessary life-style changes such as quitting an addiction can be attributed, in large part, to the helplessness they learned from childhood.

(William J. McCarthy)

8. Forty-one million Americans cannot afford health insurance in this time of global capitalism. At the same time, nine insurance executives earned more than $10 million last year, according to a recent study. If this is the celebrated triumph of capitalism over other forms of economic organization, what exactly did we win? Have we gained the world at the cost of our souls?

(Jason Reynolds)

9. The suggestion by sociobiologists that stepparent child abuse has evolutionary advantages is superficial. If there were evolutionary advantages to harming one's mate's offspring of a different parent, then by now there probably wouldn't be loving and generous stepparents around—and there are plenty. I know. I have a loving stepparent and am one.

(Ronald Cohen)

★10. The voting public is as full of bull as the politicians. As a result, we get the kind of officeholders we ask for. Show me a politician who will stand up and tell Americans the truth, and I'll show you a person who will never be elected.

(Huie Dixon)

III. The following statements represent conclusions for arguments. Each is expressed in the form of two alternatives. Select one of the alternatives for each conclusion, and then jot down several reasons that support it. Finally, incorporate your reasons into a written argument of at least 100 words that supports the conclusion. Include premise and conclusion indicators in some of your arguments, but not in all of them.

1. A constitutional amendment that outlaws flag burning should/should not be adopted.

2. Street drugs should/should not be legalized.

3. The death penalty should/should not be abolished.

4. Sanctions should/should not be imposed on students for using speech that is offensive to minorities.

5. Free health care should/should not be guaranteed to all citizens.

6. Same-sex marriages should/should not be recognized by the state.

7. The possession, ownership, and sale of handguns should/should not be outlawed.

8. Cigarettes should/should not be regulated as an addictive drug.

9. Affirmative action programs should/should not be abolished.

10. Doctors should/should not be allowed to assist terminally ill patients in committing suicide.

IV. Define the following terms:

| | |
|---|---|
| argument from example | explanation |
| conditional statement | explanandum |
| antecedent | explanans |
| consequent | illustration |
| sufficient condition | expository passage |
| necessary condition | |

V. Answer "true" or "false" to the following statements:

1. Any passage that contains an argument must contain a claim that something is supported by evidence or reasons.

2. In an argument, the claim that something is supported by evidence or reasons is always explicit.

3. Passages that contain indicator words such as "thus," "since," and "because" are always arguments.

4. In deciding whether a passage contains an argument, we should always keep an eye out for indicator words and the presence of an inferential relationship between the statements.

5. Some expository passages can be correctly interpreted as arguments.

6. Some passages containing "for example" can be correctly interpreted as arguments.

7. In deciding whether an expository passage or an illustration should be interpreted as an argument, it helps to note whether the claim being developed or illustrated is one that is accepted by everyone.

8. Some conditional statements can be reexpressed to form arguments.

9. In an explanation, the explanandum usually describes an accepted matter of fact.

10. In an explanation, the explanans is the statement or group of statements that does the explaining.

VI. Fill in the blanks with "necessary" or "sufficient" to make the following statements true. After the blanks have been filled in, express the result in terms of conditional statements.

★1. Being a tiger is a _____ condition for being an animal.

2. Being an animal is a _____ condition for being a tiger.

3. Drinking water is a _____ condition for quenching one's thirst.

★4. Having a racket is a _____ condition for playing tennis.

5. Pulling the cork is a _____ condition for drinking an expensive bottle of wine.

6. Stepping on a cat's tail is a _____ condition for making the cat yowl.

★7. Burning leaves is a _____ condition for producing smoke.

8. Paying attention is a _____ condition for understanding a lecture.

    **9.** Taking a swim in the North Sea is a _____ condition for cooling off.

★**10.** Opening a door is a _____ condition for crossing the threshold.

**VII.** Page through a book, magazine, or newspaper and find two arguments, one with indicator words, the other without. Copy the arguments as written, giving the appropriate reference. Then identify the premises and conclusion of each.

---

## 1.3     Deduction and Induction

In the previous section we saw that every argument involves an inferential claim—the claim that the conclusion is supposed to follow from the premises. The question we now address has to do with the strength of this claim. Just how strongly is the conclusion claimed to follow from the premises? If the conclusion is claimed to follow with strict certainty or necessity, the argument is said to be deductive; but if it is claimed to follow only probably, the argument is inductive.

Stated more precisely, a **deductive argument** is an argument incorporating the claim that it is *impossible* for the conclusion to be false given that the premises are true. Deductive arguments are those that involve necessary reasoning. On the other hand, an **inductive argument** is an argument incorporating the claim that it is *improbable* that the conclusion be false given that the premises are true. Inductive arguments involve probabilistic reasoning. Here are two examples:

> The meerkat is closely related to the suricat.
> The suricat thrives on beetle larvae.
> Therefore, probably the meerkat thrives on beetle larvae.

> The meerkat is a member of the mongoose family.
> All members of the mongoose family are carnivores.
> Therefore, it necessarily follows that the meerkat is a carnivore.

The first of these arguments is inductive, the second deductive.

In deciding whether an argument is inductive or deductive, we look to certain objective features of the argument. These features include (1) the occurrence of special indicator words, (2) the *actual* strength of the inferential link between premises and conclusion, and (3) the form or style of argumentation. However, we must acknowledge at the outset that many arguments in ordinary language are incomplete, and because of this, deciding whether the argument should best be interpreted as deductive or inductive may be impossible.

The occurrence of special indicator words is illustrated in the examples we just considered. The word "probably" in the conclusion of the first argument suggests that the argument should be taken as inductive, and the word "necessarily" in the conclusion of the second suggests that the second argument be taken as deductive. Additional inductive indicators are "improbable," "plausible," "implausible," "likely," "unlikely," and "reasonable to conclude." Additional deductive indicators are "certainly," "absolutely," and "definitely." (Note that the phrase "it must be the case that" is simply a conclusion indicator that can occur in either deductive or inductive argments.)

Inductive and deductive indicator words often suggest the correct interpretation. However, if they conflict with one of the other criteria (discussed shortly), we should probably ignore them. Arguers often use phrases such as "it certainly follows that" for rhetorical purposes to add impact to their conclusion and not to suggest that the argument be taken as deductive. Similarly, some arguers, not knowing the distinction between inductive and deductive, will claim to "deduce" a conclusion when their argument is more correctly interpreted as inductive.

The second factor that bears on our interpretation of an argument as inductive or deductive is the *actual* strength of the inferential link between premises and conclusion. If the conclusion actually does follow with strict necessity from the premises, the argument is clearly deductive. In such an argument it is impossible for the premises to be true and the conclusion false. On the other hand, if the conclusion does not follow with strict necessity but does follow probably, it is often best to consider the argument inductive. Examples:

> All entertainers are extroverts.
> David Letterman is an entertainer.
> Therefore, David Letterman is an extrovert.
>
> The vast majority of entertainers are extroverts.
> David Letterman is an entertainer.
> Therefore, David Letterman is an extrovert.

In the first example, the conclusion follows with strict necessity from the premises. If we assume that all entertainers are extroverts and that David Letterman is an entertainer, then it is impossible that David Letterman not be an extrovert. Thus, we should interpret this argument as deductive. In the second example, the conclusion does not follow from the premises with strict necessity, but it does follow with some degree of probability. If we assume that the premises are true, then based on that assumption it is probable that the conclusion is true. Thus, it is best to interpret the second argument as inductive.

Occasionally, an argument contains no special indicator words, and the conclusion does not follow either necessarily or probably from the premises; in other words, it does not follow at all. This situation points up the need for the third factor to be taken into account, which is the character or form of argumentation the arguer uses.

## Deductive Argument Forms

Many arguments have a distinctive character or form that indicates that the premises are supposed to provide absolute support for the conclusion. Five examples of such forms or kinds of argumentation are arguments based on mathematics, arguments from definition, and categorical, hypothetical, and disjunctive syllogisms.

An **argument based on mathematics** is an argument in which the conclusion depends on some purely arithmetic or geometric computation or measurement. For example, a shopper might place two apples and three oranges into a paper bag and then conclude that the bag contains five pieces of fruit. Or a surveyor might measure a square piece of land and, after determining that it is 100 feet on each side, conclude that it contains 10,000 square feet. Since all arguments in pure mathematics are deductive, we can usually consider arguments that depend on mathematics to be deductive as well. A noteworthy exception, however, is arguments that depend on statistics. As we will see shortly, such arguments are usually best interpreted as inductive.

An **argument from definition** is an argument in which the conclusion is claimed to depend merely on the definition of some word or phrase used in the premise or conclusion. For example, someone might argue that because Claudia is mendacious, it follows that she tells lies, or that because a certain paragraph is prolix, it follows that it is excessively wordy. These arguments are deductive because their conclusions follow with necessity from the definitions of "mendacious" and "prolix."

A *syllogism*, in general, is an argument consisting of exactly two premises and one conclusion. Categorical syllogisms will be treated in greater depth in Chapter 5, but for now we will say that a **categorical syllogism** is a syllogism in which each statement begins with one of the words "all," "no," or "some." Example:

> All ancient forests are sources of wonder.
> Some ancient forests are targets of the timber industry.
> Therefore, some sources of wonder are targets of the timber industry.

Arguments such as these are nearly always best treated as deductive.

A **hypothetical syllogism** is a syllogism having a conditional statement for one or both of its premises. Examples:

> If estate taxes are abolished, then wealth will accumulate disproportionately.
> If wealth accumulates disproportionately, then democracy will be threatened.
> Therefore, if estate taxes are abolished, then democracy will be threatened.
>
> If Fox News is a propaganda machine, then it misleads its viewers.
> Fox News is a propaganda machine.
> Therefore, Fox News misleads its viewers.

Although certain forms of such arguments can sometimes be interpreted inductively, the deductive interpretation is usually the most appropriate.

A **disjunctive syllogism** is a syllogism having a disjunctive statement (i.e., an "either . . . or . . ." statement) for one of its premises. Example:

> Either global warming will be arrested, or hurricanes will become more intense.
> Global warming will not be arrested.
> Therefore, hurricanes will become more intense.

As with hypothetical syllogisms, such arguments are usually best taken as deductive. Hypothetical and disjunctive syllogisms will be treated in greater depth in Chapter 6.

## Inductive Argument Forms

In general, inductive arguments are such that the content of the conclusion is in some way intended to "go beyond" the content of the premises. The premises of such an argument typically deal with some subject that is relatively familiar, and the conclusion then moves beyond this to a subject that is less familiar or that little is known about. Such an argument may take any of several forms: predictions about the future, arguments from analogy, inductive generalizations, arguments from authority, arguments based on signs, and causal inferences, to name just a few.

A **prediction** is an argument that proceeds from our knowledge of the past to a claim about the future. For example, someone might argue that because certain meteorological phenomena have been observed to develop over a certain region of central Missouri, a storm will occur there in six hours. Or again, one might argue that because certain fluctuations occurred in the prime interest rate on Friday, the value of the dollar will decrease against foreign currencies on Monday. Nearly everyone realizes that the future cannot be known with certainty; thus, whenever an argument makes a prediction about the future, one is usually justified in considering the argument inductive.

An **argument from analogy** is an argument that depends on the existence of an analogy, or similarity, between two things or states of affairs. Because of the existence of this analogy, a certain condition that affects the better-known thing or situation is concluded to affect the similar, lesser-known thing or situation. For example, someone might argue that because Christina's Porsche is a great handling car, it follows that Angela's Porsche must also be a great handling car. The argument depends on the existence of a similarity, or analogy, between the two cars. The certitude attending such an inference is probabilistic at best.

A **generalization** is an argument that proceeds from the knowledge of a selected sample to some claim about the whole group. Because the members of the sample have a certain characteristic, it is argued that all the members of the group have that same characteristic. For example, one might argue that because three oranges selected from a certain crate were especially tasty and juicy, all the oranges from that crate are especially tasty and juicy. Or again, one might argue that because six out of a total of nine members sampled from a certain labor union intend to vote for Johnson for union president, two-thirds of the entire membership intend to vote for Johnson. These examples illustrate the use of statistics in inductive argumentation.

An **argument from authority** is an argument that concludes something is true because a presumed expert or witness has said that it is. For example, a person might argue that earnings for Hewlett-Packard Corporation will be up in the coming quarter because of a statement to that effect by an investment counselor. Or a lawyer might argue that Mack the Knife committed the murder because an eyewitness testified to that effect under oath. Because the investment counselor and the eyewitness could be either mistaken or lying, such arguments are essentially probabilistic.

An **argument based on signs** is an argument that proceeds from the knowledge of a sign to a claim about the thing or situation that the sign symbolizes. The word "sign," as it is used here, means any kind of message (usually visual) produced by an intelligent being. For example, when driving on an unfamiliar highway one might see a sign indicating that the road makes several sharp turns one mile ahead. Based on this information, one might argue that the road does indeed make several sharp turns one mile ahead. Because the sign might be misplaced or in error about the turns, the conclusion is only probable.

A **causal inference** is an argument that proceeds from knowledge of a cause to a claim about an effect, or, conversely, from knowledge of an effect to a claim about a cause. For example, from the knowledge that a bottle of wine had been accidentally left in the freezer overnight, someone might conclude that it had frozen (cause to effect). Conversely, after tasting a piece of chicken and finding it dry and tough, one might conclude that it had been overcooked (effect to cause). Because specific instances of cause and effect can never be known with absolute certainty, one may usually interpret such arguments as inductive.

## Further Considerations

It should be noted that the various subspecies of inductive arguments listed here are not intended to be mutually exclusive. Overlaps can and do occur. For example, many causal inferences that proceed from cause to effect also qualify as predictions. The purpose of this survey is not to demarcate in precise terms the various forms of induction but rather to provide guidelines for distinguishing induction from deduction.

Keeping this in mind, we should take care not to confuse arguments in geometry, which are always deductive, with arguments from analogy or inductive generalizations. For example, an argument concluding that a triangle has a certain attribute (such as a right angle) because another triangle, with which it is congruent, also has that attribute might be mistaken for an argument from analogy. Similarly, an argument that concludes that all triangles have a certain attribute (such as angles totaling two right angles) because any particular triangle has that attribute might be mistaken for an inductive generalization. Arguments such as these, however, are always deductive, because the conclusion follows necessarily and with complete certainty from the premises.

One broad classification of arguments not listed in this survey is scientific arguments. Arguments that occur in science can be either inductive or deductive, depending on the circumstances. In general, arguments aimed at the *discovery* of a law of nature are usually considered inductive. Suppose, for example, that we want to discover a law that governs the time required for a falling body to strike the earth. We drop bodies of various weights from various heights and measure the time it takes them to fall. Comparing our measurements, we notice that the time is approximately proportional to the square root of the distance. From this we conclude that the time required for any body to fall is proportional to the square root of the distance through which it falls. Such an argument is best interpreted as an inductive generalization.

Another type of argument that occurs in science has to do with the *application* of known laws to specific circumstances. Arguments of this sort are often considered to be deductive—but only with certain reservations. Suppose, for example, that we want to apply Boyle's law for ideal gases to a container of gas in our laboratory. Boyle's law states that the pressure exerted by a gas on the walls of its container is inversely proportional to the volume. Applying this law, we conclude that when we reduce the volume of our laboratory sample by half, the pressure will double. Considered purely as a mathematical computation, this argument is deductive. But if we acknowledge the fact that the conclusion pertains to the future and the possibility that Boyle's law may not work in the future, then the argument is best considered inductive.

A final point needs to be made about the distinction between inductive and deductive arguments. There is a tradition extending back to the time of Aristotle that holds that inductive arguments are those that proceed from the particular to the general, while deductive arguments are those that proceed from the general to the particular. (A **particular statement** is one that makes a claim about one or more particular members of a class, while a **general statement** makes a claim about *all* the members of a class.) It is true, of course, that many inductive and deductive arguments do work in this way; but this fact should not be used as a criterion for distinguishing induction from deduction. As a matter of fact, there are deductive arguments that proceed from the general to the general, from the particular to the particular, and from the particular to the general, as well as from the general to the particular; and there are inductive arguments that do the same. For example, here is a deductive argument that proceeds from the particular to the general:

> Three is a prime number.
> Five is a prime number.
> Seven is a prime number.
> Therefore, all odd numbers between two and eight are prime numbers.

And here is one that proceeds from the particular to the particular:

> Gabriel is a wolf.
> Gabriel has a tail.
> Therefore, Gabriel's tail is the tail of a wolf.

Here is an inductive argument that proceeds from the general to the particular:

> All emeralds previously found have been green.
> Therefore, the next emerald to be found will be green.

The other varieties are easy to construct. Thus, the progression from particular to general, and vice versa, cannot be used as a criterion for distinguishing induction and deduction.

## Summary

To distinguish deductive arguments from inductive arguments, we attempt to evaluate the strength of the argument's inferential claim—how strongly the conclusion is claimed to follow from the premises. This claim is an objective feature of an argument, and it may or may not be related to the subjective intentions of the arguer.

To interpret an argument's inferential claim we look at three factors: special indicator words, the actual strength of the inferential link between premises and conclusion, and the character or form of argumentation. Given that we have more than one factor to look at, it is possible in a single argument for the occurrence of two of these factors to conflict with each other, leading to opposite interpretations. For example, in drawing a conclusion to a categorical syllogism (which is clearly deductive), an arguer might say "It probably follows that . . ." (which suggests induction). To help alleviate this conflict we can list the factors in order of importance:

1. Arguments in which the premises provide absolute support for the conclusion. Such arguments are always deductive.

2. Arguments having a specific deductive character or form (e.g., categorical syllogism). This factor is often of equal importance to the first, and, when present, it provides a clear-cut indication that the argument is deductive.

3. Arguments having a specific inductive character or form (e.g., a prediction). Arguments of this sort are nearly always best interpreted as inductive.

4. Arguments containing inductive indicator language (e.g., "It probably follows that . . ."). Since arguers rarely try to make their argument appear weaker than it really is, such language can usually be trusted. But if this language conflicts with one of the first two factors, it should be ignored.

5. Arguments containing deductive indicator language (e.g., "It necessarily follows that . . ."). Arguers occasionally use such language for rhetorical purposes, to make their argument appear stronger than it really is, so such language should be evaluated carefully.

6. Arguments in which the premises provide only probable support for the conclusion. This is the least important factor, and if it conflicts with any of the earlier ones, it should probably be ignored.

Unfortunately, many arguments in ordinary language are incomplete, so it often happens that none of these factors are clearly present. Determining the inductive or deductive character of such arguments may be impossible.

## EXERCISE 1.3

I. Determine whether the following arguments are best interpreted as being inductive or deductive. Also state the criteria you use in reaching your decision (i.e., the presence of indicator words, the nature of the inferential link between premises and conclusion, or the character or form of argumentation).

★1. Because triangle A is congruent with triangle B, and triangle A is isosceles, it follows that triangle B is isosceles.

2. The plaque on the leaning tower of Pisa says that Galileo performed experiments there with falling objects. It must be the case that Galileo did indeed perform those experiments there.

3. The rainfall in Seattle has been more than 15 inches every year for the past thirty years. Therefore, the rainfall next year will probably be more than 15 inches.

★4. No e-mail messages are eloquent creations. Some love letters are eloquent creations. Therefore, some love letters are not e-mail messages.

5. Amoco, Exxon, and Texaco are all listed on the New York Stock Exchange. It must be the case that all major American oil companies are listed on the New York Stock Exchange.

6. The longer a pendulum is, the longer it takes to swing. Therefore, when the pendulum of a clock is lengthened, the clock slows down.

★7. Paying off terrorists in exchange for hostages is not a wise policy, since such action will only lead them to take more hostages in the future.

8. The Matterhorn is higher than Mount Whitney, and Mount Whitney is higher than Mount Rainier. The obvious conclusion is that the Matterhorn is higher than Mount Rainier.

9. Although both front and rear doors were found open after the burglary, there were pry marks around the lock on the rear door and deposits of mud near the threshold. It must be the case that the thief entered through the rear door and left through the front.

★10. The *Encylopaedia Britannica* has an article on symbiosis. The *Encyclopedia Americana,* like the *Britannica,* is an excellent reference work. Therefore, the *Americana* probably also has an article on symbiosis.

11. Cholesterol is endogenous with humans. Therefore, it is manufactured inside the human body.

12. Either classical culture originated in Greece, or it originated in Egypt. Classical culture did not originate in Egypt. Therefore, classical culture originated in Greece.

★13. World-renowned physicist Stephen Hawking says that the condition of the universe at the instant of the Big Bang was more highly ordered than it is today. In view of Hawking's stature in the scientific community, we should conclude that this description of the universe is correct.

14. If Alexander the Great died from typhoid fever, then he became infected in India. Alexander the Great did die from typhoid fever. Therefore, he became infected in India.

15. Crater Lake, the deepest lake in the United States, was caused by a huge volcanic eruption 7700 years ago. Since human beings have lived around the mountain for more than 10,000 years, it is likely that people witnessed that eruption.

(National Park Service, "Crater Lake—Its History")

★16. Each element, such as hydrogen and iron, has a set of gaps—wavelengths that it absorbs rather than radiates. So if those wavelengths are missing from the spectrum, you know that that element is present in the star you are observing.

(Rick Gore, "Eyes of Science")

17. Because the apparent daily movement which is common to both the planets and the fixed stars is seen to travel from the east to the west, but the far slower single movements of the single planets travel in the opposite direction from west to east, it is therefore certain that these movements cannot depend on the common movement of the world but should be assigned to the planets themselves.

(Johannes Kepler, *Epitomy of Copernican Astronomy*)

18. Reserves of coal in the United States have an energy equivalent 33 times that of oil and natural gas. On a worldwide basis the multiple is about 10. By shifting to a coal-based economy, we could satisfy our energy requirements for at least a century, probably longer.

(William L. Masterson and Emil J. Slowinski, *Principles of Chemistry*)

★19. When the Romans occupied England, coal was burned. Since coal produces quite a bit of soot and sulfur dioxide, there must have been days almost 2000 years ago when the air in the larger towns was badly polluted.

(Stanley Gedzelman, *The Science and Wonders of the Atmosphere*)

20. The graphical method for solving a system of equations is an approximation, since reading the point of intersection depends on the accuracy with which the lines are drawn and on the ability to interpret the coordinates of the point.

(Karl J. Smith and Patrick J. Boyle, *Intermediate Algebra for College Students*)

21. That [the moons of Jupiter] revolve in unequal circles is manifestly deduced from the fact that at the longest elongation from Jupiter it is never possible to see two of these moons in conjunction, whereas in the vicinity of Jupiter they are found united two, three, and sometimes all four together.

(Galileo Galilei, *The Starry Messenger*)

★22. Lenses function by refracting light at their surfaces. Consequently, their action depends not only on the shape of the lens surfaces, but also on the indices of refraction of the lens material and the surrounding medium.

(Frank J. Blatt, *Principles of Physics,* 2nd ed.)

23. Given present growth rates in underdeveloped countries, the limited practice of birth control, and the difficulty of slowing the current growth momentum, it can be said with virtual certainty that none of the people now reading this book will ever live in a world where the population is not growing.

(J. John Palen, *Social Problems*)

24. The interpretation of the laws is the proper and peculiar province of the courts. A constitution is, in fact, and must be regarded by the judges, as a fundamental law. It therefore belongs to them to ascertain its meaning, as well as the meaning of any particular act proceeding from the legislative body.

(Alexander Hamilton, *Federalist Papers,* No. 78)

★25. The Simpson incident had shown me that a dog was kept in the stables, and yet, though someone had been in and had fetched out a horse, he had not barked enough to arouse the two lads in the loft. Obviously the midnight visitor was someone whom the dog knew well.

(A. Conan Doyle, *Memoirs of Sherlock Holmes*)

26. Eternity is simultaneously whole. But time has a before and an after. Therefore time and eternity are not the same thing.

(Thomas Aquinas, *Summa Theologica*)

27. Ordinary things that we encounter every day are electrically neutral. Therefore, since negatively charged electrons are a part of everything, positively charged particles must also exist in all matter.

(James E. Brady and Gerard E. Humiston, *General Chemistry*)

★28. Animals that live on plant foods must eat large quantities of vegetation, and this consumes much of their time. Meat eaters, by contrast, have no need to eat so much or so often. Consequently, meat-eating hominines [early humans] may have had more leisure time available to explore and manipulate their environment; like lions and leopards, they would have time to spend lying around and playing.

(William A. Haviland, *Cultural Anthropology*, 8th ed.)

29. [Psychologists] Wirtshafter and Davis noted that the glycerol content of the blood is related to the size of the fat cells [in the body]. Since the size of the fat cells would indicate something about the amount of stored fats, increases in blood glycerol should indicate increases in body weight.

(Herbert L. Petri, *Motivation: Theory and Research*, 2nd ed.)

30. Because the moon moves relative to the earth so that it returns to the same position overhead after about 25 hours, there are two high and two low tides at any point every 25 hours.

(Douglas C. Giancoli, *The Ideas of Physics*, 3rd ed.)

II. Define the following terms:

| | |
|---|---|
| deductive argument | argument from analogy |
| inductive argument | generalization |
| argument based on | prediction |
|     mathematics | argument from authority |
| argument from definition | argument based on signs |
| categorical syllogism | causal inference |
| hypothetical syllogism | particular statement |
| disjunctive syllogism | general statement |

III. Answer "true" or "false" to the following statements:

1. In an inductive argument, it is intended that the conclusion contain more information than the premises.

2. In a deductive argument, the conclusion is not supposed to contain more information than the premises.

3. The form of argumentation the arguer uses may allow one to determine whether an argument is inductive or deductive.

4. The actual strength of the link between premises and conclusion may allow one to determine whether an argument is inductive or deductive.

5. A geometrical proof is an example of an inductive argument.

6. Most arguments based on statistical reasoning are deductive.

7. If the conclusion of an argument follows merely from the definition of a word used in a premise, the argument is deductive.

8. An argument that draws a conclusion about a thing based on that thing's similarity to something else is a deductive argument.

9. An argument that draws a conclusion that something is true because some-one has said that it is, is a deductive argument.

10. An argument that presents two alternatives and eliminates one, leaving the other as the conclusion, is an inductive argument.

11. An argument that proceeds from knowledge of a cause to knowledge of an ef-fect is an inductive argument.

12. If an argument contains the phrase "it definitely follows that," then we know for certain that the argument is deductive.

13. An argument that predicts what will happen in the future, based on what has happened in the past, is an inductive argument.

14. Inductive arguments always proceed from the particular to the general.

15. Deductive arguments always proceed from the general to the particular.

IV. Page through a book, magazine, or newspaper and find two arguments, one in-ductive and the other deductive. Copy the arguments as written, giving the appro-priate reference. Then identify the premises and conclusion of each.

---

## 1.4    Validity, Truth, Soundness, Strength, Cogency

This section introduces the central ideas and terminology required to evaluate argu-ments. We have seen that every argument makes two basic claims: a claim that evi-dence or reasons exist and a claim that the alleged evidence or reasons support something (or that something follows from the alleged evidence or reasons). The first is a factual claim, the second an inferential claim. The evaluation of every argument centers on the evaluation of these two claims. The more important of the two is the inferential claim, because if the premises fail to support the conclusion (that is, if the reasoning is bad), an argument is worthless. Thus we will always test the inferential claim first, and only if the premises do support the conclusion will we test the factual claim (that is, the claim that the premises present genuine evidence, or are true). The material that follows considers first deductive arguments and then inductive.

### Deductive Arguments

The previous section defined a deductive argument as one incorporating the claim that it is impossible for the conclusion to be false given that the premises are true. If this claim is true, the argument is said to be valid. Thus, a **valid deductive argument** is an argument in which it is impossible for the conclusion to be false given that the premises are true. In these arguments the conclusion follows with strict necessity from the premises. Conversely, an **invalid deductive argument** is a deductive argument in which it *is* possible for the conclusion to be false given that the premises are true. In these arguments the conclusion does not follow with strict necessity from the premises, even though it is claimed to.

An immediate consequence of these definitions is that there is no middle ground between valid and invalid. There are no arguments that are "almost" valid and "almost" invalid. If the conclusion follows with strict necessity from the premises, the argument is valid; if not, it is invalid.

To test an argument for validity we begin by assuming that all the premises are true, and then we determine if it is possible, in light of that assumption, for the conclusion to be false. Here is an example:

> All television networks are media companies.
> NBC is a television network.
> Therefore, NBC is a media company.

In this argument both premises are actually true, so it is easy to *assume* that they are true. Next we determine, in light of this assumption, if it is possible for the conclusion to be false. Clearly this is not possible. If NBC is included in the group of television networks (second premise) and if the group of television networks is included in the group of media companies (first premise), it necessarily follows that NBC is included in the group of media companies (conclusion). In other words, assuming the premises to be true and the conclusion false entails a strict *contradiction*. Thus, the argument is valid.

Here is another example:

> All automakers are computer manufacturers.
> United Airlines is an automaker.
> Therefore, United Airlines is a computer manufacturer.

In this argument, both premises are actually false, but it is easy to assume that they are true. Every automaker could have a corporate division that manufactures computers. Also, in addition to flying airplanes, United Airlines could make cars. Next, in light of these assumptions, we determine if it is possible for the conclusion to be false. Again, we see that this is not possible, by the same reasoning as the previous example. Assuming the premises to be true and the conclusion false entails a contradiction. Thus, the argument is valid.

Another example:

> All banks are financial institutions.
> Wells Fargo is a financial institution.
> Therefore, Wells Fargo is a bank.

As in the first example, both premises of this argument are true, so it is easy to assume they are true. Next we determine, in light of this assumption, if it is possible for the conclusion to be false. In this case it *is* possible. If banks were included in one part of the group of financial institutions and Wells Fargo were included in another part, then Wells Fargo would *not* be a bank. In other words, assuming the premises to be true and the conclusion false does not involve any contradiction, and so the argument is invalid.

In addition to illustrating the basic idea of validity, these examples suggest an important point about validity and truth. In general, validity is not something that is uniformly determined by the actual truth or falsity of the premises and conclusion. Both the NBC example and the Wells Fargo example have actually true premises and an actually true conclusion, yet one valid and the other invalid. The United Airlines example has actually false premises and an actually false conclusion, yet the argument is

**Table 1.1  Deductive Arguments**

|  | Valid | Invalid |
|---|---|---|
| **True premises True conclusion** | All wines are beverages. Chardonnay is a wine. Therefore, chardonnay is a beverage. [sound] | All wines are beverages. Chardonnay is a beverage. Therefore, chardonnay is a wine. [unsound] |
| **True premises False conclusion** | None exist. | All wines are beverages. Ginger ale is a beverage. Therefore, ginger ale is a wine. [unsound] |
| **False premises True conclusion** | All wines are soft drinks. Ginger ale is a wine. Therefore, ginger ale is a soft drink. [unsound] | All wines are whiskeys. Chardonnay is a whiskey. Therefore, chardonnay is a wine. [unsound] |
| **False premises False conclusion** | All wines are whiskeys. Ginger ale is a wine. Therefore, ginger ale is a whiskey. [unsound] | All wines are whiskeys. Ginger ale is a whiskey. Therefore, ginger ale is a wine. [unsound] |

valid. Rather, validity is something that is determined by the *relationship* between premises and conclusion. The question is not whether the premises and conclusion are true or false, but whether the premises *support* the conclusion. In the examples of valid arguments the premises do support the conclusion, and in the invalid case they do not.

Nevertheless, there is *one* arrangement of truth and falsity in the premises and conclusion that does determine the issue of validity. Any deductive argument having actually true premises and an actually false conclusion is invalid. The reasoning behind this fact is fairly obvious. If the premises are actually true and the conclusion is actually false, then it certainly is *possible* for the premises to be true and the conclusion false. Thus, by the definition of invalidity, the argument is invalid.

The idea that any deductive argument having actually true premises and a false conclusion is invalid may be the most important point in all of deductive logic. The entire system of deductive logic would be quite useless if it accepted as valid any inferential process by which a person could start with truth in the premises and arrive at falsity in the conclusion.

Table 1.1 presents examples of deductive arguments that illustrate the various combinations of truth and falsity in the premises and conclusion. In the examples having false premises, both premises are false, but it is easy to construct other examples having only one false premise. When examining this table, note that the only combination of truth and falsity that does not allow for *both* valid and invalid arguments is true premises and false conclusion. As we have just seen, any argument having this combination is necessarily invalid.

The relationship between the validity of a deductive argument and the truth or falsity of its premises and conclusion, as illustrated in Table 1.1, is summarized as follows:

| Premises | Conclusion | Validity |
|:---:|:---:|:---:|
| T | T | ? |
| T | F | Invalid |
| F | T | ? |
| F | F | ? |

A **sound argument** is a deductive argument that is *valid* and has *all true premises.* Both conditions must be met for an argument to be sound; if either is missing the argument is unsound. Thus, an **unsound argument** is a deductive argument that is invalid, has one or more false premises, or both. Because a valid argument is one such that it is impossible for the premises to be true and the conclusion false, and because a sound argument does in fact have true premises, it follows that every sound argument, by definition, will have a true conclusion as well. A sound argument, therefore, is what is meant by a "good" deductive argument in the fullest sense of the term.

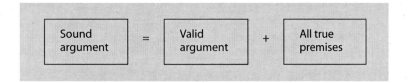

In connection with this definition of soundness, a single proviso is required: For an argument to be unsound, the false premise or premises must actually be needed to support the conclusion. An argument with a conclusion that is validly supported by true premises but with a superfluous false premise would still be sound. By similar reasoning, no addition of a false premise to an originally sound argument can make the argument unsound. Such a premise would be superfluous and should not be considered part of the argument. Analogous remarks, incidentally, extend to induction.

## Inductive Arguments

Section 1.3 defined an inductive argument as one incorporating the claim that it is improbable that the conclusion be false given that the premises are true. If this claim is true, the argument is said to be strong. Thus, a **strong inductive argument** is an inductive argument in which it is improbable that the conclusion be false given that the premises are true. In such arguments, the conclusion does in fact follow probably from the premises. Conversely, a **weak inductive argument** is an argument in which the conclusion does not follow probably from the premises, even though it is claimed to.

The procedure for testing the strength of inductive arguments runs parallel to the procedure for deduction. First we assume the premises are true, and then we determine whether, based on that assumption, the conclusion is probably true. Example:

> All dinosaur bones discovered to this day have been at least 50 million years old. Therefore, probably the next dinosaur bone to be found will be at least 50 million years old.

In this argument the premise is actually true, so it is easy to assume that it is true. Based on that assumption, the conclusion is probably true, so the argument is strong. Here is another example:

> All meteorites found to this day have contained sugar. Therefore, probably the next meteorite to be found will contain sugar.

The premise of this argument is obviously false. But if we assume the premise is true, then based on that assumption, the conclusion would probably be true. Thus, the argument is strong.

The next example is an argument from analogy:

> When a lighted match is slowly dunked into water, the flame is snuffed out. But gasoline is a liquid, just like water. Therefore, when a lighted match is slowly dunked into gasoline, the flame will be snuffed out.

In this argument the premises are actually true and the conclusion is probably false. Thus, if we assume the premises are true, then, based on that assumption, it is not probable that the conclusion is true. Thus, the argument is weak.

Another example:

> During the past fifty years, inflation has consistently reduced the value of the American dollar. Therefore, industrial productivity will probably increase in the years ahead.

In this argument, the premise is actually true and the conclusion is probably true in the actual world, but the probability of the conclusion is in no way based on the assumption that the premise is true. Because there is no direct connection between inflation and increased industrial productivity, the premise is irrelevant to the conclusion and it provides no probabilistic support for it. The conclusion is probably true independently of the premise. As a result, the argument is weak.

This last example illustrates an important distinction between strong inductive arguments and valid deductive arguments. As we will see in later chapters, if the conclusion of a deductive argument is necessarily true independently of the premises, the argument is still considered valid. But if the conclusion of an inductive argument is probably true independently of the premises, the argument is weak.

These four examples show that in general the strength or weakness of an inductive argument results not from the actual truth or falsity of the premises and conclusion, but from the probabilistic support the premises give to the conclusion. The dinosaur argument has a true premise and a probably true conclusion, and the meteorite argument has a false premise and a probably false conclusion; yet both are strong because the premise of each provides probabilistic support for the conclusion. The industrial productivity argument has a true premise and a probably true conclusion, but the argument is weak because the premise provides no probabilistic support for the conclusion. As in the evaluation of deductive arguments, the only arrangement of truth and

Table 1.2  **Inductive Arguments**

|  | **Strong** | **Weak** |
|---|---|---|
| **True premise**<br><br>**Probably true conclusion** | All previous U.S. presidents were older than 40.<br>Therefore, probably the next U.S. president will be older than 40.<br><br>[cogent] | A few U.S. presidents were lawyers.<br>Therefore, probably the next U.S. president will be older than 40.<br><br>[uncogent] |
| **True premise**<br><br>**Probably false conclusion** | None exist | A few U.S. presidents were unmarried.<br>Therefore, probably the next U.S. president will be unmarried<br><br>[uncogent] |
| **False premise**<br><br>**Probably true conclusion** | All previous U.S. presidents were TV debaters.<br>Therefore, probably the next U.S. president will be a TV debater.<br><br>[uncogent] | A few U.S. presidents were dentists.<br>Therefore, probably the next U.S. president will be a TV debater.<br><br>[uncogent] |
| **False premise**<br><br>**Probably false conclusion** | All previous U.S. presidents died in office.<br>Therefore, probably the next U.S. president will die in office.<br><br>[uncogent] | A few U.S. presidents were dentists.<br>Therefore, probably the next U.S. president will be a dentist.<br><br>[uncogent] |

falsity that establishes anything is true premises and probably false conclusion (as in the lighted match argument). Any inductive argument having true premises and a probably false conclusion is weak.

Table 1.2 presents the various possibilities of truth and falsity in the premises and conclusion of inductive arguments. Note that the only arrangement of truth and falsity that is missing for strong arguments is true premises and probably false conclusion.

The relationship between the strength of an inductive argument and the truth or falsity of its premises and conclusion, as illustrated in Table 1.2, is summarized as follows:

| Premises | Conclusion | Strength |
|---|---|---|
| T | prob. T | ? |
| T | prob. F | Weak |
| F | prob. T | ? |
| F | prob. F | ? |

Unlike the validity and invalidity of deductive arguments, the strength and weakness of inductive arguments admit of degrees. To be considered strong, an inductive argument must have a conclusion that is more probable than improbable. In other words, given that the premises are true, the likelihood that the conclusion is true must be more than 50 percent, and as the probability increases, the argument becomes stronger. For this purpose, consider the following pair of arguments:

> This barrel contains 100 apples.
> Three apples selected at random were found to be ripe.
> Therefore, probably all 100 apples are ripe.

> This barrel contains 100 apples.
> Eighty apples selected at random were found to be ripe.
> Therefore, probably all 100 apples are ripe.

The first argument is weak and the second is strong. However, the first is not absolutely weak nor the second absolutely strong. Both arguments would be strengthened or weakened by the random selection of a larger or smaller sample. For example, if the size of the sample in the second argument were reduced to seventy apples, the argument would be weakened. The incorporation of additional premises into an inductive argument will also generally tend to strengthen or weaken it. For example, if the premise "One unripe apple that had been found earlier was removed" were added to either argument, the argument would be weakened.

A **cogent argument** is an inductive argument that is *strong* and has *all true premises;* if either condition is missing, the argument is uncogent. Thus, an **uncogent argument** is an inductive argument that is weak, has one or more false premises, or both. A cogent argument is the inductive analogue of a sound deductive argument and is what is meant by a "good" inductive argument without qualification. Because the conclusion of a cogent argument is genuinely supported by true premises, it follows that the conclusion of every cogent argument is probably true.

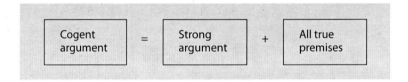

There is a difference, however, between sound and cogent arguments in regard to the true premise requirement. In a sound argument it is necessary only that the premises be true and nothing more. Given such premises and good reasoning, a true conclusion is guaranteed. In a cogent argument, on the other hand, the premises must not only be true, but they must also not ignore some important piece of evidence that entails a quite different conclusion. This is called the *total evidence requirement.* As an illustration of the need for it, consider the following argument:

> Swimming in the Caribbean is usually lots of fun. Today the water is warm, the surf
>     is gentle, and on this beach there are no dangerous currents. Therefore, it would
>     be fun to go swimming here now.

If the premises reflect all the important factors, then the argument is cogent. But if they ignore the fact that several large dorsal fins are cutting through the water (suggesting sharks), then obviously the argument is not cogent. Thus, for cogency the premises must not only be true but also not overlook some important fact that requires a different conclusion.

## Summary

For both deductive and inductive arguments, two separate questions need to be answered: (1) Do the premises support the conclusion? (2) Are all the premises true?

To answer the first question we begin by *assuming* the premises to be true. Then, for deductive arguments we determine whether, in light of this assumption, it *necessarily* follows that the conclusion is true. If it does, the argument is valid; if not, it is invalid. For inductive arguments we determine whether it *probably* follows that the conclusion is true. If it does, the argument is strong; if not, it is weak. For inductive arguments we keep in mind the requirements that the premises actually support the conclusion and that they not ignore important evidence. Finally, if the argument is either valid or strong, we turn to the second question and determine whether the premises are actually true. If all the premises are true, the argument is sound (in the case of deduction) or cogent (in the case of induction). All invalid deductive arguments are unsound, and all weak inductive arguments are uncogent.

The various alternatives open to statements and arguments may be diagrammed as follows. Note that in logic one never speaks of an argument as being "true" or "false," and one never speaks of a statement as being "valid," "invalid," "strong," or "weak."

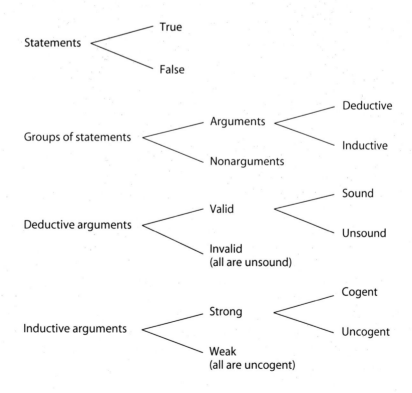

## ■ EMINENT LOGICIANS

### *Chrysippus* 280–206 B.C.

© Araldo de Luca/CORBIS

Chrysippus was born in Soli, a city located in the south east coast of Asia Minor. Early in life he moved to Athens, where he studied under the Stoic philosopher Cleanthes, who in turn was a student of Zeno of Citium, the founder of Stoicism. Upon Cleanthes' death in 232 B.C., Chrysippus took over as leader of the school, and he produced over 700 treatises that systematized Stoic teaching. All of these works have been lost, but fragments survive in the writings of Cicero, Seneca, and others. Because of his extraordinary contribution, Chrysippus is considered to be the second founder of Stoicism.

Stoicism derives its name from the Greek word *stoa,* which means porch; stoic philosophers used to gather on a porch in the Agora (marketplace) in Athens to discuss their views. The stoics prized the virtue of self-sufficiency, and they emphasized the importance of not allowing oneself to be carried away by emotions or passions such as fear or love. Emotions are considered to be false judgments about the goodness or badness of something . The proper therapy for those victimized by emotions is to persuade them that these judgments are indeed false because they constitute obstacles to true happiness.

Chrysippus is often considered to be the originator of propositional logic. Unlike Aristotelian logic, where the fundamental components are terms, in propositional logic the fundamental components are whole propositions or statements. Aristotle had overlooked this kind of logic, but his close friend and successor Theophrastus worked out some of the logic of the pure hypothetical syllogism (If *A* then *B*, if *B* then *C;* therefore if *A* then *C*). Also, Philo of Megara introduced the truth functional interpretation of the material conditional (If *A,* then *B*). Beginning at this point, Chrysippus advanced propositional logic to a high level of development.

Chrysippus divided propositions into simple and compound, and he introduced a set of connectives that were used to produce compound propositions from one or more simple propositions. The compound propositions included negation, conjunction, exclusive disjunction, and implication, and Chrysippus showed how the truth value of a compound statement is a function of the truth values of its simple components. Chrysippus also introduced a set of rules of inference including what is today called *modus ponens, modus tollens,* disjunctive syllogism, and a rule similar to De Morgan's rule. Finally, he introduced the theory of natural deduction by which the conclusion of an argument can be derived from its premises through a series of discrete steps.

The broader philosophy of Chrysippus is characterized by monism and determinism. While most of us think that the universe is made up of millions of discrete entities, Chrysippus argued that in fact only one substance exists, and what appear to be individual substances are really parts of this one primary substance. Furthermore, everything that occurs is strictly governed by fate. Yet, in the face of this rigid causal determinism Chrysippus held that humans are responsible for their actions, and he tried in many ways to prove that the two viewpoints are in fact compatible with each other.

### EXERCISE 1.4

I. The following arguments are deductive. Determine whether each is valid or invalid, and note the relationship between your answer and the truth or falsity of the premises and conclusion. Finally, determine whether the argument is sound or unsound.

★1. Since *Moby Dick* was written by Shakespeare, and *Moby Dick* is a science fiction novel, it follows that Shakespeare wrote a science fiction novel.

2. Since London is north of Paris and south of Edinburgh, it follows that Paris is south of Edinburgh.

3. If George Washington was beheaded, then George Washington died. George Washington died. Therefore, George Washington was beheaded.

★4. The longest river in South America is the Amazon, and the Amazon flows through Brazil. Therefore, the longest river in South America flows through Brazil.

5. Since the Spanish-American War occurred before the U.S. Civil War, and the U.S. Civil War occurred after the Korean War, it follows that the Spanish-American War occurred before the Korean War.

6. The Empire State Building is taller than the Statue of Liberty, and the Statue of Liberty is taller than the Eiffel Tower. Therefore, the Empire State Building is taller than the Eiffel Tower.

★7. All leopards with lungs are carnivores. Therefore, all leopards are carnivores.

8. Chicago is a city in Michigan and Michigan is part of the United States. Therefore, Chicago is a city in the United States.

9. If Senator Hillary Clinton represents California, then she represents a western state. Hillary Clinton does not represent a western state. Therefore, she does not represent California.

★10. Every province in Canada has exactly one city as its capital. Therefore, since there are thirty provinces in Canada, there are thirty provincial capitals.

11. Since the Department of Defense Building outside Washington, D.C., has the shape of a hexagon, it follows that it has seven sides.

12. Since Winston Churchill was English, and Winston Churchill was a famous statesman, we may conclude that at least one Englishman was a famous statesman.

★13. Since some fruits are green, and some fruits are apples, it follows that some fruits are green apples.

14. All physicians are individuals who have earned degrees in political science, and some lawyers are physicians. Therefore, some lawyers are persons who have earned degrees in political science.

15. The United States Congress has more members than there are days in the year. Therefore, at least two members of Congress have the same birthday.

II. The following arguments are inductive. Determine whether each is strong or weak, and note the relationship between your answer and the truth or falsity of the premise(s) and conclusion. Then determine whether each argument is cogent or uncogent.

★1. The grave marker at Arlington National Cemetery says that John F. Kennedy is buried there. It must be the case that Kennedy really is buried in that cemetery.

2. The ebb and flow of the tides has been occurring every day for millions of years. But nothing lasts forever. Therefore, probably the motion of the tides will die out within a few years.

3. The vast majority of Rose Bowl games (in Pasadena, California) have been played in freezing cold weather. Therefore, probably the next Rose Bowl game will be played in freezing cold weather.

★4. Franklin Delano Roosevelt said that we have nothing to fear but fear itself. Therefore, women have no reason to fear serial rapists.

5. Most popular film stars are millionaires. Lindsay Lohan is a popular film star. Therefore, probably Lindsay Lohan is a millionaire.

6. Constructing the great pyramid at Giza required lifting massive stone blocks to great heights. Probably the ancient Egyptians had some antigravity device to accomplish this feat.

★7. People have been listening to rock and roll music for over a hundred years. Probably people will still be listening to it a year from now.

8. Paleontologists have unearthed the fossilized bones of huge reptiles, which we have named dinosaurs. Tests indicate that these bones are more than 50 million years old. Therefore, probably dinosaurs really did roam the earth 50 million years ago.

9. The Declaration of Independence says that all men are endowed by their creator with certain unalienable rights. Therefore it probably follows that a creator exists.

★10. Coca-Cola is an extremely popular soft drink. Therefore, probably someone, somewhere, is drinking a Coke right this minute.

11. Every map of the United States shows that Alabama is situated on the Pacific coast. Therefore, Alabama must be a western state.

12. When Neil Armstrong landed on the moon, he left behind a gold-plated Schwinn bicycle, which he used to ride around on the moon's surface. Probably that bicycle is still up there on the moon.

★13. The African American athlete LaDainian Tomlinson is able to withstand tremendous impacts on the football field. However, Serena Williams, like LaDainian Tomlinson, is a great African American athlete. Therefore, Serena Williams should be able to withstand tremendous impacts on the football field.

14. Unlike monkeys, today's humans have feet that are not suited for grasping objects. Therefore, a thousand years from now, probably humans will still have feet that are not suited for grasping objects.

15. A random sample of twenty-five famous country and western singers, including Garth Brooks and Dolly Parton, revealed that every single one of them

studied music in Tasmania. Therefore, probably the majority of famous country and western singers studied music in Tasmania.

III. Determine whether the following arguments are inductive or deductive. If an argument is inductive, determine whether it is strong or weak. If it is deductive, determine whether it is valid or invalid.

★1. Since Agatha is the mother of Raquel and the sister of Tom, it follows that Tom is the uncle of Raquel.

2. When a cook cannot recall the ingredients in a recipe, it is appropriate that she refresh her memory by consulting the recipe book. Similarly, when a student cannot recall the answers during a final exam, it is appropriate that she refresh her memory by consulting the textbook.

3. The sign on the highway leading into Denver, Colorado, says that the city's elevation is 5280 feet. It must be the case that Denver is 1 mile high.

★4. Since Christmas is always on a Thursday, it follows that the day after Christmas is always a Friday.

5. This figure is a Euclidean triangle. Therefore, the sum of its angles is equal to two right angles.

6. By accident Karen baked her brownies two hours longer than she should have. Therefore, they have probably been ruined.

★7. After taking LSD, Alice said she saw a flying saucer land in the shopping center parking lot. Since Alice has a reputation for always telling the truth, we must conclude that a flying saucer really did land there.

8. Since Phyllis is the cousin of Denise, and Denise is the cousin of Harriet, it follows necessarily that Harriet is the cousin of Phyllis.

9. The picnic scheduled in the park for tomorrow will most likely be cancelled. It's been snowing for six days straight.

★10. Circle A has exactly twice the diameter of circle B. From this we may conclude that circle A has exactly twice the area of circle B.

11. Robert has lost consistently at blackjack every day for the past several days. Therefore, it is very likely that he will win today.

12. Since John loves Nancy and Nancy loves Peter, it follows necessarily that John loves Peter.

★13. This cash register drawer contains over 100 coins. Three coins selected at random were found to have dates earlier than 1945. Therefore, probably all of the coins in the drawer have dates earlier than 1945.

14. The Japanese attack on Pearl Harbor happened in either 1941 or 1951. But it didn't happen in 1941. Therefore, it happened in 1951.

15. Harry will never be able to solve that difficult problem in advanced calculus in the limited time allowed. He has never studied anything beyond algebra, and in that he earned only a C−.

★16. Since $x + y = 10$, and $x = 7$, it follows that $y = 4$.

17. If acupuncture is hocus pocus, then acupuncture cannot relieve chronic pain. But acupuncture can relieve chronic pain. Therefore, acupuncture is not hocus pocus.

18. If inflation heats up, then interest rates will rise. If interest rates rise, then bond prices will decline. Therefore, if inflation heats up, then bond prices will decline.

★19. Statistics reveal that 86 percent of those who receive flu shots do not get the flu. Jack received a flu shot one month ago. Therefore, he should be immune, even though the flu is going around now.

20. Since Michael is a Pisces, it necessarily follows that he was born in March.

IV. Define the following terms:

| | |
|---|---|
| valid argument | strong argument |
| invalid argument | weak argument |
| sound argument | cogent argument |
| unsound argument | uncogent argument |

V. Answer "true" or "false" to the following statements:

1. Some arguments, while not completely valid, are almost valid.
2. Inductive arguments admit of varying degrees of strength and weakness.
3. Invalid deductive arguments are basically the same as inductive arguments.
4. If a deductive argument has true premises and a false conclusion, it is necessarily invalid.
5. A valid argument may have a false premise and a false conclusion.
6. A valid argument may have a false premise and a true conclusion.
7. A sound argument may be invalid.
8. A sound argument may have a false conclusion.
9. A strong argument may have false premises and a probably false conclusion.
10. A strong argument may have true premises and a probably false conclusion.
11. A cogent argument may have a probably false conclusion.
12. A cogent argument must be inductively strong.
13. If an argument has true premises and a true conclusion, we know that it is a perfectly good argument.
14. A statement may legitimately be spoken of as "valid" or "invalid."
15. An argument may legitimately be spoken of as "true" or "false."

## 1.5　　Argument Forms: Proving Invalidity

This section explores the idea that the validity of a deductive argument is determined by the **argument form**. This idea was suggested in the arguments about wines and beverages presented in Table 1.1 in the previous section. All the arguments in the valid column have the same form, and all the arguments in the invalid column have the same form.

Yet, in the exercises at the end of that section we saw many cases of valid deductive arguments that did not have any recognizable form. How can we reconcile this fact with the claim that validity is determined by form? The answer is that these arguments are incomplete, so the form is not explicit. But once such arguments are completed and correctly phrased (which we address later in this book), the form becomes apparent. For example, consider the following valid argument:

Geese are migratory waterfowl, so they fly south for the winter.

This argument is missing a premise:

Migratory waterfowl fly south for the winter.

The argument can now be rephrased to make its form apparent:

All geese are migratory waterfowl.
All migratory waterfowl are birds that fly south for the winter.
Therefore, all geese are birds that fly south for the winter.

The form of the argument is

All *A* are *B*.
All *B* are *C*.
_____
All *A* are *C*.

This form is valid, and it captures the reasoning process of the argument. If we assume that the *A*s (whatever they might be) are included in the *B*s, and that the *B*s (whatever they might be) are included in the *C*s, then the *A*s must necessarily be included in the *C*s. This necessary relationship between the *A*s, *B*s, and *C*s is what makes the argument valid. This is what we mean when we say that the validity of a deductive argument is determined by its form.

Since validity is determined by form, it follows that any argument that has this valid form is a valid argument. Thus, we might substitute "daisies" for *A*, "flowers" for *B*, and "plants" for *C* and obtain the following valid argument:

All daisies are flowers.
All flowers are plants.
Therefore, all daisies are plants.

Any argument such as this that is produced by uniformly substituting terms or statements in place of the letters in an argument form is called a **substitution instance** of that form.

Let us now consider an invalid argument form:

All *A* are *B*.
All *C* are *B*.
_____
All *A* are *C*.

In this argument form, if we assume that the *A*s are in the *B*s and that the *C*s are in the *B*s, it does not *necessarily* follow that the *A*s are in the *C*s. It would not follow if the

As were in one part of the *B*s and the *C*s were in another part, as the following diagram illustrates:

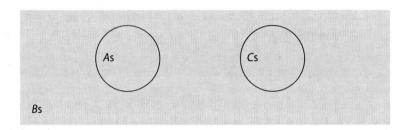

This diagram suggests that we can prove the form invalid if we can find a substitution instance having actually true premises and an actually false conclusion. In such a substitution instance the *A*s and the *C*s would be separated from each other, but they would both be included in the *B*s. If we substitute "cats" for *A*, "animals" for *B*, and "dogs" for *C*, we have such a substitution instance:

| All *A* are *B*. | All cats are animals. | True |
|---|---|---|
| All *C* are *B*. | All dogs are animals. | True |
| All *A* are *C*. | Therefore, all cats are dogs. | False |

This substitution instance proves the form invalid, because it provides a concrete example of a case where the *A*s are in the *B*s, the *C*s are in the *B*s, but the *A*s are *not* in the *C*s.

Now, since the form is invalid, can we say that any argument that has this form is invalid? Unfortunately, the situation with invalid forms is not quite as simple as it is with valid forms. Every substitution instance of a valid form is a valid argument, but it is not the case that every substitution instance of an invalid form is an invalid argument. The reason is that some substitution instances of invalid forms are also substitution instances of valid forms.* However, we can say that any substitution instance of an invalid form is an invalid argument *provided* that it is not a substitution instance of any valid form. Thus we will say that an argument actually *has* an invalid form if it is a substitution instance of that form and it is not a substitution instance of any valid form.

The fact that some substitution instances of invalid forms are also substitution instances of valid forms means simply that we must exercise caution in identifying the

---

*For example, the following valid argument is a substitution instance of the invalid form we have been discussing:

All bachelors are persons.
All unmarried men are persons.
Therefore, all bachelors are unmarried men.

However, because "bachelors" is equivalent in meaning to "unmarried men," the argument is also a substitution instance of this valid form:

All *A* are *B*.
All *A* are *B*.
All *A* are *A*.

form of an argument. However, cases of ordinary language arguments that can be interpreted as substitution instances of both valid and invalid forms are so rare that this
book chooses to ignore them. With this in mind, consider the following argument:

> All romantic novels are literary pieces.
> All works of fiction are literary pieces.
> Therefore, all romantic novels are works of fiction.

This argument clearly has the invalid form just discussed. This invalid form captures the reasoning process of the argument, which is obviously defective. Therefore,
the argument is invalid, and it is invalid precisely because it has an invalid form.

## Counterexample Method

A substitution instance having true premises and a false conclusion (like the cats-and-
dogs example just constructed) is called a counterexample, and the method we have
just used to prove the romantic-novels argument invalid is called the **counterexample
method.** It consists of isolating the form of an argument and then constructing a substitution instance having true premises and a false conclusion. This proves the form
invalid, which in turn proves the argument invalid. The counterexample method can
be used to prove the invalidity of any invalid argument, but it cannot prove the validity of any valid argument. Thus, before the method is applied to an argument, the argument must be known or suspected to be invalid in the first place. Let us apply the
counterexample method to the following invalid categorical syllogism:

> Since some employees are not social climbers and all vice presidents are employees,
> we may conclude that some vice presidents are not social climbers.

This argument is invalid because the employees who are not social climbers might
not be vice presidents. Accordingly, we can *prove* the argument invalid by constructing
a substitution instance having true premises and a false conclusion. We begin by isolating the form of the argument:

> Some E are not S.
> All V are E.
> —————————
> Some V are not S.

Next, we select three terms to substitute in place of the letters that will make the
premises true and the conclusion false. The following selection will work:

> E = animals
> S = mammals
> V = dogs

The resulting substitution instance is this:

> Some animals are not mammals.
> All dogs are animals.
> Therefore, some dogs are not mammals.

The substitution instance has true premises and a false conclusion and is therefore, by definition, invalid. Because the substitution instance is invalid, the form is invalid, and therefore the original argument is invalid.

In applying the counterexample method to categorical syllogisms, it is useful to keep in mind the following set of terms: "cats," "dogs," "mammals," "fish," and "animals." Most invalid syllogisms can be proven invalid by strategically selecting three of these terms and using them to construct a counterexample. Because everyone agrees about these terms, everyone will agree about the truth or falsity of the premises and conclusion of the counterexample. Also, in constructing the counterexample, it often helps to begin with the conclusion. First, select two terms that yield a false conclusion, and then select a third term that yields true premises. Another point to keep in mind is that the word "some" in logic always means "at least one." For example, the statement "Some dogs are animals" means "At least one dog is an animal"—which is true. Also note that this statement does not imply that some dogs are not animals.

Not all deductive arguments, of course, are categorical syllogisms. Consider, for example, the following hypothetical syllogism:

> If the government imposes import restrictions, the price of automobiles will rise. Therefore, since the government will not impose import restrictions, it follows that the price of automobiles will not rise.

This argument is invalid because the price of automobiles might rise even though import restrictions are not imposed. It has the following form:

> If G, then P.
> Not G.
> _____
> Not P.

This form differs from the previous one in that its letters stand for complete statements. G, for example, stands for "The government imposes import restrictions." If we make the substitution

> G = Abraham Lincoln committed suicide.
> P = Abraham Lincoln is dead.

we obtain the following substitution instance:

> If Abraham Lincoln committed suicide, then Abraham Lincoln is dead.
> Abraham Lincoln did not commit suicide.
> Therefore, Abraham Lincoln is not dead.

Since the premises are true and the conclusion false, the substitution instance is clearly invalid. Therefore, the form is invalid, and this proves the original argument invalid.

When applying the counterexample method to an argument having a conditional statement as a premise (such as the one just discussed), it is recommended that the statement substituted in place of the conditional statement express some kind of necessary connection. In the Lincoln example, the first premise asserts the necessary connection between suicide and death. There can be no doubt about the truth of such a statement. Furthermore, if it should turn out that the conclusion is a conditional state-

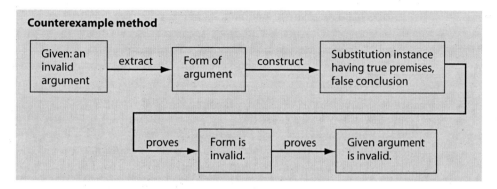

**Counterexample method**

ment, note that one sure way of producing a false conditional statement is by joining a true antecedent with a false consequent. For example, the conditional statement "If Lassie is a dog, then Lassie is a cat" is clearly false.

Being able to identify the form of an argument with ease requires a familiarity with the basic deductive argument forms. The first task consists in distinguishing the premises from the conclusion. Always write the premises first and the conclusion last. The second task involves distinguishing what we may call "form words" from "content words." To reduce an argument to its form, leave the form words as they are, and replace the content words with letters. For categorical syllogisms, the words "all," "no," "some," "are," and "not" are form words, and for hypothetical syllogisms the words "if," "then," and "not" are form words. Additional form words for other types of arguments are "either," "or," "both," and "and." For various kinds of hybrid arguments, a more intuitive approach may be needed. Here is an example:

> All movie stars are actors who are famous, because all movie stars who are famous are actors.

If we replace "movie stars," "actors," and "famous" with the letters *M*, *A*, and *F*, this argument has the following form:

> All *M* who are *F* are *A*.
> _____
> All *M* are *A* who are *F*.

Here is one possible substitution instance for this form:

> All humans who are fathers are men.
> Therefore, all humans are men who are fathers.

Because the premise is true and the conclusion false, the form is invalid and so is the original argument.

Using the counterexample method to prove arguments invalid requires a little ingenuity because there is no rule that will automatically produce the required term or statement to be substituted into the form. Any term or statement will work, of course, provided that it yields a substitution instance that has premises that are indisputably true and a conclusion that is indisputably false. Ideally, the truth value of these statements should be known to the average individual; otherwise, the substitution instance cannot be depended on to prove anything. If, for example, *P* in the earlier hypothetical syllogism had been replaced by the statement "George Wilson is dead," the substitution instance would be useless, because nobody knows whether this statement is true or false.

The counterexample method is useful only for proving invalidity, because the only arrangement of truth and falsity that proves anything is true premises and false conclusion. If a substitution instance is produced having true premises and a true conclusion, it does *not* prove that the argument is valid. Furthermore, the method is useful only for deductive arguments because the strength and weakness of inductive arguments is only partially dependent on the form of the argument. Accordingly, no method that relates exclusively to the form of an inductive argument can be used to prove the argument weak.

## EXERCISE 1.5

I.  Use the counterexample method to prove the following categorical syllogisms invalid. In doing so, follow the suggestions given in the text.

★1. All galaxies are structures that contain black holes in the center, so all galaxies are quasars, since all quasars are structures that contain black holes in the center.

2. Some evolutionists are not people who believe in the Bible, for no creationists are evolutionists, and some people who believe in the Bible are not creationists.

3. No patents are measures that discourage research and development, and all patents are regulations that protect intellectual property. Thus, no measures that discourage research and development are regulations that protect intellectual property.

★4. Some farm workers are not people who are paid decent wages, because no illegal aliens are people who are paid decent wages, and some illegal aliens are not farm workers.

5. Some politicians are people who will stop at nothing to win an election, and no people who will stop at nothing to win an election are true statesmen. Hence, no politicians are true statesmen.

6. All meticulously constructed timepieces are true works of art, for all Swiss watches are true works of art and all Swiss watches are meticulously constructed timepieces.

★7. No patrons of fast-food restaurants are health-food addicts. Consequently, no patrons of fast-food restaurants are connoisseurs of fine desserts, since no connoisseurs of fine desserts are health-food addicts.

8. Some toxic dumps are sites that emit hazardous wastes, and some sites that emit hazardous wastes are undesirable places to live near. Thus, some toxic dumps are undesirable places to live near.

9. All persons who assist others in suicide are people guilty of murder. Accordingly, some individuals motivated by compassion are not persons guilty of murder, inasmuch as some people who assist others in suicide are individuals motivated by compassion.

★10. Some school boards are not groups that oppose values clarification, because some school boards are not organizations with vision, and some groups that oppose values clarification are not organizations with vision.

II. Use the counterexample method to prove each of the following arguments invalid.

★1. If animal species are fixed and immutable, then evolution is a myth. Therefore, evolution is not a myth, since animal species are not fixed and immutable.

2. If carbon dioxide is present in the atmosphere, then plants have a source of carbon. Hence, since plants have a source of carbon, carbon dioxide is present in the atmosphere.

3. If human rights are recognized, then civilization flourishes. If equality prevails, then civilization flourishes. Thus, if human rights are recognized, then equality prevails.

★4. If energy taxes are increased, then either the deficit will be reduced or conservation will be taken seriously. If the deficit is reduced, then inflation will be checked. Therefore, if energy taxes are increased, then inflation will be checked.

5. All homeless people who are panhandlers are destitute individuals. Therefore, all homeless people are destitute individuals.

6. Some wrestlers are colorful hulks, since some wrestlers are colorful and some wrestlers are hulks.

★7. All community colleges with low tuition are either schools with large enrollments or institutions supported by taxes. Therefore, all community colleges are institutions supported by taxes.

8. All merchandisers that are retailers are businesses that are inventory rotators. Therefore, all merchandisers are inventory rotators.

9. All diabetes victims are either insulin takers or glucose eliminators. Accordingly, some diabetes victims are glucose eliminators, since some diabetes victims are insulin takers.

★10. All FHA loans are living-standard enhancers for the following reasons. All reverse mortgages that are FHA loans are either living-standard enhancers or home equity depleters, and all reverse mortgages are home equity depleters.

---

## 1.6        Extended Arguments

The logical analysis of extended arguments, such as those found in editorials, essays, and lengthy letters to newspaper editors, involves numerous difficulties. Such arguments are often mixed together with fragments of reports, pieces of expository writing, illustrations, explanations, and statements of opinion. Proper analysis involves weeding out the extraneous material and isolating premises and conclusions. Another problem stems from the fact that lengthy arguments often involve complex arrangements of subarguments that feed into the main argument in various ways. Distinguishing one subargument from another is often a complicated task. And then there are some argumentative passages that involve completely separate strands of argumentation leading to separate conclusions. Again, distinguishing the strands and assigning premises to the right conclusion not only is problematic but often involves an element of creativity on the part of the analyst.

To facilitate the analysis of extended arguments, we will assign numerals to the various statements in the passage and use arrows to represent the inferential links. Example:

① The contamination of underground aquifers represents a pollution problem of
catastrophic proportions. ② Half the nation's drinking water, which comes from
these aquifers, is being poisoned by chemical wastes dumped into the soil for
generations.

This argument is diagrammed as follows:

The diagram says that statement ②, the premise, supports statement ①, the conclusion.

In extended arguments we can identify two distinct patterns of argumentation,
which we will name the vertical pattern and the horizontal pattern. The *vertical pattern* consists of a series of arguments in which a conclusion of a logically prior argument becomes a premise of a subsequent argument. Example:

① The selling of human organs, such as hearts, kidneys, and corneas, should be outlawed. ② Allowing human organs to be sold will inevitably lead to a situation in
which only the rich will be able to afford transplants. This is so because ③ whenever something scarce is bought and sold as a commodity, the price always goes
up. ④ The law of supply and demand requires it.

This argument is diagrammed as follows:

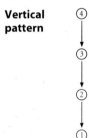

**Vertical
pattern**

The diagram says that statement ①, which is the main conclusion, is supported by ②,
which in turn is supported by ③, which in turn is supported by ④.

The *horizontal pattern* consists of a single argument in which two or more premises
provide independent support for a single conclusion. If one of the premises were omitted, the other(s) would continue to support the conclusion in the same way. Example:

① The selling of human organs, such as hearts, kidneys, and corneas, should be outlawed. ② If this practice is allowed to get a foothold, people in desperate financial
straits will start selling their own organs to pay their bills. Alternately, ③ those
with a criminal bent will take to killing healthy young people and selling their organs on the black market. ④ In the final analysis, the buying and selling of human
organs comes just too close to the buying and selling of life itself.

The diagram for this argument is as follows:

**Horizontal pattern**

This diagram says that statements ②, ③, and ④ support ① independently.

Two variations on the horizontal and vertical patterns occur when two or more premises support a conclusion *conjointly,* and when one or more premises support *multiple* conclusions. The first variation occurs when the premises depend on one another in such a way that if one were omitted, the support that the others provide would be diminished or destroyed. The following argument illustrates the occurrence of conjoint premises:

> ① Getting poor people off the welfare rolls requires that we modify their behavior patterns. ② The vast majority of people on welfare are high school dropouts, single parents, or people who abuse alcohol and drugs. ③ These behavior patterns frustrate any desire poor people may have to get a job and improve their condition in life.

Statement ① is the conclusion. Taken separately, statements ② and ③ provide little or no support for ①, but taken together they do provide support. That is, ② and ③ support ① *conjointly.* This relationship between the premises is illustrated by the use of the brace in the following diagram:

**Conjoint premises**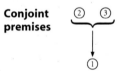

The next example illustrates the occurrence of a multiple conclusion:

> ① Dropping out of school and bearing children outside of marriage are two of the primary causes of poverty in this country. Therefore, ② to eliminate poverty we must offer incentives for people to get high school diplomas. Also, ③ we must find some way to encourage people to get married before they start having children.

In this passage statement ① supports both ② and ③. Since no single argument can have more than one conclusion, the passage is correctly evaluated as consisting of two arguments. For our purposes, however, we will treat it as if it were a single argument by joining the two conclusions with a brace:

**Multiple conclusion**

Our symbolism is now sufficiently developed to analyze most arguments found in editorials and letters to the editor of newspapers and magazines. Consider the following argument, taken from a newspaper editorial:

> ① Government mandates for zero-emission vehicles won't work because ② only electric cars qualify as zero-emission vehicles, and ③ electric cars won't sell. ④ They are too expensive, ⑤ their range of operation is too limited, and ⑥ recharging facilities are not generally available.
>
> (William Campbell, "Technology Is Not Good Enough")

We immediately see that ① is the main conclusion, and ② and ③ support ① conjointly. Also, ④, ⑤, and ⑥ support ③ independently. The argument pattern is as follows:

The next argument is taken from a letter to the editor:

> ① Rhinos in Kenya are threatened with extinction because ② poachers are killing them for their horn. Since ③ the rhino has no natural predators, ④ it does not need its horn to survive. Thus ⑤ there should be an organized program to capture rhinos in the wild and remove their horn. ⑥ Such a program would eliminate the incentive of the poachers.
>
> (Pamela C. Wagner, "Rhino Poaching")

First we search for the final conclusion. We select ⑤, because it is the ultimate point that the passage attempts to establish. Next we survey the premise and conclusion indicators. From this, we see that ② supports ① and ③ supports ④. Finally, we see that ①, ④, and ⑥ support ⑤. Yet these supporting statements depend on one another for their effect. Thus, they support the final conclusion conjointly. The argument pattern is as follows:

The next argument is taken from a magazine article:

> ① Skating is a wonderful form of exercise and relaxation, but ② today's rollerbladers are a growing menace and ③ something should be done to control them. ④ Rollerbladers are oblivious to traffic regulations as ⑤ they breeze through red lights and ⑥ skim down the wrong way on one-way streets. ⑦ They pose a threat to pedestrians because ⑧ a collision can cause serious injury. ⑨ Rollerbladers are

even a hazard to shopkeepers as ⑩ they zoom through stores and ⑪ damage merchandise.

(Joan Schmidt, "Hell—On Wheels")

After reading the argument, we see that ① is merely an introductory sentence, and ② and ③ together compose the main conclusion. Also, ④, ⑦, and ⑨ support the main conclusion independently, while ⑤ and ⑥ support ④ independently, ⑧ supports ⑦, and ⑩ and ⑪ support ⑨ independently. The diagram is as follows:

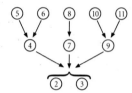

The next argument is taken from the science column of a newspaper:

> ① We can expect small changes to occur in the length of our calendar year for an indefinite time to come. ② This is true for two reasons. ③ First, the rotation of the earth exhibits certain irregularities. ④ And why is this so? ⑤ The rotation of any body is affected by its distribution of mass, and ⑥ the earth's mass distribution is continually subject to change. For example, ⑦ earthquakes alter the location of the tectonic plates. Also, ⑧ the liquid core of the earth sloshes as the earth turns, and ⑨ rainfall redistributes water from the oceans. The second reason is that ⑩ the motion of the tides causes a continual slowing down of earth's rotation. ⑪ Tidal motion produces heat, and ⑫ the loss of this heat removes energy from the system.

(Isaac Asimov, "As the World Turns")

Preliminary analysis reveals that the final conclusion is ①. Also, ② tells us that the supporting statements are divided into two basic groups, but since ② does not add any support, we can leave it out of the diagram. In the first group, ⑤ and ⑥ support ③ conjointly, while ⑦, ⑧, and ⑨ support ⑥ independently. ④ will not appear in the diagram, because it serves merely as a premise indicator. In the second group, ⑪ and ⑫ support ⑩ conjointly. Thus, the argument pattern is as follows:

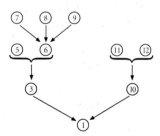

Our last example is taken from a letter to the editor of a newspaper:

> ① Community college districts save a great deal of money by hiring untenured part-time instructors, but ② the extensive use of these instructors is a disadvantage to

the students. ③ Most part-time instructors are paid only 60 percent of what a full-time teacher earns, and as a result, ④ they are forced to teach five or six courses just to survive. ⑤ This detracts from the opportunity to consult with students outside the classroom. To make matters worse, ⑥ many part-timers are not even given office space. Furthermore, ⑦ the lower pay demoralizes the part-timer, and ⑧ the lack of tenure makes for constant financial insecurity. ⑨ Obviously these conditions render the instructor less receptive to student needs. Lastly, because ⑩ these part-timers are burning the candle from both ends, ⑪ they have no spare energy to improve their courses, and ⑫ many lack the enthusiasm to motivate their students. As a result, ⑬ the educational process is impaired.

(Gordon Dossett et al., "Part-Time College Instructors")

Preliminary analysis reveals that the main conclusion is not ① but ②. Also, we see three main reasons why part-timers are a disadvantage to students: They have little opportunity to consult with students, they are less receptive to student needs, and the educational process is impaired by ⑪ and ⑫. In the first main branch, the indicator "as a result" shows that ③ supports ④, and ④ and ⑥ independently support ⑤. In the second branch, ⑦ and ⑧ independently support ⑨. In the third, ⑩ supports both ⑪ and ⑫, which in turn support ⑬ independently. Here is the argument pattern:

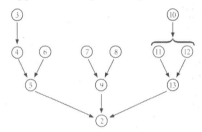

I.  The following arguments were abstracted from newspaper articles, editorials, and letters to the editor. Use the method presented in this section to construct argument patterns. If a statement is redundant or plays no role in the argument, do not include it in the pattern.

★1.  ① The conditions under which many food animals are raised are unhealthy for humans. ② To keep these animals alive, large quantities of drugs must be administered. ③ These drugs remain in the animals' flesh and are passed on to the humans who eat it.

(Philip D. Oliver, "We Can Eat Ribs and Still Be Humane")

2.  ① The development of carbon-embedded plastics, otherwise called "composits," is an important new technology because ② it holds the key for new aircraft and spacecraft designs. This is so because ③ these composits are not only stronger than steel but lighter than aluminum.

(Thomas H. Maugh II, "Composits—The Lightweight Champs of Aircraft Industry")

3. ① Homework stifles the thrill of learning in the mind of the student. ② It in-
stills an oppressive learn-or-else discipline. ③ It quenches the desire for
knowledge and the love of truth. For these reasons ④ homework should never
be assigned.

(Colman McCarthy, "Homework's Tyranny Hobbles
Promising Minds")

★4. ① When parents become old and destitute, the obligation of caring for them
should be imposed on their children. ② Clearly, children owe a debt to their
parents. ③ Their parents brought them into the world and cared for them
when they were unable to care for themselves. ④ This debt could be appropriately discharged by having grown children care for their parents.

(Gary Jones, "The Responsibility of Parents")

5. ① Defending the war on drugs may not be fashionable, but the fact remains
that ② hardcore drugs should remain illegal. ③ As long as hardcore drugs are
illegal, they are harder to get, and ④ the social stigma of being arrested deters
many users.

(Charles Van DeVenter, "I'm Proof: The War on Drugs Is Working")

6. ① The rain forest of Brazil produces oxygen for the whole world, yet ② it
yields no monetary return to that country. Given that ③ the industrialized
nations consume the most oxygen, ④ those nations ought to pay Brazil an
annual fee for the use of its rain forest.

(Diane B. Robinson, letter to the editor)

★7. ① It appears that animals may be able to predict earthquakes. ② Prior to a
major quake in China, hundreds of snakes suddenly appeared from hiberna-
tion and froze to death in the snow, ③ fish were seen leaping from rivers and
lakes, and ④ cows and horses refused to enter barns. Also, ⑤ prior to a quake
in Fremont, California, a flood of callers reported strange behavior from their
pets and domestic animals.

(Michael Bowker, "Can Animals Really Predict Earthquakes?")

8. ① Contributions to relief organizations are often wasted. ② Food sent to war
torn countries rarely reaches its destination, because ③ food distribution is
controlled by the warring groups, and ④ these groups sell the food to buy
weapons and ammunition.

(Michael Maren, "The Faces of Famine")

9. ① Research leading to the development of a scramjet engine is worthwhile. ②
Commercial aircraft incorporating such an engine could cross the Pacific in
as little as two hours. ③ This would relieve the fatigue of flights from New
York to Tokyo. Also, ④ such an engine could power future orbiting spacecraft.

(T. A. Heppenheimer, "A Plane for Space")

★10. ① There is a lot of pressure on untenured college teachers to dumb down
their courses. ② Administrators tend to rehire teachers who bring in more

money, and ③ teachers who dumb down their classes do precisely this. Why? Because ④ easier classes attract more students, and ⑤ more students means more money for the school.

(Lynne Drury Lerych, "Meeting the Bottom Line in the College Biz")

II. The following arguments gradually increase in difficulty. Use the method presented in this section to construct argument patterns. If a statement is redundant or plays no role in the argument, do not include it in the pattern.

★1. ① Many people believe that the crime of bribery cannot extend to campaign contributions. ② From a legal standpoint, however, countless campaign contributions are in fact bribes. ③ A bribe is anything of value or advantage given with the intent to unlawfully influence the person to whom it is given in his official capacity. ④ A campaign contribution is certainly something of value or advantage. Furthermore, ⑤ every contribution from a lobbyist or special interest group is given with the intent to influence voting, and ⑥ thousands of such contributions are made in every important election.

(Daniel Hays Lowenstein, "Can Candidates Run for Political Office Without Taking Bribes?")

2. ① America's farm policy desperately needs revamping. ② Seventy-three cents of every farm program dollar ends up in the pockets of the nation's super-farmers. As a result, ③ the mid-sized family farms are being squeezed out of existence. Also, ④ our farm policy courts environmental disaster. ⑤ Federal subsidies encourage farmers to use enormous amounts of fertilizer and pesticides. ⑥ These chemicals percolate down through the soil and pollute limited groundwater.

(Osha Gray Davidson, "Rise of America's Rural Ghetto")

3. ① Society values white lives more than black lives. This is clear from the fact that ② killers of whites are much more likely to be sentenced to death than killers of blacks. ③ Of the 1788 people currently on death row, 1713 were convicted of killing a white person. Yet ④ blacks are six times more likely to be murder victims than whites are. ⑤ In Florida, no one has ever been executed for murdering a black person, but ⑥ dozens have been executed for murdering white people.

(*Los Angeles Times* editorial, "Death and Race")

★4. ① Powerful new particle accelerators are important in high-energy physics, and ② they are worth their cost because ③ they will allow scientists to produce and capture significant quantities of Z particles. ④ Z particles result from the collision of positrons and electrons, and ⑤ particle accelerators are needed to achieve significant numbers of these collisions. ⑥ Z particles are thought to be the bearers of the weak nuclear force, and ⑦ learning the nature of this force may lead to the development of entirely new sources of energy.

(Lee Dye, "Linear Collider: Bold Gamble in Atomic Physics")

5. ① For years our country has been providing Japan unlimited access to our technology while getting little in return. ② Currently 7,000 Japanese graduate students study science and engineering in the U.S., ③ while only 1,000 Americans are engaged in similar studies in Japan. Also, ④ our government laboratories are open to the Japanese, but ⑤ Japanese laboratories are not open to Americans. ⑥ To remedy this imbalance, Japan should subsidize our universities, and also ⑦ it should help defray the costs of our laboratories.

(William C. Norris, "Technology Must Travel 2-Way Street")

6. ① All men crave material success because ② it serves as an insurance policy against sexual rejection. This is true because ③ women love men who are successful. ④ Both men and women want power, and ⑤ success is the form of power women feel most deprived of. Thus, ⑥ women try to achieve it vicariously through men. ⑦ As the 5-foot 6-inch Dustin Hoffman once put it, "When I was in high school, women wouldn't touch me with a 10-foot pole. Now I can't keep them away with a 10-foot pole."

(Warren Farrell, "Success Story: From Frog to Prince")

★7. ① Cigarette consumption could be easily reduced by simply outlawing tailor-made cigarettes. ② The manufacture of tailor-made cigarettes to American standards is a high-tech industry. ③ It cannot be done in small illicit labs like the processing of PCP, cocaine or heroin. ④ The availability of quality tobacco for hand-rolling would discourage the development of an illegal tailor-made market. ⑤ Most people would not pay the premium prices demanded by an illicit market for a product of unknown quality. ⑥ They could roll a high-quality product for themselves. ⑦ Truly addicted persons would continue to smoke no matter how inconvenient. But ⑧ most would give it up as too much bother before it became a deeply ingrained habit.

(Richard Sand, "An Easy Way to Reduce Cigarette Consumption")

8. ① Flesh food is not a necessity in the human diet, as ② nutritionally adequate alternatives are readily available. ③ Many people in the world thrive on a nonmeat diet. ④ Indeed, vegetarian Seventh-Day Adventists in this country live an average of six years longer than their meat-eating counterparts. ⑤ The National Academy of Science warns that our fat-laden diet is directly responsible for much of the heart disease and cancer that afflict so many. ⑥ At a time when people are starving in certain parts of the world, it should be noted that a steer must consume sixteen pounds of grain and soy to produce one pound of meat. ⑦ The grain and soybeans we feed our meat-producing animals would feed every hungry mouth in the world many times over. ⑧ Cattle are competing with humans for food. ⑨ Clearly, a reassessment of the whole concept of killing and eating animals is in order.

(Suzanne Sutton, "Killing Animals for Food—Time for a Second Look")

9. ① The argument has been made that to cut down on teenage drunk driving we should increase the federal excise tax on beer. ② Such a measure, however, would almost certainly fail to achieve its intended result. ③ Teenagers are notoriously insensitive to cost. ④ They gladly accept premium prices for the latest style in clothes or the most popular record albums. And then, ⑤ those who drink and drive already risk arrest and loss of driving privileges. ⑥ They would not think twice about paying a little more for a six-pack. Finally, ⑦ the situation is not as bleak as it has been made to appear. ⑧ The fatality rate for teenage drivers is lower today than it has been in years.

(James C. Sanders, "Increased U.S. Tax on Beer")

★10. ① It has been widely acknowledged that the quality of undergraduate education in this country is diminishing. ② An often unrecognized cause of this malady is the exploitative way that universities as employers treat their part-time and temporary faculty members. ③ In many universities there are no formal guidelines for evaluating the work of these instructors. As a result, ④ poor instructors who solicit the favor of the department chairman are often retained over better ones who do not. ⑤ Another factor is the low pay given to these instructors. ⑥ In order to survive, many of them must accept heavy teaching loads spread out over three or four institutions. ⑦ The quality of instruction can only suffer when faculty members stretch themselves so thin. Lastly, because ⑧ part-time and temporary faculty are rarely members of the faculty senate, ⑨ they have no voice in university governance. But ⑩ without a voice, the shoddy conditions under which they work are never brought to light.

(Michael Schwalbe, "Part-Time Faculty Members Deserve a Break")

11. ① Doctors who attend elderly people in nursing homes often prescribe tranquilizers to keep these people immobile. ② This practice is often unwarranted, and ③ it often impairs the health of the patients. ④ These tranquilizers often have damaging side effects in that ⑤ they accentuate the symptoms of senility, and ⑥ they increase the likelihood of a dangerous fall because ⑦ they produce unsteadiness in walking. Furthermore, since ⑧ these medications produce immobility, ⑨ they increase the risk of bedsores. ⑩ Doctors at the Center for Aging and Health say that physicians who care for the elderly are simply prescribing too much medication.

(Hal Willard, "At 90, the Zombie Shuffle")

12. ① All of us have encountered motorists who will go to any length to get a parking spot within 20 feet of the door they expect to enter. ② This obsession with good parking spots transcends all logic. ③ It might take 5 minutes to secure the ideal spot in a store parking lot, ④ while a more distant spot that is immediately available is only a 40-second walk from the door. ⑤ Waiting for that ideal spot also results in frenzied nerves and skyrocketing blood pressure. ⑥ Inevitably the occupant of the desired space will preen her hair before departing, and ⑦ all the while the cars backed up behind the waiting driver are blaring their horns. ⑧ Parking a little farther away is usually easier and safer

because ⑨ you can pull out more quickly, and ⑩ it avoids damage to car doors by adjacent parkers.

(Gwinn Owens, "A Ridiculous Addiction")

★13. ① The state has a right to intervene on behalf of unborn children, and ② this right should be implemented immediately. ③ While it may be true that a mere fetus has no rights, ④ surely a born child does have rights, and ⑤ these rights project backward to the time it was in the womb. This is true because ⑥ what happens to the child in the womb can have an impact throughout the child's life. ⑦ It is well known that alcohol and drug abuse by expectant mothers cause birth defects, and ⑧ these defects are not correctable after birth. ⑨ Granted, an expectant mother has the right to treat her own body as she chooses, but ⑩ this right does not extend to her unborn child. ⑪ Once a pregnant woman decides to give birth, she effectively transfers part of her rights over to her unborn child. ⑫ Unfortunately, however, the unborn child is incapable of securing these rights for itself. Thus, ⑬ the intervention of a higher power is justified.

(Alan Dershowitz, "Drawing the Line on Prenatal Rights")

14. ① A manned trip to Mars is a justified scientific goal because ② it affords a unique opportunity to explore the origins of the solar system and the emergence of life. However, ③ from a scientific standpoint, an initial landing on the tiny Martian moons, Phobos and Deimos, would be more rewarding than a landing on the planet itself. Because ④ the Martian terrain is rugged, ⑤ humans would not be able to venture far, ⑥ nor could they operate a robot vehicle without the use of a satellite, since ⑦ Mars's mountains would block their view. ⑧ Explorers on Phobos and Deimos could easily send robot vehicles to the planet's surface. ⑨ Using Mars's moons as a base would also be better than unmanned exploration directed from the Houston space center. Because ⑩ the distance is so great, ⑪ radio signals to and from Mars can take as long as an hour. Thus, ⑫ driving an unmanned rover from Earth, step by step, would be a time-consuming operation. ⑬ Sample returns to Earth would take months instead of hours, and ⑭ follow-on missions would be years apart instead of days, further slowing the process of exploration.

(S. Fred Singer, "The Case for Going to Mars")

15. ① There are lots of problems with the U.S. airline system, but ② deregulation isn't one of them. ③ Airline deregulation has delivered most of what it promised when enacted in 1978. ④ It has held down fares, ⑤ increased competition, ⑥ and raised the industry's efficiency. ⑦ Despite claims to the contrary, airline safety has not suffered. And, ⑧ with some exceptions, service to some cities and towns has improved. ⑨ On average, fares are lower today than in 1980. ⑩ Morrison and Winston estimate that fares are 20% to 30% below what they would be under regulation. ⑪ Competition has increased because ⑫ prior to deregulation airlines had protected routes. ⑬ After deregulation this changed. ⑭ Efficiency has also improved. ⑮ After deregulation the percentage of occupied seats jumped by 10% and miles traveled by 32%. ⑯ Despite fears that

airlines would cut unprofitable service to small communities, most smaller cities and towns experienced a 20% to 30% increase in flight frequency. Lastly, ⑰ travel on U.S. airlines remains among the safest forms of transportation. ⑱ Between 1975 and 1985, deaths resulting from crashes totaled fewer than 3000.

(Robert J. Samuelson, "Let's Not Regulate the Deregulated Airlines")

III. Turn to the editorial pages of a newspaper and select an editorial that contains an argument. Keep in mind that some editorials are really reports and contain no arguments at all. Also, few editorials are as neat and straightforward as the selections presented in Parts I and II of this exercise. Guest editorials on the opinion-editorial page (usually opposite the editorial page) are often better written than those on the editorial page. Analyze the argument (or arguments) according to the method presented in this section. Begin by placing a numeral at the beginning of each statement. Compound statements having components that are claimed to be true may be broken up into parts and the parts enumerated accordingly. Numerals should usually be placed after genuine premise and conclusion indicators even when they occur in the middle of a statement. Do *not,* however, break up conditional statements into antecedent and consequent. Proceed to identify the main conclusion (or conclusions) and determine how the other statements provide support. Any statement that does not play a direct role in the argument should be left out of the final argument pattern.

## Summary

Logic is the study of the evaluation of arguments, which are lists of statements consisting of one or more premises and one conclusion. Premises can be distinguished from conclusion by the occurrence of indicator words ("hence," "therefore," "since," and so on) or an inferential relation among the statements. Because not all groups of statements are arguments, it is important to be able to distinguish arguments from nonarguments. This is done by attending to indicator words, the presence of an inferential relation among the statements, and typical kinds of nonarguments. Typical nonarguments include warnings, loosely associated statements, reports, expository passages, illustrations, conditional statements, and explanations.

Arguments are customarily described as deductive or inductive. Deductive arguments are those in which the conclusion is claimed to follow necessarily from the premises, while inductive arguments are those in which the conclusion is claimed to follow only probably from the premises. The two can be distinguished by attending to special indicator words ("it necessarily follows that," "it probably follows that," and so on), the actual strength of the inferential relation, and typical forms or styles of deductive and inductive argumentation. Typical deductive arguments include arguments based on mathematics, arguments from definition, and categorical, hypothetical, and disjunctive syllogisms. Typical inductive arguments include predictions, arguments from analogy, generalizations, arguments from authority, arguments based on signs, and causal inferences.

The evaluation of arguments involves two steps: evaluating the link between premises and conclusion, and evaluating the truth of the premises. Deductive arguments in which the conclusion actually follows from the premises are said to be valid, and those that also have true premises are said to be sound. Inductive arguments in which the conclusion actually follows from the premises are said to be strong, and those that also have true premises are said to be cogent. The terms "true" and "false" apply not to arguments, but to statements. The truth and falsity of premises and conclusion is only indirectly related to validity, but any deductive argument having true premises and a false conclusion is invalid.

The validity of a deductive argument is determined by the form of the argument. An argument form that allows for a substitution instance having true premises and a false conclusion is an invalid form, and any argument having that form is an invalid argument. This fact leads to the counterexample method for proving invalidity. This method consists in identifying the form of a given invalid argument and then constructing a counterexample having premises that are indisputably true and a conclusion that is indisputably false.

The structure of longer arguments may be disclosed by the application of a method consisting of arrows and braces that show how the various premises support intermediate conclusions, and how the latter in turn support the main conclusion. Four basic argument patterns are the vertical pattern, horizontal pattern, conjoint premises, and multiple conclusion.

# Answers to Selected Exercises

## Exercise 1.1

I.

1. P:    Titanium combines readily with oxygen, nitrogen, and hydrogen, all of which have an adverse effect on its mechanical properties.

   C:    Titanium must be processed in their absence.

4. P:    When individuals voluntarily abandon property, they forfeit any expectation of privacy in it that they might have had.

   C:    A warrantless search and seizure of abandoned property is not unreasonable under the Fourth Amendment.

7. $P_1$:   After October 1963, when Hurricane Flora devastated the island and killed more than a thousand people, the Cuban government overhauled its civil defense system.

   $P_2$:   It was so successful that when six powerful hurricanes thumped Cuba between 1996 and 2002 only 16 people died.

   $P_3$:   And when Hurricane Ivan struck Cuba in 2004 there was not a single casualty, but the same storm killed at least 70 people in other Caribbean countries.

   C:    Cuba's record on disaster prevention is impressive.

10. $P_1$:   Punishment, when speedy and specific, may suppress undesirable behavior.

    $P_2$:   Punishment cannot teach or encourage desirable alternatives.

    C:    It is crucial to use positive techniques to model and reinforce appropriate behavior that the person can use in place of the unacceptable response that has to be suppressed.

13. $P_1$:   Private property helps people define themselves.

    $P_2$:   Private property frees people from mundane cares of daily subsistence.

    $P_3$:   Private property is finite.

    C:    No individual should accumulate so much property that others are prevented from accumulating the necessities of life.

16. $P_1$:   The nations of planet earth have acquired nuclear weapons with an explosive power equal to more than a million Hiroshima bombs.

    $P_2$:   Studies suggest that explosion of only half these weapons would produce enough soot, smoke, and dust to blanket the earth, block out the sun, and bring on a nuclear winter that would threaten the survival of the human race.

    C:    Radioactive fallout isn't the only concern in the aftermath of nuclear explosions.

19. $P_1$:   Antipoverty programs provide jobs for middle-class professionals in social work, penology, and public health.

    $P_2$:   Such workers' future advancement is tied to the continued growth of bureaucracies dependent on the existence of poverty.

    C:    Poverty offers numerous benefits to the nonpoor.

22. P:   Take the nurse who alleges that physicians enrich themselves in her hospital through un-necessary surgery; the engineer who discloses safety defects in the braking systems of a fleet of new rapid-transit vehicles; the Defense Department official who alerts Congress to military graft and overspending: All know that they pose a threat to those whom they de-nounce and that their own careers may be at risk.

    C:   The stakes in whistle-blowing are high.

25. $P_1$:   It is generally accepted that by constantly swimming with its mouth open, the shark is simply avoiding suffocation.

    $P_2$:   This assures a continuous flow of oxygen-laden water into the shark's mouth, over its gills, and out through the gill slits.

    C:   Contrary to the tales of some scuba divers, the toothy, gaping grin on the mouth of an approaching shark is not necessarily anticipatory.

28. $P_1$:   Anyone familiar with our prison system knows that there are some inmates who behave little better than brute beasts.

    $P_2$:   If the death penalty had been truly effective as a deterrent, such prisoners would long ago have vanished.

    C:   The very fact that these prisoners exist is a telling argument against the efficacy of capital punishment as a deterrent.

## II.

1. College sports are as much driven by money as are professional sports.

4. Business majors are robbing themselves of the true purpose of collegiate academics, a sacrifice that outweighs the future salary checks.

7. The religious intolerance of television preachers must not be tolerated.

10. Protecting the environment requires that we limit population growth.

## Exercise 1.2

## I.

1. Nonargument; explanation.

4. Nonargument; illustration.

7. Argument (conclusion: If stem-cell research is restricted, then people will die prematurely).

10. Nonargument; report.

13. Nonargument; opinion.

16. Nonargument; piece of advice.

19. Argument (conclusion: For organisms at the sea surface, sinking into deep water usually means death).

22. Argument (conclusion: Atoms can combine to form molecules whose properties generally are very different from those of the constituent atoms).

25. Nonargument; explanation.

28. Argument (conclusion: A person never becomes truly self-reliant).

31. This passage could be both an argument and an explanation (conclusion: In areas where rats are a problem, it is very difficult to exterminate them with bait poison).

34. Nonargument; loosely associated statements.

## II.

1. Nonargument.

4. Nonargument.

7. Argument (conclusion: The poor quality of parenting and the lack in continuity of adult care provided to many U.S. children contribute to a passivity and a sense of helplessness that hobbles individuals for the remainder of their lives).

10. Nonargument.

**VI.**

1. Sufficient: If something is a tiger, then it is an animal.
4. Necessary: If a person has no racket, then he/she cannot play tennis. *Or,* If a person plays tennis, then he/she has a racket.
7. Sufficient: If leaves burn, then smoke is produced.
10. Necessary: If a person does not open the door, then he/she cannot cross the threshold. *Or,* If a person crosses the threshold, then he/she has opened the door.

## Exercise 1.3

**I.**

1. Deductive (argument based on mathematics; also, conclusion follows necessarily from the premises).
4. Deductive (categorical syllogism; also, conclusion follows necessarily from the premises).
7. Inductive (causal inference; also, conclusion follows only probably from the premise).
10. Inductive (argument from analogy; also, conclusion follows only probably from the premise).
13. Inductive (argument from authority; also, conclusion follows only probably from the premise).
16. Deductive (conclusion follows necessarily from the premise).
19. Inductive (causal inference; also, conclusion follows only probably from the premises).
22. Deductive (conclusion follows necessarily from the premise; this example might also be interpreted as an argument from definition—the definition of "refraction").
25. Inductive (causal inference: The dog's familiarity with the visitor caused the dog to be silent).
28. Inductive (causal inference; also, the word "may" suggests a probabilistic inference).

## Exercise 1.4

**I.**

1. Valid, unsound; false premises, false conclusion.
4. Valid, sound; true premises, true conclusion.
7. Invalid, unsound; true premise, true conclusion.
10. Valid, unsound; false premise, false conclusion.
13. Invalid, unsound; true premises, true conclusion.

**II.**

1. Strong, cogent; true premise, probably true conclusion.
4. Weak, uncogent; true premise, probably false conclusion.
7. Strong, uncogent; false premise, probably true conclusion.
10. Strong, cogent; true premise, probably true conclusion.
13. Weak, uncogent; true premises, probably false conclusion.

**III.**

| | | |
|---|---|---|
| 1. Deductive, valid. | 7. Inductive, weak. | 13. Inductive, weak. |
| 4. Deductive, valid. | 10. Deductive, invalid. | 16. Deductive, invalid. |
| | | 19. Inductive, strong. |

## Exercise 1.5

**I.**

1. All *G* are *S*.              All cats are animals. (T)
   All *Q* are *S*.              All dogs are animals. (T)
   All *G* are *Q*.              All cats are dogs. (F)

**4.** No *I* are *P*.
Some *I* are not *F*.
Some *F* are not *P*.

No fish are mammals. (T)
Some fish are not cats. (T)
Some cats are not mammals. (F)

**7.** No *P* are *H*.
No *C* are *H*.
No *P* are *C*.

No dogs are fish. (T)
No mammals are fish. (T)
No dogs are mammals. (F)

**10.** Some *S* are not *O*.
Some *G* are not *O*.
Some *S* are not *G*.

Some dogs are not fish. (T)
Some animals are not fish. (T)
Some dogs are not animals. (F)

**II.**

**1.** If *A* then *E*.
Not *A*.
Not *E*.

If George Washington was assassinated, then
George Washington is dead. (T)
George Washington was not assassinated. (T)
George Washington is not dead. (F)

**4.** If *E*, then either *D* or *C*.
If *D*, then *I*.
If *E*, then *I*.

If Tom Cruise is a man, then he is either
a mouse or a human. (T)
If Tom Cruise is a mouse, then he has a tail. (T)
If Tom Cruise is a man, then he has a tail. (F)

**7.** All *C* with *L* are either
*S* or *I*.
All *C* are *I*.

All cats with fur are either mammals or dogs. (T)
All cats are dogs. (F)

**10.** All *R* that are *F* are either
*L* or *H*.
All *R* are *H*.
All *F* are *L*.

All cats that are mammals are either
dogs or animals. (T)
All cats are animals. (T)
All mammals are dogs. (F)

**Exercise 1.6**

**I.**

1.

4.

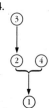

7.

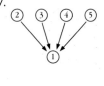

10.

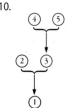

**II.**

1.

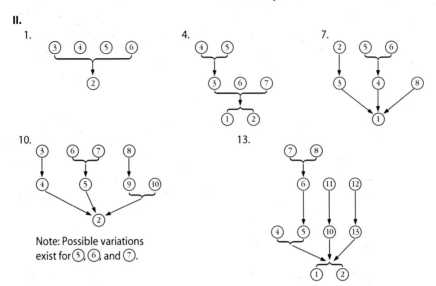

4.

7.

10.

Note: Possible variations
exist for ⑤, ⑥, and ⑦.

13.

# 2

# Language: Meaning and Definition

## 2.1    Varieties of Meaning

Ordinary language, as most of us are at least vaguely aware, serves various functions in our day-to-day lives. The twentieth-century philosopher Ludwig Wittgenstein thought the number of these functions to be virtually unlimited. Thus, among many other things, language is used to

| | |
|---|---|
| ask questions | tell jokes |
| tell stories | flirt with someone |
| tell lies | give directions |
| guess at answers | sing songs |
| form hypotheses | issue commands |
| launch verbal assaults | greet someone |

For our purpose, two linguistic functions are particularly important: (1) to convey information and (2) to express or evoke feelings. Consider, for example, the following statements:

The death penalty, which is legal in thirty-six states, has been carried out most often in Georgia; however, since 1977 Texas holds the record for the greatest number of executions.

The death penalty is a cruel and inhuman form of punishment in which hapless prisoners are dragged from their cells and summarily slaughtered only to satiate the bloodlust of a vengeful public.

The first statement is intended primarily to convey information about the death penalty, while the second is intended to persuade us that the death penalty is bad. The second accomplishes this function by engaging our feelings and not, as in an argument, by establishing the truth of a claim.

These statements accomplish their respective functions through the distinct kinds of terminology in which they are phrased. Terminology that conveys information is said to have **cognitive meaning,** and terminology that expresses or evokes feelings is said to have **emotive meaning.** Thus, in the first statement the words "legal," "thirty-six," "most often," "Georgia," "record," and so on have primarily a cognitive meaning, while in the second statement the words "cruel," "inhuman," "hapless," "dragged," "slaughtered," "bloodlust," and "vengeful" have a strong emotive meaning. Of course, these latter words have cognitive meaning as well. "Cruel" means tending to hurt others, "inhuman" means inappropriate for humans, "hapless" means unfortunate, and so on.

The emotively charged statement about the death penalty illustrates two important points. The first is that statements of this sort usually have *both* cognitive meaning and emotive meaning. Therefore, since logic is concerned chiefly with cognitive meaning, we must be able to distinguish and disengage the cognitive meaning of such statements from the emotive meaning. The second point is that part of the cognitive meaning of such statements is a value claim. A **value claim** is a claim that something is good, bad, right, wrong, or better or worse, more important or less important than some other thing. For example, the statement about the death penalty asserts the value claim that the death penalty is wrong or immoral. Such value claims are often the most important part of the cognitive meaning of emotive statements. Thus, for the purposes of logic, we must be able to disengage the value claims of emotively charged statements from the emotive meaning and treat these claims as separate statements.

These observations suggest the reason that people use emotive terminology as often as they do: Value claims as such normally require evidence to support them. For example, the claim that the death penalty is immoral cannot simply stand by itself. It cries out for reasons to support it. But when value claims are couched in emotive terminology, the emotive "clothing" tends to obscure the fact that a value claim is being made, and it simultaneously gives psychological momentum to that claim. As a result, readers and listeners are inclined to swallow the value claim whole without any evidence. Furthermore, the intellectual laziness of many speakers and writers, combined with their inability to supply supporting reasons for their value claims, reinforces the desirability of couching such claims in emotive terminology.

Many people, for example, will refer to someone as "crazy," "stupid," or "weird" when they want to express the claim that what that person is doing is bad or wrong and when they are unable or unwilling to give reasons for this claim. Also, many people will use such words as "awesome" or "fantastic" to express the claim that something is good. Those who happen to be listening, especially if they are friendly with the speaker, will often accept these claims without hesitation.

For a subtler example of emotive terminology, consider the word "harvest." This word evokes feelings associated with honest, hardworking farmers being rewarded for their labor in planting and tending their crops. To capitalize on this positive feeling, wood products companies speak of harvesting the trees in 200-year-old forests, even though they had nothing to do with planting them, and surgeons speak of harvesting the organs from the bodies of donors and the tissue from aborted fetuses. In all of these cases, the use of the word "harvest" is specifically calculated to elicit a favorable or agreeable response from the listener.

Let us now consider emotive terminology as it occurs in arguments. In arguments, emotive terminology accomplishes basically the same function as it does in statements. It allows the arguer to make value claims about the subject matter of the argument without providing evidence, and it gives the argument a kind of steamroller quality by which it tends to crush potential counterarguments before the reader or listener has a chance to think of them. This steamroller quality also tends to paralyze the logical thought processes of readers or listeners so that they are not able to see illogical arguments in their true light. These effects of emotive terminology can be avoided if the reader or listener will disengage the value claims and other cognitive meanings from the emotive meaning of the language and reexpress them as distinct premises.

Consider, for example, the following emotively charged argument taken from the letters to the editor section of a newspaper:

> Now that we know that the rocks on the moon are similar to those in our backyard and that tadpoles can exist in a weightless environment, and now that we have put the rest of the world in order, can we concentrate on the problems here at home? Like what makes people hungry and why is unemployment so elusive?
>
> (Robert J. Boland)

The conclusion of this argument is that our government should take money that has been spent on the space program and on international police actions and redirect it to solving domestic problems. The author minimizes the importance of the space program by covertly suggesting that it amounts to nothing more than work on ordinary rocks and tadpoles (which by themselves are relatively insignificant), and he exaggerates the scope of the international effort by covertly suggesting that it has solved every problem on earth but our own. Also, the phrase "put . . . in order" suggests that the international effort has been no more important than restoring order to a room in one's house. We might rephrase the argument in emotively neutral language, making the implicit suggestions and value claims explicit, as follows:

> The space program has been confined to work on ordinary rocks and tadpoles.
> Ordinary rocks and tadpoles are less important than domestic hunger and unemployment.
> Our international efforts have restored order to every nation on earth but our own.
> These efforts have been directed to problems that are less important than our own domestic problems.
> Therefore, our government should redirect funds that have been spent on these projects to solving our own domestic problems.

By restructuring the argument in this way, we can more easily evaluate the degree to which the premises support the conclusion. Inspection of the premises reveals that the first, third, and possibly fourth premises are false. Thus, the actual support provided by the premises is less than what we might have first expected. If the argument were to be rephrased a second time so that the premises turned out true (for example, the first premise might read "*Part* of the space program has been devoted to research on ordinary rocks and tadpoles"), the support given to the conclusion would still be weaker than the author intended.

Now that we have distinguished emotive meaning from cognitive meaning, let us explore some of the ways that cognitive meanings can be defective. Two of them are vagueness and ambiguity. A **vague expression** is one that allows for borderline cases in which it is impossible to tell if the expression applies or does not apply. Vague expressions often allow for a continuous range of interpretations. The meaning is hazy, obscure, and imprecise. For example, words such as "love," "happiness," "peace," "excessive," "fresh," "rich," "poor," "normal," "conservative," and "polluted" are vague. We can rarely tell with any precision whether they apply to a given situation or not. How fresh does something have to be in order to be called fresh?

Vagueness can also affect entire statements. Such vagueness may arise not so much from the individual words as from the way in which the words are combined. For example, suppose someone were to say, "Today our job situation is more transparent." First, what is the meaning of "job situation"? Does it refer to finding a job, keeping a job, filling a job, completing a job, or bidding on a job? And what exactly does it mean for a job situation to be "transparent"? Does it mean that the job is more easily perceived or comprehended? That the job is more easily completed? That we can anticipate our future job needs more clearly? Or what else?

Not all cases of vagueness, however, are problematic. To describe an acquaintance as "tall" or "thin" often causes no trouble in ordinary conversation. Indeed, it may be burdensome to describe this person in more precise language. Trouble arises only when the language is not sufficiently precise for what the situation demands.

The other way in which cognitive meanings can be defective is ambiguity. An **ambiguous expression** is one that can be interpreted as having more than one clearly distinct meaning in a given context. For example, words such as "light," "proper," "critical," "stress," "mad," "inflate," "chest," "bank," "sound," and "race" can be used ambiguously. Thus, if one were to describe a beer as a light pilsner, does this mean that the beer is light in color, light in calories, or light in taste? If one were to describe an action as proper, does this mean proper in a moral sense or proper in the sense of being socially acceptable? Or if one were to describe a person as critical, does this mean that the person is essential for a certain task or that the person tends to criticize others?

As is the case with vagueness, ambiguity can also affect entire statements. Such ambiguity often results from the way in which certain words are combined. For example, there was a newspaper headline that read, "Tuna are biting off the Washington coast." Does this mean that the tuna are nibbling away at the coastline or that fishermen are catching them off the coast? Presumably it means the latter. Another headline read, "College students are turning to vegetables." Does this mean that the students are metamorphosing into vegetables or that they are incorporating more vegetables into their diet? Again, the intended meaning is probably the latter.

The difference between ambiguity and vagueness is that vague terminology allows for a relatively continuous range of interpretations, whereas ambiguous terminology allows for multiple discrete interpretations. A vague expression creates a blur of meaning, whereas an ambiguous expression mixes up otherwise clear meanings. However, many forms of expression are ambiguous in one context and vague in another. For example, the word "slow" in one context could mean either mentally retarded or physically slow, but when the word refers to physical slowness, it could be vague. How slow is slow? Similar remarks apply to "light," "fast," and "rich."

Ambiguity and vagueness are important in logic because there are countless occasions in which the evaluation of an argument leads to the observation, "Well, that depends on what you mean by . . ." Certain phraseology in the argument is vague or ambiguous, and its meaning must be clarified before any evaluation can proceed. For example, Scientologists argue that their organization should be exempt from paying taxes because, they claim, Scientology is a religion. Evaluating their argument requires that we clarify the meaning of "religion." Pro-life advocates argue that abortion is wrong because it results in the killing of human beings. But what is the meaning of "human being"? And some feminists argue that leering glances constitute sexual harassment. To evaluate their arguments we must clarify the meaning of "leering glances" and "sexual harassment."

The role of vagueness and ambiguity in arguments may be conveniently explored in the context of conflicting arguments between individuals. Such conflicts are called disputes:

> CLAUDIA: Mrs. Wilson abuses her children. And how do I know that? I saw her spank one of her kids the other day after the kid misbehaved.
> JANE: Don't be silly. Kids need discipline, and by disciplining her children, Mrs. Wilson is showing that she loves them.

Here the problem surrounds the vagueness of the words "abuse" and "discipline." When does discipline become abuse? The line separating the two is hazy at best, but unless it is clarified, disputes of this sort will never be resolved.

Another example:

> BRENDA: I'm afraid that Smiley is guilty of arson. Last night he confided to me that he was the one who set fire to the old schoolhouse.
> WARREN: No, you couldn't be more mistaken. In this country no one is guilty until proven so in a court of law, and Smiley has not yet even been accused of anything.

In this case the dispute arises over the ambiguity of the word "guilty." Brenda is using the word in the moral sense. Given that Smiley has admitted to setting fire to the old schoolhouse, it is very likely that he did indeed set fire to it and therefore is guilty of arson in the moral sense of the term. Warren, on the other hand, is using the word in the legal sense. Because Smiley has not been convicted in a court of law, he is not legally guilty of anything.

Disputes that arise over the meaning of language are called *verbal disputes*. But not all disputes are of this sort. Some disputes arise over a disagreement about facts, and these are called *factual disputes*. Example:

> KEITH: I know that Freddie stole a computer from the old schoolhouse. Barbara told me that she saw Freddie do it.
> PHYLLIS: That's ridiculous! Freddie has never stolen anything in his life. Barbara hates Freddie, and she is trying to pin the theft on him only to shield her criminal boyfriend.

Here the dispute centers on the factual issues of whether Barbara told the truth and whether Freddie stole the computer.

In dealing with disputes, the first question is whether the dispute is factual, verbal, or some combination of the two. If the dispute is verbal, then the second question to be answered is whether the dispute concerns ambiguity or vagueness.

## EXERCISE 2.1

I. The following selection is taken from a speech delivered by George C. Wallace, former Governor of Alabama, on July 4, 1964. In this speech Wallace attacked

Lyndon Johnson's signing of the Civil Rights Act. The speech is liberally sprinkled with emotive terminology. Make a list of what you consider to be the twenty-five most highly charged words or phrases, and then indicate whether they are intended to evoke a favorable or an unfavorable attitude from the listener.

We come here today in deference to the memory of those stalwart patriots who on July 4, 1776, pledged their lives, their fortunes, and their sacred honor to establish and defend the proposition that governments are created by the people, empowered by the people, derive their just powers from the consent of the people, and must forever remain subservient to the will of the people.

Today, 188 years later, we celebrate that occasion and find inspiration and determination and courage to preserve and protect the great principles of freedom enunciated in the Declaration of Independence.

It is therefore a cruel irony that the President of the United States has only yesterday signed into law the most monstrous piece of legislation ever enacted by the United States Congress.

It is a fraud, a sham, and a hoax.

This bill will live in infamy. To sign it into law at any time is tragic. To do so upon the eve of the celebration of our independence insults the intelligence of the American people.

It dishonors the memory of countless thousands of our dead who offered up their very lives in defense of principles which this bill destroys.

Never before in the history of this nation have so many human and property rights been destroyed by a single enactment of the Congress. It is an act of tyranny. It is the assassin's knife stuck in the back of liberty.

With this assassin's knife and a blackjack in the hand of the federal force-cult, the left-wing liberals will try to force us back into bondage. Bondage to a tyranny more brutal than that imposed by the British Monarchy which claimed power to rule over the lives of our forefathers under sanction of the omnipotent black-robed despots who sit on the bench of the United States Supreme Court.

This bill is fraudulent in intent, in design and in execution.

It is misnamed. Each and every provision is mistitled. It was rammed through the Congress on the wave of ballyhoo, promotions, and publicity stunts reminiscent of P. T. Barnum.

It was enacted in an atmosphere of pressure, intimidation, and even cowardice, as demonstrated by the refusal of the United States Senate to adopt an amendment to submit the bill to a vote of the people.

To illustrate the fraud—it is not a civil rights bill. It is a federal penal code. It creates federal crimes which would take volumes to list and years to tabulate because it affects the lives of 192 million American citizens. Every person in every walk and station of life and every aspect of our daily lives become subject to the criminal provisions of this bill.

It threatens our freedom of speech, of assembly, of association, and makes the exercise of these freedoms a federal crime under certain conditions.

It affects our political rights, our right to trial by jury, our right to the full use and enjoyment of our private property, the freedom from search and seizure of our private property and possessions, the freedom from harassment by federal police and, in short, all the rights of individuals inherent in a society of free men.

Ministers, lawyers, teachers, newspapers, and every private citizen must guard his speech and watch his actions to avoid the deliberately imposed booby traps put into this bill. It is designed to make federal crimes of our customs, beliefs, and traditions. Therefore, under the fantastic powers of the federal judiciary to punish for contempt of court and under their fantastic powers to regulate our most intimate aspects of our lives by injunction, every American citizen is in jeopardy and must stand guard against these despots.

II. The following selections were taken from the letters to the editor section of a newspaper. Each can be interpreted as expressing one or more arguments. Begin by identifying the conclusion of each. Then disengage the covert assumptions, value claims, and other cognitive assertions from the emotive language and translate them into emotively neutral premises. Use the two examples in the text as models. Finally, evaluate the restructured arguments. Some may turn out to be good ones.

★1. Why don't animal lovers do something about these dog sled races? Have you ever witnessed a race on television? Talk about torture. It's sickening to watch the dogs, panting and their tongues hanging out, pull a heavily laden sled with a driver through snow and ice in bitter cold.

(Joe Shapiro)

2. How anyone who has seen even one photo of the fly-covered, starving children in Somalia can still believe in a loving, everpresent, omnipotent God is beyond intelligent reasoning.

(William Blanchard)

3. The creationists have no right to impose their mistaken, ignorant, superstitious beliefs on others. They claim the constitutional right to the free exercise of religion. How about the rights of the majority of people who want their children taught the scientific truth about evolution—not fallacious myths and superstitions from primitive societies.

(Andrew M. Underhill, Jr.)

★4. God, guts, and guns made this great country of ours free, and you can bet your buns it will take more of the same to keep it that way. One of the very last things in this world we need is handgun control.

(R. Kinzie)

5. The insanity plea should be done away with; criminals should lose this easy way out. Killers can theoretically spend as little as six months in a mental hospital, then be released. It's time to take a stand for safety and put psychotic killers in prison.

(Keith Aikens)

6. Until now, the protest against the holocaust in our own nation has been vocal but far too small. The massacre of an unwanted generation through abortion and infanticide has sounded an alarm that should wake up every Christian. Helpless and guiltless little infants are mercilessly butchered daily in hospitals and clinics across our land. For the love of God, let us all urge the passage of the Human Life Bill, now before Congress.

(Jim Key)

★7. It's time to challenge all this nonsense about the "celebration of diversity" in our society. The more the schizophrenics preach the glories of diversity, the more we pull apart. This is not to deny appreciation of the ethnic roots, rituals, and foods, which add color to life. But to lay undue emphasis upon diversification results in destruction of the "social glue" that binds us together. Our forefathers framed one nation, indivisible. In the misguided effort to "celebrate" the uniqueness of every disparate culture and subculture, we betray our heritage and dilute our identities as Americans.

(Ruth M. Armstrong)

8. A kind and loving God surely favors the pro-choice attitude. He wants his world inhabited by happy, well-fed children with parents who love and care for them.

Our burgeoning population in Third World nations with constant famine and disease, and many other human miseries, could be relieved if the Catholic Church were to adjust more of its ancient policies to our current civilization.

(Art Bates)

9. Thousands of years of organized religion have done nothing to solve any problems and have almost always exacerbated them by promoting fear, superstition, and irrational mythologies. Kneeling in prayer to some supernatural entity seeking "divine guidance" or, even more implausibly, "divine intervention," is not only a waste of time, it is counterproductive because it lulls the supplicant into inactivity.

We must stand up, open our eyes and face life's challenges head-on in a problem-solving approach that is reality-based, empirical, and above all, rational.

(James W. Baugh)

★10. Liberalism has turned our welfare system from a social safety net into a hammock. We hand out money with few questions asked. When welfare recipients are asked for some contribution to our society in return, liberals scream that it's unconstitutional.

Liberalism has transformed our criminal justice system into one that cares more about the criminal's past childhood problems than for the victim. Liberalism in its never-ending quest for "social justice" has sacrificed the rights of the majority while continuing to push the rights of a few to new limits.

Liberalism has turned our school system from one of excellence to one where condoms and metal detectors are more important than prayer.

(Marc Sexton)

III. Determine whether the following disputes are verbal, factual, or some combination of the two. If verbal, discuss whether the dispute arises from vagueness or ambiguity.

★1. FRANK: Look at that huge tree that fell last night. It must have made a tremendous crash when it came down.

SHIRLEY: No, I'm afraid you're quite wrong. Sound is a perception, and perceptions depend on a perceiver. Therefore, since nobody was around here last night, there was no crash.

2. VICKIE: Yesterday I visited the exhibition of the work of Jean Michel Basquiat at the Central Gallery. What an interesting artist he is!

   BARBARA: Don't be ridiculous! That's not art—it's just graffiti.

3. PHIL: That was a great basketball game last night. Shaquille O'Neal scored 37 points.

   ARTHUR: Your statistics are all wet. O'Neal scored only 34 points.

★4. ROGER: I think modern society is becoming more and more violent every day. Just look at the increase in murder, rape, and robbery. Violence is clearly an evil that must be eradicated.

   MARK: You might be right about the increase in crime, but the idea that violence is an evil is nonsense. Violence is quite natural. The universe was created in a tremendously violent big bang, the nuclear reactions that bring us sunlight are extremely violent, and insects and animals kill and devour one another all the time.

5. KATHY: I was saddened to hear about the death of your uncle. He was such a wonderful man. You must be consoled knowing that he's enjoying his heavenly reward.

   ANNE: Thanks, but I'm afraid I don't know what you mean. If death is the end of life, how could my uncle be alive right now in heaven?

6. HEIDI: This morning I heard a lecture on the life of Jane Austen. She was such a wonderfully educated woman.

   DAVID: That's not true at all. Jane Austen dropped out of school when she was only eleven, and she never even attended high school, much less college or graduate school.

★7. LESLIE: Your friend Paul told us that he would be visiting his parents in Knoxville this weekend. Therefore, he must not be at home.

   DIANA: I agree that Paul is probably not at home, but you didn't hear him right. He said that his parents live in Nashville.

8. KARL: There's a euthanasia measure on the ballot today, and I think I'll vote for it. It seems reasonable that terminally ill patients should be allowed to be disconnected from life-support systems so that they can die peacefully and naturally.

   SERGIO: You must be crazy! Euthanasia means giving people lethal injections, and that's clearly murder.

9. CHERYL: Tomorrow I'm going to the Metallica concert. Their music is fabulous.

   OLIVER: You call that music? Really it's just noise, and incredibly loud noise at that.

★10. CAROL: Nelson could not have fought in the battle of Trafalgar, because that battle occurred in 1806, and Nelson died in 1804.

   JUSTIN: Your knowledge of history is atrocious! Nelson did fight in Trafalgar, and the date was October 21, 1805.

11. ERIC: I've just signed up for Philosophy 502—Dr. Peterson's class in metaphysics. I know I'm going to enjoy it because I've always been fascinated by magic and ghosts.

    LEAH: I'm afraid you're in for a surprise.

12. HAROLD: Professor Steinbeck is the most intelligent man I know. His lecture series on matter and consciousness was simply brilliant.

    JOYCE: Steinbeck is actually an idiot. Yesterday I watched while he tried to get his car started. When it wouldn't start, he opened the hood, and he didn't even notice that someone had stolen the battery.

★13. THOMAS: George Foreman committed those crimes of child abuse through his own free choice. Nobody put a gun to his head. Therefore, he should be punished for them.

    EMILIE: That's not true. It's been established that Foreman was severely abused himself when he was a child, and such children have an irresistible obsession to abuse others when they grow up.

14. ANTHONY: The sun is much smaller than the earth. You see, it's just a small thing up there in the sky. Therefore, since the sun's gravitational attraction is proportional to its mass, the sun's gravity is less than the earth's.

    CINDY: You are as stupid as they come. I agree the mass of the sun is less than that of the earth, but its volume is greater. Therefore, since gravitational attraction is proportional to volume, the sun's gravity is greater than the earth's.

15. MINDY: President Clinton should have been removed from office because he lied about having sexual relations with Monica Lewinsky.

    KAREN: Don't be silly. President Clinton had only oral sex with Lewinsky, and oral sex does not constitute sexual relations.

★16. FRED: Today's professional athletes are overpaid. Many of them make millions of dollars a year.

    SHAWN: I don't think they are overpaid at all. Just look at the owners of some of these teams. They make ten times as much as the athletes do.

17. BRIAN: That new morning-after pill, RU-486, causes abortion. Therefore, since abortion is wrong, you should never take that pill.

    ELAINE: How ignorant you are! RU-486 merely prevents implantation of the fertilized ovum. Therefore, since the woman never gets pregnant, there is no abortion.

18. PENNY: In my mind, the use of marijuana should be legalized. After all, caffeine and alcohol are no less of a drug than marijuana, and it's not illegal to enjoy a glass of beer or drink a cup of coffee.

    SAM: Your conclusion is way off. Beer and coffee are not drugs; they're foods.

★19. JERRY: In spite of the great strides technology has made in this country, poverty remains a terrible problem. Why, some people earn less than $10,000 per year. The government should do something about it.

FRANKIE: I hardly think that $10,000 per year constitutes poverty. Why, in many Third World countries the majority of inhabitants earn less than $1,000 per year.

20. JOSEPH: Adult human beings have the right to marry whomever they please, as long as that person is not a close relative. From this it follows that homosexuals have the right to marry someone of their own sex.

STEPHEN: Your argument makes no sense. Rights are created by laws, and since there is no federal or state law that gives homosexuals the right to marry, they have no such right.

## 2.2 The Intension and Extension of Terms

The main task of logic is the evaluation of arguments. However, as we saw in the previous section, there are countless arguments in which this task leads to the observation, "Well, that depends on what you mean by . . ." Such an observation usually indicates that the meaning of certain words in the argument is vague or ambiguous. Clearing up the problem often involves supplying a definition. Thus, the study of meaning and definition is closely related to the main task of logic. In this section we continue our inquiry into aspects of linguistic meaning, and the results of this inquiry provide the basis for the theory of definition in the next section.

The basic units of any ordinary language are *words*. Our main concern in this chapter, however, is not with words in general but with terms. A **term** is any word or arrangement of words that may serve as the subject of a statement. Terms consist of proper names, common names, and descriptive phrases. Here are some examples:

| Proper names | Common names | Descriptive phrases |
|---|---|---|
| Napoleon | animal | first president of the United |
| North Dakota | restitution | States |
| The United States | house | author of *Hamlet* |
| Senate | activity | books in my library |
| Gore Vidal | person | officers in the Swiss Navy |
| Robinson Crusoe | | blue things |
| | | those who study hard |

Words that are not terms include verbs, nonsubstantive adjectives, adverbs, prepositions, conjunctions, and all nonsyntactic arrangements of words. The following words or phrases are not terms; none can serve as the subject of a statement:

| | |
|---|---|
| dictatorial | moreover |
| runs quickly | craves |
| above and beyond | cabbages into again the forest |

The last example is a nonsyntactic arrangement.

At this point it is important to distinguish the *use* of a word from the *mention* of a word. Without this distinction any word can be imagined to serve as the subject of a statement and, therefore, to count as a term. The word "wherever," for example, is not a term, but "wherever" (in quotes) can serve as the subject of a statement, such as

" 'Wherever' is an eight-letter word." But in this statement, it is not the word itself that is the subject but rather the *quoted* word. The word is said to be *mentioned*—not *used*. On the other hand, "wherever" is *used* in this statement: "I will follow you wherever you go." In distinguishing terms from nonterms one must be sure that the word or group of words can be *used* as the subject of a statement.

The previous section of this chapter explored the cognitive meaning of language in general. The cognitive meaning of terms comprises two kinds: intensional and extensional. The **intensional meaning,** or **intension,** consists of the qualities or attributes that the term *connotes,* and the **extensional meaning,** or **extension,** consists of the members of the class that the term *denotes.* For example, the intensional meaning of the term "cat" consists of the attributes of being furry, of having four legs, of moving in a certain way, of emitting certain sounds, and so on, while the extensional meaning consists of cats themselves—all the cats in the universe. The term connotes the attributes and denotes the cats.

The intensional meaning of a term is otherwise known as the **connotation,** and the extensional meaning is known as the **denotation.** *Intension* and *extension* are roughly equivalent to the more modern terms *sense* and *reference,* respectively. Also, note that logic uses the terms *connotation* and *denotation* differently from the way they are used in grammar. In grammar, *connotation* refers to the subtle nuances of a word, whereas *denotation* refers to the word's direct and specific meaning.

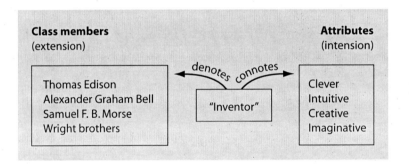

Exactly how a term connotes a set of attributes allows for at least two different interpretations. Some philosophers take an objective approach and hold that a term connotes whatever attributes something must have in order to be denoted by the term. Others take what might be called a subjective approach and hold that a term connotes the attributes that occur in the minds of the people who use that term. This book takes the latter approach.

In connection with this approach, however, we encounter the problem of terms connoting different things to different people. Thus, to a cat lover the term "cat" might connote the attributes of being cuddly and adorable, while to someone who hates cats it might connote the attributes of being obnoxious and disgusting. To avoid this problem, we restrict the meaning of connotation to what is usually called the conventional connotation. The **conventional connotation** of a term includes the attributes that the term *commonly* calls forth in the minds of competent speakers of the language. Under this interpretation, the connotation of a term remains more or less the same from person to person and from time to time.

The denotation of a term also typically remains the same from person to person, but it may change over time. The denotation of "currently living cat," for example, is constantly fluctuating as some cats die and others are born. The denotation of the term "cat," on the other hand, is presumably constant because it denotes all cats—past, present, and future.

Sometimes the denotation of a term can change radically with the passage of time. The terms "currently living dodo bird" and "current king of France," for example, at one time denoted actually existing entities, but today all such entities have perished. Accordingly, these terms now have what is called **empty extension.** They are said to denote the empty (or "null") class, the class that has no members. Other terms with empty extension include "unicorn," "leprechaun," "gnome," "elf," and "griffin." While these terms have empty extension, however, they do not have empty intension. "Currently living dodo bird" and "current king of France," as well as "unicorn," "elf," and "griffin," connote a variety of intelligible attributes.

The fact that some terms have empty extension leads us to an important connection between extension and intension—namely, that *intension determines extension.* The intensional meaning of a term serves as the criterion for deciding what the extension consists of. Because we know the attributes connoted by the term "unicorn," for example, we know that the term has empty extension. That is, we know that there are no four-legged mammals having a single straight horn projecting from their forehead. Similarly, the intension of the word "cat" serves as the criterion for determining what is and what is not a member of the class of cats.

One kind of term that raises problems for the intension-determines-extension rule is proper names. For example, the name "David" might not appear to have any intension, but it denotes the person who has this name. Although philosophers have disagreed about this, it would seem that proper names must have some kind of intension or we would not know what persons, if any, they denote. One possible solution to this problem is that names are shorthand symbols for descriptions or bundles of descriptions. For example, "David" could be shorthand for "the person who lives next door" or "the person who works at the corner store and who drives a green Chevy."

Another possible solution to the problem of proper names is that the intension of proper names consists of the causal chain of events leading from the point at which the name is first assigned to the point at which a certain person learns about the name. Thus, the first link in such a chain might be the baptismal event at which the name "David" is given to a certain infant, the second link would be the event in which a certain third party is informed of the first event, and so on. This entire chain of events extending through the linguistic community would then constitute the intension of "David." Thus, we conclude that for all terms, including proper names, intension determines extension.

The distinction between intension and extension may be further illustrated by comparing the way in which these concepts can be used to give order to random sequences of terms. Terms may be put in the order of increasing intension, increasing extension, decreasing intension, and decreasing extension. A series of terms is in the order of **increasing intension** when each term in the series (except the first) connotes more attributes than the one preceding it. In other words, each term in the series after the first is *more specific* than the one preceding it. (A term is specific to the degree that it connotes more attributes.) The order of **decreasing intension** is the reverse of that of increasing intension.

A series of terms is in the order of **increasing extension** when each term in the series (except the first) denotes a class having more members than the class denoted by the term preceding it. In other words, the class size gets larger with each successive term. **Decreasing extension** is, of course, the reverse of this order. Examples:

| increasing intension: | animal, mammal, feline, tiger |
| increasing extension: | tiger, feline, mammal, animal |
| decreasing intension: | tiger, feline, mammal, animal |
| decreasing extension: | animal, mammal, feline, tiger |

These examples illustrate a fact pertaining to most such series: The order of increasing intension is usually the same as that of decreasing extension. Conversely, the order of decreasing intension is usually the same as that of increasing extension. There are some exceptions, however. Consider the following series:

> unicorn; unicorn with blue eyes; unicorn with blue eyes and green horn; unicorn with blue eyes, green horn, and a weight of over 400 pounds

Each term in this series has empty extension; so, while the series exhibits the order of increasing intension, it does not exhibit the order of decreasing extension. Here is another, slightly different, example:

> living human being; living human being with a genetic code; living human being with a genetic code and a brain; living human being with a genetic code, a brain, and a height of less than 100 feet

In this series none of the terms has empty extension, but each term has exactly the *same* extension as the others. Thus, while the intension increases with each successive term, once again the extension does not decrease.

## EXERCISE 2.2

I. The following exercises deal with words and terms.

1. Determine which of the following words or groups of words are terms and which are nonterms.

| | |
|---|---|
| extortion | Thomas Jefferson |
| laborious | Empire State Building |
| cunningly | annoy |
| practitioner | render satisfactory |
| seriousness | graceful dancer |
| forever | wake up |
| whoever studies | not only |
| interestingly impassive | tallest man on the squad |
| scarlet | mountaintop |
| reinvestment | between |
| therefore | since |

2. Name some of the attributes connoted by the following terms. Express your answer with adjectives or adjectival phrases. Example: The term "elephant" connotes the attributes of being large, having tusks, having a trunk.

| | | | |
|---|---|---|---|
| drum | wolf | fanatic | riot |
| politician | Mona Lisa | carrot | piano |
| devil | Statue of Liberty | | |

3. Name three items denoted by the terms in the following left-hand column and all items denoted by the terms in the right-hand column.

| | |
|---|---|
| newspaper | tallest mountain on earth |
| scientist | prime number less than 10 |
| manufacturer | governor of New York |
| river | language of Canada |
| opera | Scandinavian country |

4. Put the following sequences of terms in the order of increasing intension:

★a. conifer, Sitka spruce, tree, spruce, plant

b. Italian sports car, car, vehicle, Maserati, sports car

c. doctor of medicine, person, brain surgeon, professional person, surgeon

d. wallaby, marsupial, mammal, animal, kangaroo

e. parallelogram, polygon, square, rectangle, quadrilateral

5. Construct a series of four terms that exhibits increasing intension but nondecreasing extension.

II. Answer "true" or "false" to the following statements:

1. All words have an intensional meaning and an extensional meaning.

2. The intensional meaning of a term consists of the attributes connoted by the term.

3. The extensional meaning of a term consists of the members of the class denoted by the term.

4. The extension of a term always remains the same with the passage of time.

5. Some terms have empty intension.

6. Some terms have empty extension.

7. The intension of a term determines the extension.

8. The intension of a term determines how specific the term is.

9. The order of increasing intension is always the same as that of decreasing extension.

10. "Leprechaun" and "unicorn" have the same extension.

## 2.3    Definitions and Their Purposes

Over the years philosophers have held various conflicting views about the purpose of definitions. For example, Plato claimed that definitions were intended to explicate the meaning of certain eternal essences or forms, such as justice, piety, and virtue. For most logicians today, however, definitions are intended exclusively to explicate the meaning of *words*. In conformity with this latter position, we may define **definition** as a group of words that assigns a meaning to some word or group of words. Accordingly, every definition consists of two parts: the definiendum and the definiens. The **definiendum** is the word or group of words that is supposed to be defined, and the **definiens** is the word or group of words that does the defining. For example, in the definition "'Tiger' means a large, striped, ferocious feline indigenous to the jungles of India and Asia," the word "tiger" is the definiendum, and everything after the word "means" is the definiens. The definiens is not itself the meaning of the definiendum; rather, it is the group of words that symbolizes (or that is supposed to symbolize) the *same* meaning as the definiendum. Because we presumably know in advance what the definiens symbolizes, we are led, via the definition, to understand what the definiendum symbolizes. It is in this way that the definition "assigns" a meaning to its definiendum.

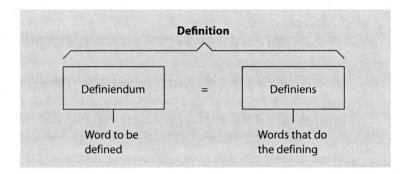

Once it has been decided that definitions explicate the meaning of words, other disagreements emerge among the philosophers. Some argue that since a definition is merely a rule that allows one set of words (the definiens) to be used in place of another set (the definiendum), definitions communicate no information at all about the subject matter of the definiendum. Others take the opposite tack and argue that since definitions result in a clarification of language, they provide a means for the discovery of deeper philosophical truths. It seems, however, that neither of these approaches is able to make good sense of all the various kinds of definitions that are actually employed in ordinary usage. As a result, instead of beginning their analysis of definitions with a set of a priori criteria, many logicians take a pragmatic approach and begin with a survey of the various kinds of definitions that are actually used and of the functions that they actually serve. This is the approach taken here.

## Stipulative Definitions

A **stipulative definition** assigns a meaning to a word for the first time. This may involve either coining a new word or giving a new meaning to an old word. The purpose of a stipulative definition is usually to replace a more complex expression with a simpler one.

The need for a stipulative definition is often occasioned by some new phenomenon or development. For example, a few years ago the attempt was made at a certain zoo to crossbreed tigers and lions. Because of the genetic similarity of the two species, the attempt succeeded. Offspring were produced from a male tiger and a female lion and from a male lion and a female tiger. When the offspring were born, it became appropriate to give them names. Of course, the names "offspring of male tiger and female lion" and "offspring of male lion and female tiger" could have been used, but these names were hardly convenient. Instead, the names "tigon" and "liger" were selected. Any two new words would have sufficed equally well for naming the offspring— "topar" and "largine" for example—but "tigon" and "liger" were considered more appropriate, for obvious reasons. "Tigon" was taken to mean the offspring of a male tiger and a female lion, and "liger" the offspring of a male lion and a female tiger. These assignments of meanings were accomplished through stipulative definitions.

Another use for stipulative definitions is to set up secret codes. For example, during World War II, "Tora, Tora, Tora" was the code name Admiral Yamamoto transmitted to the war office in Tokyo signaling that the Japanese fleet had not been spotted in the hours preceding the bombing of Pearl Harbor; "Operation Barbarossa" was the name the Germans gave to the invasion of Russia; and "Operation Overlord" was the name the allied forces gave to the planned invasion of Normandy. More recently, "Operation Desert Storm" was the code name given to the military invasion of Iraq; the campaign in Afghanistan, at least in its early phase, was called "Operation Enduring Freedom." Law enforcement organizations have adopted similar code names for sting operations against organized crime.

Because people are continually coming up with new creations, whether it be food concoctions, inventions, modes of behavior, or kinds of apparel, stipulative definitions are continually being introduced to name them. The invention of computers provides a prime example. Today we have dozens of new terms or new uses of old terms that did not exist a few years ago: "cyberspace," "e-mail," "browser," "hacker," "dot-com," "hardware," "software," "download," "website," "webmaster," "server," "boot," "bar code," "mouse," "modem," "cookies," and "spam"—to name just a few. Earlier, in the area of biology, when a certain excretion of the pancreas was refined to its pure form, the word "insulin" was chosen to name it, and the word "penicillin" was chosen for an antibacterial substance produced by certain *Penicillium* molds. In mathematics, the symbol "$10^5$" was chosen as a simple substitute for "$10 \times 10 \times 10 \times 10 \times 10$."

Because a stipulative definition is a completely arbitrary assignment of a meaning to a word for the first time, there can be no such thing as a "true" or "false" stipulative definition. Furthermore, for the same reason, a stipulative definition cannot provide any new information about the subject matter of the definiendum. The fact that the word "tigon" was selected to replace "offspring of a male tiger and a female lion" tells us nothing new about the nature of the animal in question. One stipulative definition may, however, be more or less convenient or more or less appropriate than another.

Stipulative definitions are misused in verbal disputes when one person covertly uses a word in a peculiar way and then proceeds to assume that everyone else uses that word in the same way. Under these circumstances that person is said to be using the word "stipulatively." In such cases the assumption that other persons use the word in the same way is rarely justified.

## Lexical Definitions

A **lexical definition** is used to report the meaning that a word already has in a language. Dictionary definitions are all instances of lexical definitions. Thus, in contrast with a stipulative definition, which assigns a meaning to a word for the first time, a lexical definition may be true or false depending on whether it does or does not report the way a word is actually used. Because words are frequently used in more than one way, lexical definitions have the further purpose of eliminating the ambiguity that would otherwise arise if one of these meanings were to be confused with another.

As we saw in the first section of this chapter, an expression is *ambiguous* when it can be interpreted as having two or more clearly distinct meanings in a given context. Words such as "light," "mad," and "bank" can be used ambiguously. Because a lexical definition lists the various meanings that a word can have, a person who consults such a definition is better prepared to avoid ambiguous constructions of his or her own and to detect those of others. Undetected ambiguity causes the most trouble. In many cases the problem lies not with the obvious differences in meaning that words such as "light" and "bank" may have but with the subtle shadings of meaning that are more likely to be confused with one another. For example, if a woman is described as "nice," any number of things could be intended. She could be fastidious, refined, modest, pleasant, attractive, or even lewd. A good lexical definition will distinguish these various shadings and thereby guard against the possibility that two such meanings will be unconsciously jumbled together into one.

## Precising Definitions

The purpose of a **precising definition** is to reduce the vagueness of a word. As we saw in the first section of this chapter, an expression is *vague* if there are borderline cases in which it is impossible to tell if the word applies or does not apply. Words such as "fresh," "rich," and "poor" are vague. Once the vagueness of such words is reduced by a precising definition, one can reach a decision as to the applicability of the word to a specific situation. For example, if legislation were ever introduced to give direct financial assistance to the poor, a precising definition would have to be supplied specifying exactly who is poor and who is not. The definition " 'Poor' means having an annual income of less than $4,000 and a net worth of less than $20,000" is an example of a precising definition.

Whenever words are taken from ordinary usage and used in a highly systematic context such as science, mathematics, medicine, or law, they must always be clarified by means of a precising definition. The terms "force," "energy," "acid," "element," "number," "equality," "contract," and "agent" have all been given precising definitions by specific disciplines.

Sometimes the substance of a court trial may revolve around the precise usage of a term. A trial in California addressed the question of whether a man who had ridden a bicycle while intoxicated violated the motor vehicle code. The question concerned

## ■ EMINENT LOGICIANS

### *Peter Abelard* 1079–1142

Generally considered the greatest logician of the Middle Ages, Peter Abelard was born in the village of Le Pallet in the Brittany region of France. His parents were members of the French nobility, and as their eldest son, Abelard was slated to inherit substantial wealth and noble standing. However, he gave up claim to this inheritance and the knighthood that went with it, choosing instead the life of a scholar.

When he was only a teenager, Abelard went off to Paris to study philosophy with William of Champeaux at the cathedral school of Notre-Dame. He proved to be a brilliant student and arrogant to a fault. He openly challenged the views of his teacher and seized on every opportunity to debate William in public. Later, he set up a rival school, describing its founder as the "only remaining philosopher in the world." Gradually, he became renowned throughout all of Europe, and he was eventually appointed to the faculty of Notre-Dame, where he attracted hundreds of students eager to learn from this illustrious master.

Around this time Abelard's attentions were drawn to Heloise, the beautiful and brilliant young niece of a prominent Parisian canon named Fulbert. Making the acquaintance of Fulbert's young protégé proved a daunting task, since her uncle kept her closely guarded. Nonetheless, Abelard persuaded Fulbert to allow him to move into his house and tutor the gifted niece, who, though only in her teens, had already mastered Greek and Hebrew. Fulbert saw this as a way of providing Heloise with a first-rate higher education, but for Abelard it provided quite a different opportunity. He later compared Fulbert's credulity in allowing him access to his charge as akin to placing a lamb in the care of a devouring wolf.

The tutoring sessions rapidly turned toward seduction, with Heloise a receptive student. Before long Heloise became pregnant and gave birth to a son. A publicly avowed marriage might have abated the ensuing social scandal, but scholars and clerics were not supposed to marry. The couple decided to marry secretly, and Heloise fled to a convent to shield herself from the scandal mongers who persecuted the couple for being ostensibly unwed. Meanwhile, a furious Fulbert plotted to punish Abelard, and he hired a gang of marauders to break into Abelard's lodgings in the middle of the night and castrate him.

After the castration, Abelard took refuge in one monastery after another. His arrogance made him ill suited for monastic life, though, as he went out of his way to provoke the other monks. Much later, he returned to Paris where he taught until he was silenced by the church for alleged heresy. At one point he was forced to burn one of his own books. Throughout all of these calamities, Abelard remained devoted to his scholarly endeavors. He developed a truth-functional propositional logic and a theory of entailment, and he wrote prolifically in the areas of metaphysics, ethics, and philosophy of language. He is buried alongside Heloise in the Père-Lachaise cemetery in Paris. Today, their grave site is visited by people seeking solace from the frustrations of love.

whether, for these purposes, a bicycle could be considered a "vehicle." The court decided in the affirmative, and the decision amounted to an incremental extension of an already existent precising definition of the word "vehicle."

Another example involves the practice of surgical transplantation of vital organs. Before a heart transplant can be conducted, the donor must be dead; otherwise, the surgeon will be accused of murder. If the donor is dead for too long, however, the success of the transplant will be imperiled. But exactly when is a person considered to be dead? Is it when the heart stops beating, when the person stops breathing, when rigor mortis sets in, or some other time? The question involves the meaning of the term "moment of death." The courts have decided that "moment of death" should be taken to mean the moment the brain stops functioning, as measured by an electroencephalograph. This decision amounts to the acceptance of a precising definition for "moment of death."

A precising definition differs from a stipulative definition in that the latter involves a purely arbitrary assignment of meaning, whereas the assignment of meaning in a precising definition is not at all arbitrary. A great deal of care must be taken to ensure that the assignment of meaning in a precising definition is appropriate and legitimate for the context within which the term is to be employed.

## Theoretical Definitions

A **theoretical definition** assigns a meaning to a word by suggesting a theory that gives a certain characterization to the entities that the term denotes. Such a definition provides a way of viewing or conceiving these entities that suggests deductive consequences, further investigation (experimental or otherwise), and whatever else would be entailed by the acceptance of a theory governing these entities. The definition of the term "heat" found in texts dealing with the kinetic theory of heat provides a good example: "'Heat' means the energy associated with the random motion of the molecules of a substance." This definition does more than merely assign a meaning to a word; it provides a way of conceiving the physical phenomenon that is heat. In so doing, it suggests the deductive consequence that as the molecules of a substance speed up, the temperature of the substance increases. In addition, it suggests a number of experiments—experiments investigating the relationship between molecular velocity and the phenomena of radiation, gas pressure, molecular elasticity, and molecular configuration. In short, this definition of "heat" provides the impetus for an entire theory about heat.

Other examples of theoretical definitions are the definition of "light" as a form of electromagnetic radiation and the definition of "force," "mass," and "acceleration" in Newton's second law of motion as expressed in the equation "$F = MA$." The latter is a kind of contextual definition in which each term is defined in terms of the other two. Both definitions entail numerous deductive consequences about the phenomena involved and suggest numerous avenues of experimental investigation.

Not all theoretical definitions are associated with science. Many terms in philosophy, such as "substance," "form," "cause," "change," "idea," "good," "mind," and "God," have been given theoretical definitions. In fact, most of the major philosophers in history have given these terms their own peculiar theoretical definitions, and this fact accounts in part for the unique character of their respective philosophies. For example,

Gottfried Wilhelm Leibniz's definition of "substance" in terms of what he called "monads" laid the foundation for his metaphysical theory, and John Stuart Mill's definition of "good" as the greatest happiness of the greatest number provided the underpinnings for his utilitarian theory of ethics.

Like stipulative definitions, theoretical definitions are neither true nor false, strictly speaking. The reason is that theoretical definitions function as proposals to see or interpret some phenomenon in a certain way. Since proposals have no truth value, neither do theoretical definitions. They may, however, be more or less interesting or more or less fruitful, depending on the deductive consequences they entail and on the outcome of the experiments they suggest.

## Persuasive Definitions

The purpose of a **persuasive definition** is to engender a favorable or unfavorable attitude toward what is denoted by the definiendum. This purpose is accomplished by assigning an emotionally charged or value-laden meaning to a word while making it appear that the word really has (or ought to have) that meaning in the language in which it is used. Thus, persuasive definitions amount to a certain synthesis of stipulative, lexical, and, possibly, theoretical definitions backed by the rhetorical motive to engender a certain attitude. As a result of this synthesis, a persuasive definition masquerades as an honest assignment of meaning to a term while condemning or blessing with approval the subject matter of the definiendum. Here are some examples of opposing pairs of persuasive definitions:

> "Abortion" means the ruthless murdering of innocent human beings.
> "Abortion" means a safe and established surgical procedure whereby a woman is relieved of an unwanted burden.

> "Liberal" means a drippy-eyed do-gooder obsessed with giving away other people's money.
> "Liberal" means a genuine humanitarian committed to the goals of adequate housing and health care and of equal opportunity for all of our citizens.

> "Capitalism" means the economic system in which individuals are afforded the God-given freedom to own property and conduct business as they choose.
> "Capitalism" means the economic system in which humanity is sacrificed to the wanton quest for money, and mutual understanding and respect are replaced by alienation, greed, and selfishness.

> "Taxation" means the procedure by means of which our commonwealth is preserved and sustained.
> "Taxation" means the procedure used by bureaucrats to rip off the people who elected them.

The objective of a persuasive definition is to influence the attitudes of the reader or listener; thus, such definitions may be used with considerable effectiveness in political speeches and editorial columns. While persuasive definitions may, like lexical definitions, be evaluated as either true or false, the primary issue is neither truth nor falsity but the effectiveness of such definitions as instruments of persuasion.

## EXERCISE 2.3

I. Determine whether the following definitions are stipulative, lexical, precising, theoretical, or persuasive.

★1. "Blind" means, for federal income tax purposes, either the inability to see better than 20/200 in the better eye with glasses or having a field of vision of 20 degrees or less.

2. "Football" means a sport in which modern-day gladiators brutalize one another while trying to move a ridiculously shaped "ball" from one end of the playing field to the other.

3. "Wristovision" means a miniature television set that can be worn on the wrist.

★4. "Diffident" means lacking confidence in oneself; characterized by modest reserve.

5. "Magnetism" means a property of certain substances such as iron, cobalt, and nickel that arises from the spin of the electrons in the unfilled inner shell of the atoms that compose the substance.

6. "Fiduciary" means having to do with a confidence or trust; a person who holds something in trust.

★7. "Politician" means a person of unquestioned honesty and integrity whom the people, in their collective wisdom, have duly elected to guide the ship of state and protect it from the reefs and shoals that threaten it on every side.

8. "Intoxicated," for purposes of driving a car in many states, means having a blood-alcohol content of 0.1 percent (.001) or greater.

9. "Gweed" means a thoroughly immature person who feigns intellectual prowess; a total loser.

★10. "Sound" means a compression wave, in air or some other elastic medium, having a frequency ranging (for humans) from 20 to 20,000 vibrations per second.

11. "Radioactive area" means, for purposes of the U.S. Nuclear Regulatory Commission, any area accessible to individuals in which there exists radiation at such levels that a major portion of the body could receive in any one hour a dose in excess of 5 millirems or in any five consecutive days a dose in excess of 100 millirems.

12. "Neurosis" means a chronic emotional disturbance that arises from suppressed or forgotten emotional stress (such as resentment, hostility, aggression, or guilt) experienced in early childhood.

★13. "Scaling" means a sport in which people race four-wheel-drive vehicles up the face of boulder-strewn hillsides.

14. "Smoker" means a rude and disgusting individual who callously emits noxious tobacco fumes into the air, threatening the health and comfort of everyone in the vicinity.

15. "Diadem" means an ornamental headband worn as a badge of royalty; a crown.

★16. "Psychiatry" means the fortuitous melding of modern medicine with psychology that promises relief to thousands of poor, desperate souls who suffer the pains of emotional disorder.

17. "Gene" means the hereditary unit that occupies a fixed chromosomal locus, which through transcription has a specific effect on phenotype and which can mutate to various allelic forms.

18. "Subgression" means moving oneself and one's family to a subterranean bomb shelter for the purpose of escaping nuclear attack.

★19. "Intractable" means not easily governed; obstinate; unruly; not disposed to be taught.

20. "Recession" means, for purposes of the National Bureau of Economic Research, two consecutive quarters of negative growth in real GNP or in aggregate output for the entire economy.

21. "Gravity" means a force that results from the universal attraction that every particle of matter has for every other particle, and which varies directly with the mass of the particles and inversely with the square of the distance between them.

★22. "Assault" means, for legal purposes, an intentional and unprivileged act resulting in the apprehension of an immediate harmful or offensive contact.

23. "Television" means the electronic medium that keeps an entire nation of viewers in a state of seminarcosis by feeding them a steady stream of inane drivel.

24. "Obelisk" means an upright, four-sided pillar that terminates in a pyramid; a dagger.

★25. "Aereomobile" means a vehicle that is normally driven on the ground but that has the capability of flying through the air to avoid traffic congestion.

II. The following exercises involve constructing definitions:

1. Invent stipulative definitions for two new words that you wish to introduce into the language for the first time.

2. Construct lexical definitions for "capital" and "depression," and indicate two different meanings for each.

3. Construct precising definitions for "middle-aged" and "alcoholic." Interpret both words as relating to people and specify the purpose for which the definitions are to be used.

4. Construct theoretical definitions for "energy" and "atom."

5. Construct opposing pairs of persuasive definitions for "conservative" and "socialism."

III. Answer "true" or "false" to the following statements:

1. From the standpoint of logic, many definitions are concerned not with words but with things.

2. The definiendum is the word or term that is supposed to be defined.

3. The definiens is the word or group of words that assigns a meaning to the word being defined.

4.  A stipulative definition is either true or false.

5.  A lexical definition reports the way a word is actually used in a language.

6.  One of the purposes of a lexical definition is to guard against the ambiguous use of a word.

7.  The meaning given to a word by a precising definition is completely arbitrary.

8.  Theoretical definitions are either true or false, just as are lexical definitions.

9.  Theoretical definitions provide a theoretical characterization of the entity or entities denoted by the word being defined.

10. The purpose of a persuasive definition is to influence attitudes.

## 2.4    Definitional Techniques

In the previous section we presented a survey of some of the kinds of definitions actually in use and the functions they are intended to serve. In this section we will investigate some of the techniques used to produce these definitions. These techniques may be classified in terms of the two kinds of meaning, intensional and extensional, discussed in Section 2.2.

### Extensional (Denotative) Definitions

An **extensional (denotative) definition** is one that assigns a meaning to a term by indicating the members of the class that the definiendum denotes. There are at least three ways of indicating the members of a class: pointing to them, naming them individually, and naming them in groups. The three kinds of definitions that result are called, respectively, demonstrative or ostensive definitions, enumerative definitions, and definitions by subclass.

**Demonstrative (ostensive) definitions** are probably the most primitive form of definition. All one need know to understand such a definition is the meaning of pointing. As the following examples illustrate, such definitions may be either partial or complete, depending on whether all or only some of the members of the class denoted by the definiendum are pointed to:

> "Chair" means this and this and this—as you point to several chairs, one after the other.

> "Washington Monument" means that—as you point to it.

If you were attempting to teach a foreigner your own native language, and neither of you understood a word of each other's language, demonstrative definition would almost certainly be one of the methods you would use.

Because demonstrative definitions are the most primitive, they are also the most limited. In addition to the limitations affecting all extensional definitions (which will be discussed shortly), there is the obvious limitation that the required objects be available for being pointed at. For example, if one wishes to define the word "sun" and it happens to be nighttime, or the word "dog" and none happens to be in the vicinity, a demonstrative definition cannot be used.

Demonstrative definitions differ from the other kinds of definitions in that the definiens is constituted at least in part by a gesture—the gesture of pointing. Since the definiens in any definition is a group of words, however, a gesture, such as pointing, must count as a word. While this conclusion may appear strange at first, it is supported by the fact that the "words" in many sign languages consist exclusively of gestures.

**Enumerative definitions** assign a meaning to a term by naming the members of the class the term denotes. Like demonstrative definitions, they may also be either partial or complete. Examples:

> "Actress" means a person such as Nicole Kidman, Emma Thompson, or Natalie Portman.

> "Baltic state" means Estonia, Latvia, or Lithuania.

Complete enumerative definitions are usually more satisfying than partial ones because they identify the definiendum with greater assurance. Relatively few classes, however, can be completely enumerated. Many classes, such as the class of real numbers greater than 1 but less than 2, have an infinite number of members. Others, such as the class of stars and the class of persons, while not infinite, have still too many members to enumerate. Therefore, anything approximating a complete enumerative definition of terms denoting these classes is clearly impossible. Then there are others—the class of insects and the class of trees, for example—the vast majority of whose members have no names. For terms that denote these classes, either a demonstrative definition or a definition by subclass is the more appropriate choice.

A **definition by subclass** assigns a meaning to a term by naming subclasses of the class denoted by the term. Such a definition, too, may be either partial or complete, depending on whether the subclasses named, when taken together, include all the members of the class or only some of them. Examples:

> "Tree" means an oak, pine, elm, spruce, maple, and the like.

> "Flower" means a rose, lily, daisy, geranium, zinnia, and the like.

> "Cetacean" means either a whale, a dolphin, or a porpoise.

> "Fictional work" means either a poem, a play, a novel, or a short story.

The first two are partial, the second two complete. As with definitions by enumeration, complete definitions by subclass are more satisfying than partial ones; but because relatively few terms denote classes that admit of a conveniently small number of subclasses, complete definitions by subclass are often difficult, if not impossible, to provide.

Extensional definitions are chiefly used as techniques for producing lexical and stipulative definitions. Lexical definitions are aimed at communicating how a word is actually used, and one of the ways of doing so is by identifying the members of the class that the word denotes. Dictionaries frequently include references to the individual members (or to the subclasses) of the class denoted by the word being defined. Sometimes they even include a kind of demonstrative definition when they provide a picture of the object that the word denotes. Not all lexical definitions have to occur in dictionaries, however. A lexical definition can just as well be spoken, as when one person attempts to explain orally to another how a word is used in a language. Such attempts, incidentally, often have recourse to all three kinds of extensional definition.

Stipulative definitions are used to assign a meaning to a word for the first time. This task may be accomplished by all three kinds of extensional definition. For example, a biologist engaged in naming and classifying types of fish might assign names to the specific varieties by pointing to their respective tanks (demonstrative definition), and then she might assign a class name to the whole group by referring to the names of the specific varieties (definition by subclass). An astronomer might point via his telescope to a newly discovered comet and announce, "That comet will henceforth be known as 'Henderson's Comet'" (demonstrative definition). The organizer of a children's game might make the stipulation: "John, Mary, and Billy will be called 'Buccaneers,' and Judy, George, and Nancy will be 'Pirates'" (enumerative definition).

Although it is conceivable that extensional definitions could also serve as techniques for theoretical and persuasive definitions (though this would be highly unusual), extensional definitions by themselves cannot properly serve as precising definitions for the following reason. The function of a precising definition is to clarify a vague word, and vagueness is a problem affecting intensional meaning. Because the intension is imprecise, the extension is indefinite. To attempt to render the intension precise by exactly specifying the extension (as with an extensional definition) would be tantamount to having extension determine intension—which cannot be done.

The principle that intension determines extension, whereas the converse is not true, underlies the fact that all extensional definitions suffer serious deficiencies. For example, in the case of the demonstrative definition of the word "chair," if all the chairs pointed to are made of wood, observers might get the idea that "chair" means "wood" instead of something to sit on. Similarly, they might get the idea that "Washington Monument" means "tall" or "pointed" or any of a number of other things. From the definition of "actress," readers or listeners might think that "actress" means "woman"—which would include countless individuals who have nothing to do with the stage or screen. From the definition of "tree" they might get the idea that "tree" means "firmly planted in the ground," which would also include the pilings of a building. And they might think that "cetacean" means "aquatic animal," which includes salmon, tuna, squid, manatees, and so on. In other words, it makes no difference how many individuals or subclasses are named in an extensional definition, there is no assurance that listeners or readers will get the *intensional* meaning. Extensions can *suggest* intensions, but they cannot *determine* them.

## Intensional (Connotative) Definitions

An **intensional definition** is one that assigns a meaning to a word by indicating the qualities or attributes that the word connotes. Because at least four strategies may be used to indicate the attributes a word connotes, there are at least four kinds of intensional definitions: synonymous definition, etymological definition, operational definition, and definition by genus and difference.

A **synonymous definition** is one in which the definiens is a single word that connotes the same attributes as the definiendum. In other words, the definiens is a synonym of the word being defined. Examples:

"Physician" means doctor.

"Intentional" means willful.

"Voracious" means ravenous.

"Observe" means see.

When a single word can be found that has the same intensional meaning as the word being defined, a synonymous definition is a highly concise way of assigning a meaning. Many words, however, have subtle shades of meaning that are not connoted by any other single word. For example, the word "wisdom" is not exactly synonymous with either "knowledge," "understanding," or "sense"; and "envious" is not exactly synonymous with either "jealous" or "covetous."

An **etymological definition** assigns a meaning to a word by disclosing the word's ancestry in both its own language and other languages. Most ordinary English words have ancestors either in old or middle English or in some other language such as Greek, Latin, or French, and the current English meaning (as well as spelling and pronunciation) is often closely tied to the meaning (and spelling and pronunciation) of these ancestral words. For example, the English word "license" is derived from the Latin verb *licere,* which means to be permitted, and the English word "captain" derives from the Latin noun *caput,* which means head.

Etymological definitions have special importance for at least two reasons. The first is that the etymological definition of a word often conveys the word's root meaning or seminal meaning from which all other associated meanings are derived. Unless one is familiar with this root meaning, one often fails to place other meanings in their proper light or to grasp the meaning of the word when it is used in its most proper sense. For example, the word "principle" derives from the Latin word *principium,* which means beginning or source. Accordingly, the "principles of physics" are those fundamental laws that provide the "source" of the science of physics. The English word "efficient" derives from the Latin verb *efficere,* which means to bring about. Thus, the "efficient cause" of something (such as the motion of a car) is the agent that actually brings that thing about (the engine).

The second reason for the importance of etymological definitions is that if one is familiar with the etymology of one English word, one often has access to the meaning of an entire constellation of related words. For example, the word "orthodox" derives from the two Greek words *ortho,* meaning right or straight, and *doxa,* meaning belief or opinion. From this, one might grasp that "orthopedic" has to do with straight bones (originally in children—*pais* in Greek means child), and that "orthodontic" has to do with straight teeth (*odon* in Greek means tooth). Similarly, if one is familiar with the etymological definition of "polygon" (from the Greek words *poly,* meaning many, and *ganos* meaning angle), one might grasp the meanings of "polygamy" (from *gamos,* meaning marriage) and "polygraph" (from *graphein,* meaning to write). A polygraph is a lie detector that simultaneously records pulse rate, blood pressure, respiration, and so on.

An **operational definition** assigns a meaning to a word by specifying certain experimental procedures that determine whether or not the word applies to a certain thing. Examples:

One substance is "harder than" another if and only if one scratches the other when the two are rubbed together.

A subject has "brain activity" if and only if an electroencephalograph shows oscillations when attached to the subject's head.

A "potential difference" exists between two conductors if and only if a voltmeter
shows a reading when connected to the two conductors.

A solution is an "acid" if and only if litmus paper turns red when dipped into it.

Each of these definitions prescribes an operation to be performed. The first prescribes
that the two substances in question be rubbed together, the second that the electroencephalograph be connected to the patient's head and observed for oscillations, the
third that the voltmeter be connected to the two conductors and observed for deflec-
tion, and the fourth that the litmus paper be placed in the solution and observed for
color change. Unless it specifies such an operation, a definition cannot be an operational definition. For example, the definition "A solution is an 'acid' if and only if it has
a pH of less than 7," while good in other respects, is not an operational definition, because it prescribes no operation.

Operational definitions were invented for the purpose of tying down relatively ab-
stract concepts to the solid ground of empirical reality. In this they succeed fairly well;
yet, from the standpoint of ordinary language usage, they involve certain deficiencies.
One of these deficiencies concerns the fact that operational definitions usually convey
only *part* of the intensional meaning of a term. Certainly "brain activity" means more
than oscillations on an electroencephalograph, just as "acid" means more than blue litmus paper turning red. This deficiency becomes more acute when one attempts to apply
operational definitions to terms outside the framework of science. For example, no adequate operational definition could be given for such words as "love," "respect," "freedom,"
and "dignity." Within their proper sphere, however, operational definitions are quite useful and important. Interestingly Einstein developed his special theory of relativity in partial response to the need for an operational definition of simultaneity.

A **definition by genus and difference** assigns a meaning to a term by identifying a
genus term and one or more difference words that, when combined, convey the meaning of the term being defined. Definition by genus and difference is more generally ap-
plicable and achieves more adequate results than any of the other kinds of intensional
definition. To explain how it works, we must first explain the meanings of the terms
*genus, species,* and *specific difference.*

In logic, *genus* and *species* have a somewhat different meaning than they have in biology. In logic, *genus* simply means a relatively larger class, and *species* means a relatively smaller subclass of the genus. For example, we may speak of the genus animal
and the species mammal, or of the genus mammal and the species feline, or of the
genus feline and the species tiger, or the genus tiger and the species Bengal tiger. In
other words, genus and species are merely relative classifications.

The *specific difference,* or *difference,* is the attribute or attributes that distinguish the
various species within a genus. For example, the specific difference that distinguishes
tigers from other species in the genus feline would include the attributes of being large,
striped, ferocious, and so on. Because the specific difference is what distinguishes the
species, when a genus is qualified by a specific difference, a species is identified. Definition by genus and difference is based on this fact. It consists of combining a term denoting a genus with a word or group of words connoting a specific difference so that
the combination identifies the meaning of the term denoting the species.

Let us construct a definition by genus and difference for the word "ice." The first step is to identify a genus of which ice is the species. The required genus is water. Next we must identify a specific difference (attribute) that makes ice a special form of water. The required difference is frozen. The completed definition may now be written out:

| Species | | Difference | Genus |
|---------|---|-----------|-------|
| "Ice" | means | frozen | water. |

A definition by genus and difference is easy to construct. Simply select a term that is more general than the term to be defined, then narrow it down so that it means the same thing as the term being defined. Examples:

| Species | | Difference | Genus |
|---------|---|-----------|-------|
| "Daughter" | means | female | offspring. |
| "Husband" | means | married | man. |
| "Doe" | means | female | deer. |
| "Fawn" | means | very young | deer. |
| "Skyscraper" | means | very tall | building. |

Other examples are more sophisticated:

> "Tent" means a collapsible shelter made of canvas or other material that is stretched and sustained by poles.

"Tent" is the species, "shelter" is the genus, and "collapsible" and "made of canvas . . ." the difference.

Definition by genus and difference is the most effective of the intensional definitions for producing the five kinds of definition discussed in Section 2.3. Stipulative, lexical, precising, theoretical, and persuasive definitions can all be constructed according to the method of genus and difference. Lexical definitions are typically definitions by genus and difference, but they also often include etymological definitions. Operational definition can serve as the method for constructing stipulative, lexical, precising, and persuasive definitions, but because of the limitations we have noted, it typically could not be used to produce a *complete* lexical definition. Other techniques would have to be used in addition. Synonymous definition may be used to produce only lexical definitions. Since, in a synonymous definition, the definiendum must have a meaning before a synonym can be found, this technique cannot be used to produce stipulative definitions, and the fact that the definiens of such a definition contains no more information than the definiendum prohibits its use in constructing precising, theoretical, and persuasive definitions.

This account of definitions is inevitably incomplete. At the beginning of the chapter we saw that all words—not just terms—stand in need of definitions, but the account given here is based on the intension and extension of *terms*. Nevertheless, many of the techniques developed here can be applied to words in general, and even to symbols. For example, Chapters 6 and 8 will present definitions of various symbols that are used in modern logic to connect one statement with another and to translate ordinary language statements into symbolic form. When logicians introduced these symbols many years ago, they did it through stipulative definitions. Also, as we will see in Chapter 6, some of these symbols are defined by certain tables, called *truth tables,*

Table 2.1  Correlation of Definitional Techniques with Types of Definition

| This technique | Can produce this type of definition | | | | |
|---|---|---|---|---|---|
| | **Stipulative** | **Lexical** | **Precising** | **Theoretical** | **Persuasive** |
| **Demonstrative** | yes | yes | no | (unusual) | (unusual) |
| **Enumerative** | yes | yes | no | (unusual) | (unusual) |
| **Subclass** | yes | yes | no | (unusual) | (unusual) |
| **Synonymous** | no | yes | no | no | no |
| **Etymological** | yes | yes | no | no | no |
| **Operational** | (limited) | yes | yes | (unusual) | (unusual) |
| **Genus & Difference** | yes | yes | yes | yes | yes |

which establish each symbol's meaning under all possible arrangements of truth values. These definitions are probably best described as extensional, and they are similar in some ways to demonstrative definitions and enumerative definitions.

The applicability of the seven definitional techniques in producing the five kinds of definition is summarized in Table 2.1.

## EXERCISE 2.4

I. Determine whether the following are demonstrative definitions, enumerative definitions, definitions by subclass, synonymous definitions, etymological definitions, operational definitions, or definitions by genus and difference.

★1. "Plant" means something such as a tree, a flower, a vine, or a cactus.

2. "Hammer" means a tool used for pounding.

3. A triangle is "equilateral" if and only if a compass, when placed sequentially on two vertices and properly adjusted, strikes through the other two vertices.

★4. "State" means something such as Ohio, Arkansas, Minnesota, and Tennessee.

5. "Angel" is a word that originates from the Greek word *angelos,* which means messenger.

6. "Neophyte" means beginner.

★7. "House" means this:

8. "Painting" means something like da Vinci's *Mona Lisa,* van Gogh's *Starry Night,* Botticelli's *Birth of Venus,* or Rembrandt's *Night Watch.*

9. "Dessert" means something such as pie, cake, cookies, or ice-cream sundaes.

★10. "Hot" means, for an electric iron, that your wetted finger sizzles when placed momentarily in contact with it.

11. "Universe" originates from the Latin word *universus,* which means whole or entire.

12. "Mountain" means something such as Everest, Rainier, Whitney, or McKinley.

★13. "Hurricane" means a storm having winds of at least 73 miles per hour that originates at sea.

14. A substance is "translucent" if and only if when held up to a strong light some of the light comes through.

15. "Insect" means something such as a fly, an ant, a wasp, or a caterpillar.

★16. "Poignant" is a word derived from the Latin word *pungere*, which means to prick, pierce, or sting.

17. "Facade" means face.

18. "Prime number" means a number greater than one that is divisible only by itself and one.

★19. "Language" means something such as French, German, Spanish, or English.

20. "Tree" means this, and this, and this (as you point to several trees).

21. "Oak" means a tree that bears acorns.

★22. "Rapier" means sword.

23. An "electric current" flows in a circuit if and only if an ammeter connected in series with the circuit shows a reading.

24. "Philosopher" means someone such as Plato, Aristotle, Descartes, or Kant.

★25. "Professional person" means a person such as a doctor, a lawyer, a professor, or an architect.

26. "Error" means mistake.

27. "Tale" is a word that derives from the Old English word *talu*, which means talk.

★28. "Truck" means a vehicle used for hauling.

29. "Done" means, in reference to a baking cake, that a wooden toothpick poked into the center comes out clean.

30. "Musical composition" means something such as a symphony, a concerto, a sonata, or a toccata.

II. The following exercises involve constructing definitions.

1. Construct a partial enumerative definition for the following terms by naming three members of the class the term denotes. Then find a nonsynonymous term that these members serve equally well to define. Example: "Poet" means a person such as Wordsworth, Coleridge, or Shelley. A nonsynonymous term is "Englishman."

   ★a. skyscraper

   b. corporation

   c. island

   d. composer

   e. novel

2. Construct a complete enumerative definition for the following terms:

   a. ocean

   b. continent

3. Construct a definition by subclass for the following terms by naming three subclasses of the class the term denotes. Then find a nonsynonymous term that these subclasses serve equally well to define.

⋆a. animal

b. fish

c. vehicle

d. gemstone

e. polygon

4. Construct a complete definition by subclass for the following terms:

a. quadrilateral

b. circulating American coin

5. Construct synonymous definitions for the following terms:

⋆a. intersection

b. fabric

c. nucleus

d. abode

e. wedlock

f. cellar

g. summit

h. apparel

6. Construct operational definitions for the following words:

⋆a. genius

b. ferromagnetic

c. fluorescent

d. alkaline

e. polarized (light)

7. Construct definitions by genus and difference for the following terms. In each definition identify the genus term.

⋆a. drake

b. biologist

c. felony

d. widow

e. library

8. Consult a dictionary to find the etymological roots of the following words, and then explain how they relate to the conventional meaning of these words.

⋆a. morphology

b. isomorphic

c. isotropic

     d. phototropic

     e. photography

     f. lithography

     g. lithology

     h. psychology

III. Answer "true" or "false" to the following statements:

1. The technique of extensional definition may be used to produce precising definitions.

2. The technique of extensional definition may be used to produce stipulative and lexical definitions.

3. Most extensional definitions convey the precise intensional meaning of a term.

4. An intensional definition conveys the meaning of a term by indicating the members of the class the term denotes.

5. In a synonymous definition the definiens must be a single word.

6. The technique of synonymous definition may be used to construct precising definitions.

7. Operational definitions typically convey the entire intensional meaning of a word.

8. The species is a subclass of the genus.

9. The specific difference is an attribute or set of attributes that identifies a species.

10. Definition by genus and difference may be used to produce stipulative, lexical, precising, theoretical, and persuasive definitions.

---

## 2.5     Criteria for Lexical Definitions

Because the function of a lexical definition is to report the way a word is actually used in a language, lexical definitions are the ones we most frequently encounter and are what most people mean when they speak of the "definition" of a word. Accordingly, it is appropriate that we have a set of rules that we may use in constructing lexical definitions of our own and in evaluating the lexical definitions of others. While some of these rules apply to the other kinds of definitions as well, the unique functions that are served by stipulative, precising, theoretical, and persuasive definitions prescribe different sets of criteria.

### Rule 1: A Lexical Definition Should Conform to the Standards of Proper Grammar

A definition, like any other form of expression, should be grammatically correct. Examples of definitions that are grammatically *incorrect* are as follows:

Vacation is when you don't have to go to work or school.

Furious means if you're angry at someone.

Cardiac is like something to do with the heart.

The corrected versions are these:

"Vacation" means a period during which activity is suspended from work or school.

"Furious" means a condition of being very angry.

"Cardiac" means pertaining to, situated near, or acting on the heart.

Technically the definiendum should be put in quotation marks or italics, but this convention is not always followed.

### Rule 2: A Lexical Definition Should Convey the Essential Meaning of the Word Being Defined

The word "human" is occasionally defined as featherless biped. Such a definition fails to convey the essential meaning of "human" as the word is used in ordinary English. It says nothing about the important attributes that distinguish humans from the other animals—namely, the capacity to reason and to use language on a sophisticated level. A more adequate definition would be "'Human' means the animal that has the capacity to reason and to speak."

If a lexical definition is to be given in terms of an operational definition or in terms of any of the forms of extensional definition, it should usually be supplemented by one of the other forms of intensional definition, preferably definition by genus and difference. As noted, from the standpoint of ordinary language usage an operational definition often conveys only part of the intensional meaning of a word, and this part frequently misses the essential meaning altogether. As for extensional definitions, at best they can only *suggest* the essential meaning of a word; they cannot *determine* it precisely. As a result, no adequate lexical definition can consist exclusively of extensional definitions.

### Rule 3: A Lexical Definition Should Be Neither Too Broad nor Too Narrow

If a definition is too broad, the definiens includes too much; if it is too narrow, the definiens includes too little. If, for example, "bird" were defined as any warm-blooded animal having wings, the definition would be too broad because it would include bats, and bats are not birds. If, on the other hand, "bird" were defined as any warm-blooded, feathered animal that can fly, the definition would be too narrow because it would exclude ostriches, which cannot fly.

The only types of lexical definitions that tend to be susceptible to either of these deficiencies are synonymous definitions and definitions by genus and difference. With synonymous definitions, one must be careful that the definiens really is a synonym of the definiendum. For example, the definition "'king' means ruler" is too broad because many rulers are not kings. "Ruler" is not genuinely synonymous with "king." As for definitions by genus and difference, one must ensure that the specific difference narrows the genus in exactly the right way. Both of the given definitions of "bird" are definitions by genus and difference in which the specific difference fails to restrict the genus in exactly the right manner.

### Rule 4: A Lexical Definition Should Avoid Circularity

A definition is *circular* when the definiendum is defined in terms of itself, or virtually in terms of itself. Sometimes the problem of circularity appears in connection with *pairs* of definitions. The following pair is circular:

> "Science" means the activity engaged in by scientists.

> "Scientist" means anyone who engages in science.

At other times a definition may be intrinsically circular. Of the following, the first is a synonymous definition, the second a definition by genus and difference:

> "Soporific" means soporiferous.

> "Jewelers' rouge" means rouge used by a jeweler.

In the first example, the definiendum is virtually the same word as the definiens. As a result, anyone who does not already know the meaning of "soporific" would probably not know the meaning of "soporiferous," either. In the second example, "jewelers' rouge" is clearly defined in terms of itself. The corrected definitions are as follows:

> "Soporific" means tending to cause sleep.

> "Jewelers' rouge" means a very fine polishing compound.

Certain operational definitions also run the risk of circularity:

> "Time" means whatever is measured by a clock.

Surely a person would have to know what "time" means before he or she could understand the purpose of a clock.

## Rule 5: A Lexical Definition Should Not Be Negative When It Can Be Affirmative

Of the following two definitions, the first is affirmative, the second negative:

> "Concord" means harmony.

> "Concord" means the absence of discord.

Some words, however, are intrinsically negative. For them, a negative definition is quite appropriate. Examples:

> "Bald" means lacking hair.

> "Darkness" means the absence of light.

## Rule 6: A Lexical Definition Should Avoid Figurative, Obscure, Vague, or Ambiguous Language

A definition is *figurative* if it involves metaphors or tends to paint a picture instead of exposing the essential meaning of a term. Examples:

> "Architecture" means frozen music.

> "Camel" means a ship of the desert.

A definition is *obscure* if its meaning is hidden as a result of defective or inappropriate language. One source of obscurity is overly technical language. Compare these two definitions:

> "Bunny" means a mammalian of the family Leporidae of the order Lagomorpha whose young are born furless and blind.
>
> "Bunny" means a rabbit.

The problem lies not with technical language as such but with *needlessly* technical language. Because "bunny" is very much a nontechnical term, no technical definition is needed. On the other hand, some words are intrinsically technical, and for them only a technical definition will suffice. Example:

> "Neutrino" means a quasi-massless lepton obeying Fermi-Dirac statistics and having one-half quantum unit of spin.

A definition is *vague* if it lacks precision or if its meaning is blurred—that is, if there is no way of telling exactly what class of things the definiens refers to. Example:

> "Democracy" means a kind of government where the people are in control.

This definition fails to identify the people who are in control, how they exercise their control, and what they are in control of.

A definition is *ambiguous* if it lends itself to more than one distinct interpretation. Example:

> "Triangle" means a figure composed of three straight lines in which all the angles are equal to two right angles.

Does this mean that each angle separately is equal to two right angles or that the angles taken together are equal to two right angles? Either interpretation is possible given the ambiguous meaning of "all the angles are equal to two right angles."

### Rule 7: A Lexical Definition Should Avoid Affective Terminology

*Affective terminology* is any kind of word usage that plays on the emotions of the reader or listener. It includes sarcastic and facetious language and any other kind of language that could influence attitudes. Examples:

> "Communism" means that "brilliant" invention of Karl Marx and other foolish political visionaries in which the national wealth is supposed to be held in common by the people.
>
> "Theism" means belief in that great Santa Claus in the sky.

The second example also violates Rule 6 because it contains a metaphor.

### Rule 8: A Lexical Definition Should Indicate the Context to Which the Definiens Pertains

This rule applies to any definition in which the context of the definiens is important to the meaning of the definiendum. For example, the definition "'Deuce' means a tie in points toward a game or in games toward a set" is practically meaningless without any reference to tennis. Whenever the definiendum is a word that means different things in different contexts, a reference to the context is important. Examples:

"Strike" means (in baseball) a pitch at which a batter swings and misses.
"Strike" means (in bowling) the act of knocking down all the pins with the first ball
   of a frame.
"Strike" means (in fishing) a pull on a line made by a fish in taking the bait.

It is not always necessary to make *explicit* reference to the context, but at least the phraseology of the definiens should indicate the context.

## EXERCISE 2.5

Criticize the following definitions in light of the eight rules for lexical definitions:

★1. A sculpture is a three-dimensional image made of marble.

2. "Elusory" means elusive.

3. "Birdie" means sinking the ball in one stroke under par.

★4. A cynic is a person who knows the price of everything and the value of nothing.

(Oscar Wilde)

5. "Semantics" is when somebody studies words.

6. "iPod" means a handheld electronic device weighing about six ounces and featuring a single click-wheel on one side.

★7. A theist is anyone who is not an atheist or an agnostic.

8. "Intelligence" means whatever is measured by an IQ test.

9. A symphony is a musical piece written for full orchestra.

★10. Feminism is a militant movement originated by a group of deviant women for the purpose of undermining the natural distinction between the sexes.

11. "Wood" means fibrous, lignified cellulose.

12. Logic is the study of arguments including definitions.

★13. "Truculent" is if you're cruel or fierce.

14. A house is a structure made of wood or stone intended for human habitation.

15. Satire is a kind of glass, wherein beholders do generally discover everybody's face but their own.

(Jonathan Swift)

★16. A carpenter's square is a square used by a carpenter.

17. "Safety" means a play in which a player grounds the ball behind his own goal line when the ball was caused to cross the goal line by his own team.

18. Puberty: the time in life in which the two sexes begin first to be acquainted.

(Johnson's Dictionary)

★19. "Normal" means an attribute possessed by people who are able to get on in the world.

20. An organic substance is any substance that is not inorganic.

21. Faith is the bird that sings when the dawn is still dark.

(Rabindranath Tagore)

★22. "Schooner" means sort of like a sailboat.

23. "Faith" means reason succumbing to insecurity.

24. "Gammon" means, in backgammon, a victory in which one player defeats another before he can remove any of his men from the board.

★25. A cello is a stringed musical instrument played with a bow.

26. Tobacco is a plant grown in the southeastern United States that, when enjoyed in the form of cigars and cigarettes, produces a most delightful and satisfying taste and aroma.

27. History is the unfolding of miscalculations.

(Barbara Tuchman)

★28. "Clock" means a manufactured device featuring two pointers that rotate past a set of numerals ranging from 1 to 12.

29. "Soap" means saponified glyceride.

30. Mackerel: a sea-fish.

(Johnson's Dictionary)

★31. "Anchorperson" means an electronic media guru who has great looks but less-than-average intelligence and who brings canned news to people incapable of reading a newspaper.

32. "Diet" means like when you cut back on your calories.

33. Animal: a living creature corporeal, distinct, on the one side, from pure spirit, on the other, from pure matter.

(Johnson's Dictionary)

★34. "Pen" means an instrument used for writing on paper.

35. Wine is an alcoholic beverage made from grapes.

## Summary

Terminology that conveys information is said to have cognitive meaning, and terminology that expresses or evokes feelings is said to have emotive meaning. Statements expressed in emotive terminology often make value claims; when these statements occur in arguments, it is appropriate to disengage the value claims from the emotive language and express them as separate premises. Two ways in which cognitive meanings can be defective are vagueness and ambiguity. Vagueness involves a blur of meaning, whereas ambiguity involves a mix-up of otherwise clear meanings.

A term is a word or group of words that can serve as the subject of a statement. All terms have intensional meaning (intension or connotation), and those terms that refer to actually existing things also have extensional meaning (extension or denotation). The intensional meaning of a term consists of the attributes that the term connotes, and the extensional meaning consists of the members of the class that the term denotes. Terms that refer to nonexistent things are said to have empty extension.

A definition is a group of words that assigns a meaning to a word or group of words. The definiendum is the word or group of words being defined, and the definiens is the word or group of words that does the defining. Because definitions can serve different purposes, there are different kinds of definitions. Stipulative definitions assign a meaning to a word when it first comes into use, lexical definitions report the meaning that a word already has within a given linguistic community, precising definitions reduce the vagueness of a word, theoretical definitions suggest a theory that gives a certain characterization to the entities that the term denotes, and persuasive definitions are used to influence the attitude of people in the community toward the things the word denotes.

The two kinds of meaning that words have, intensional and extensional, can be used as the basis for producing definitions. Extensional definitions assign a meaning to a word by identifying the things that the word denotes, and intensional definitions accomplish the same purpose by identifying the attributes that the word connotes.

Among the extensional definitions, demonstrative definitions "point" to the things in question, enumerative definitions name various individuals in the class, and definitions by subclass identify subclasses of those things. Among the intensional definitions, synonymous definitions equate the word being defined with another word that connotes the same attributes, etymological definitions disclose the word's ancestry, operational definitions specify experimental procedures for determining whether the word applies to a certain thing, and definitions by genus and difference identify a larger class of things and then narrow it down so that it matches the class that the word refers to.

There are rules that govern the construction of lexical definitions. Such definitions should conform to grammatical standards; convey the essential meaning of the word being defined; be neither too broad nor too narrow; avoid circularity; avoid negative, figurative, obscure, vague, ambiguous, and affective language; and indicate the context to which the defininiens pertains.

# Answers to Selected Exercises

## Exercise 2.1

II.

1. In dog sled races the dogs are tortured.
   Torturing animals is morally wrong.
   Therefore, dog sled races are morally wrong.

4. Free ownership of guns is as noble as belief in God and intestinal fortitude.
   Belief in God and intestinal fortitude made our country great and free.
   Continued belief in God and intestinal fortitude are necessary to keep our country the way it is.
   Free ownership of guns is no less important than God and intestinal fortitude.
   Therefore, gun control is wrong.

7. The celebration of cultural diversity causes social fragmentation.
   The celebration of cultural diversity is symptomatic of a split personality.
   The people who set this country up framed one nation, indivisible.
   The celebration of cultural diversity works against the intention of these people.
   The celebration of cultural diversity erodes national identity.
   Therefore, the celebration of cultural diversity is wrong.

10. Liberalism has excessively enlarged the welfare system.
    Liberalism has made welfare recipients indolent and irresponsible.
    The liberals refuse to acknowledge or correct the defects in this system.
    Liberalism has made the criminal justice system too sensitive to the criminal and too insensitive to the victim of crime.
    Liberalism has given more rights to the criminal than to the ordinary citizen.
    Liberalism has promoted sex and violence in the school system.
    Liberals have opposed prayer in the schools.
    Therefore, liberalism is bad.

**III.**

1. Probably verbal; ambiguity. Does "sound" designate a subjective perception or an objective disturbance of the air (or some other medium)?

4. Probably verbal; ambiguity. By "violence" do we mean intentional hostility exerted by one human against another, or the operation of blind physical forces? Possibly a combination of verbal and factual. Is human violence caused by the operation of physical forces just as other physical events are?

7. Factual. Did Paul go to Knoxville or Nashville?

10. Factual. When was the Battle of Trafalgar fought, and when did Nelson die?

13. Probably a combination of verbal (ambiguity) and factual. First, does "freedom" mean the absence of external constraint only, or the absence of both internal and external constraint? Second, given the former, is it appropriate to punish the perpetrator of evil acts even though those acts might be internally compelled?

16. Verbal; vagueness. What is the meaning of "overpaid"?

19. Verbal; vagueness. What is the meaning of "poverty"?

## Exercise 2.2

**I.**

4a. Plant, tree, conifer, spruce, Sitka spruce.

## Exercise 2.3

**I.**

1. Precising definition.

4. Lexical definition.

7. Persuasive definition.

10. Theoretical definition.

13. Stipulative definition.

16. Persuasive definition.

19. Lexical definition.

22. Precising definition.

25. Stipulative definition.

## Exercise 2.4

**I.**

1. Definition by subclass.

4. Enumerative definition.

7. Demonstrative definition.

10. Operational definition.

13. Definition by genus and difference.

16. Etymological definition.

19. Enumerative definition.

22. Synonymous definition.

25. Definition by subclass.

28. Definition by genus and difference.

**II.**

1a. "Skyscraper" means the Empire State Building, Chrysler Building, Sears Tower, and so on. Nonsynonymous term: building.

3a. "Animal" means a horse, bear, lion, and so on. Nonsynonymous term: mammal.

5a. "Intersection" means crossing.

6a. A person is a "genius" if and only if that person can earn a score of 140 on an IQ test.

7a. "Drake" means a male duck.

8a. "Morphology" is derived from the Greek words *morphe*, meaning "form," and *logos*, meaning reason, speech, or account. The morphology of something (such as an animal or a plant) gives an account or explanation of the form or structure of that thing.

## Exercise 2.5

1. Rule 3: too narrow; the definiens excludes images made of bronze, wood, plaster, and so on.

4. Rule 6: figurative language.

7. Rule 5: negative.

10. Rule 7: affective terminology.
13. Rule 1: improper grammar.
16. Rule 4: circular.
19. Rule 6: vague.
22. Rule 1: improper grammar; Rule 6: vague; Rule 3: too broad (the definiens also includes ketches, sloops, and yawls).
25. Rule 3: too broad (the definiens also describes violins, violas, and string basses).
28. Rule 2: fails to convey the essential meaning; the definition says nothing about the purpose of a clock, which is to tell the time; also too narrow: the definiens excludes twenty-four-hour clocks and clocks without twelve numerals on their face.
31. Rule 7: affective terminology.
34. Rule 3: both too narrow and too broad; the definiens excludes instruments used for writing on canvas, glass, metal, plastic, and so on, and it includes pencils, crayons, and so on.

# 3

# Informal Fallacies

## 3.1 Fallacies in General

A **fallacy** is a defect in an argument that consists in something other than false premises alone. The fallacies introduced in this chapter involve defective patterns of arguing that occur so often they have been given specific names. Such defects comprise either mistakes in reasoning or the creation of an illusion that makes a bad argument appear good. The term *non sequitur* ("it does not follow") is another name for fallacy. Both deductive and inductive arguments may contain fallacies; if they do, they are either unsound or uncogent, depending on the kind of argument. Conversely, if an argument is unsound or uncogent, it has one or more false premises or it contains a fallacy (or both).

Fallacies are usually divided into two groups: formal and informal. A **formal fallacy** is one that may be identified by merely examining the form or structure of an argument. Fallacies of this kind are found only in deductive arguments that have identifiable forms. Chapter 1 presented some of these forms: categorical syllogisms, disjunctive syllogisms, and hypothetical syllogisms. The following categorical syllogism contains a formal fallacy:

> All bullfights are grotesque rituals.
> All executions are grotesque rituals.
> Therefore, all bullfights are executions.

This argument has the following form:

> All *A* are *B*.
> All *C* are *B*.
> ———————
> All *A* are *C*.

By merely examining this form, one can see that it is invalid. The fact that *A*, *B*, and *C* stand respectively for "bullfights," "grotesque rituals," and "executions" is irrelevant in detecting the fallacy. The problem may be traced to the second premise. If the letters *C* and *B* are interchanged, the form becomes valid, and the original argument, with the same change introduced, also becomes valid (but unsound).

Here is an example of a formal fallacy that occurs in a hypothetical syllogism:

If apes are intelligent, then apes can solve puzzles.
Apes can solve puzzles.
Therefore, apes are intelligent.

This argument has the following form:

If *A* then *B*.
*B*.
_____
*A*.

In this case, if *A* and *B* are interchanged in the first premise, the form becomes valid, and the original argument, with the same change, also becomes valid. This fallacy and the one that precedes it will be discussed in later chapters.

In distinguishing formal from informal fallacies, remember that formal fallacies occur only in deductive arguments. Thus, if a given argument is inductive, it cannot contain a formal fallacy. Also, keep an eye out for standard deductive argument forms such as categorical syllogisms and hypothetical syllogisms. If such an argument is invalid because of an improper arrangement of terms or statements, it commits a formal fallacy. Section 1.5 investigated some of these forms and gave instruction on distinguishing the form from the content of an argument. All of the exercises at the end of that section commit formal fallacies.

**Informal fallacies** are those that can be detected only by examining the content of the argument. Consider the following example:

The Brooklyn Bridge is made of atoms.
Atoms are invisible.
Therefore, the Brooklyn Bridge is invisible.

To detect this fallacy one must know something about bridges—namely, that they are large visible objects, and even though their atomic components are invisible, this does not mean that the bridges themselves are invisible.

Or consider this example:

A chess player is a person.
Therefore, a bad chess player is a bad person.

To detect this fallacy one must know that the meaning of the word "bad" depends on what it modifies, and that being a bad chess player is quite different from being a bad person.

The various informal fallacies accomplish their purpose in so many different ways that no single umbrella theory covers them all. Some fallacies work by getting the reader or listener to feel various emotions, such as fear, pity, or camaraderie, and then attaching a certain conclusion to those emotions. Others attempt to discredit an opposing argument by associating it with certain pejorative features of its author. And then there are those that appeal to various dispositions on the part of the reader or listener, such as superstition or mental laziness, to get him or her to accept a conclusion. By studying the typical ways in which arguers apply these techniques, one is less likely to be fooled by the fallacious arguments posed by others or to stumble blindly into fallacies when constructing arguments for one's own use.

Since the time of Aristotle, logicians have attempted to classify the various informal fallacies. Aristotle himself identified thirteen and separated them into two groups. The work of subsequent logicians has produced dozens more, rendering the task of classifying them even more difficult. The presentation that follows divides twenty-two informal fallacies into five groups: fallacies of relevance, fallacies of weak induction, fallacies of presumption, fallacies of ambiguity, and fallacies of grammatical analogy. The final section of the chapter considers the related topics of detecting and avoiding fallacies in the context of ordinary language.

## EXERCISE 3.1

Determine whether the fallacies committed by the following arguments are formal fallacies or informal fallacies.

★1. If Rasputin was really mad, then he deceived Czar Nicholas II. Rasputin was not really mad. Therefore, he did not deceive Czar Nicholas II.

2. Everything that runs has feet. The Columbia River runs very swiftly. Therefore, the Columbia River has feet.

3. All people who believe we create our own reality are people who lack social responsibility. All people governed by selfish motives are people who lack social responsibility. Therefore, all people who believe we create our own reality are people governed by selfish motives.

★4. The ship of state is like a ship at sea. No sailor is ever allowed to protest orders from the captain. For the same reason, no citizen should ever be allowed to protest presidential policies.

5. Renowned violinist Pinchas Zukerman has said, "When it comes to vodka, Smirnoff plays second fiddle to none." We must therefore conclude that Smirnoff is the best vodka available.

6. If the Chinese government systematically kills its unwanted orphans, then the Chinese government is immoral. The Chinese government is indeed immoral. Therefore, the Chinese government systematically kills its unwanted orphans.

★7. Sarah Jessica Parker, Ben Affleck, and Julia Roberts are Democrats. Therefore, it must be the case that all Hollywood stars are Democrats.

8. Venezuelan President Hugo Chavez argues that the United States has no right to decide what's good or bad for the whole world. But who is this Chavez? He's nothing but an autocratic demagogue who assaults democracy at every opportunity. Clearly his arguments are nonsense.

9. If plastic guns are sold to the public, then terrorists will carry them aboard airliners undetected. If plastic guns are sold to the public, then airline hijackings will increase. Therefore, if terrorists carry plastic guns aboard airliners undetected, then airline hijackings will increase.

★10. Some corporate mergers are arrangements that produce layoffs. Some arrangements that produce layoffs are occasions of economic unrest. Therefore, some corporate mergers are occasions of economic unrest.

## 3.2          Fallacies of Relevance

The **fallacies of relevance** share the common characteristic that the arguments in which they occur have premises that are *logically* irrelevant to the conclusion. Yet the premises may appear to be *psychologically* relevant, so the conclusion may *seem* to follow from the premises, even though it does not follow logically. In a good argument the premises provide genuine evidence in support of the conclusion. In an argument that commits a fallacy of relevance, on the other hand, the connection between premises and conclusion is emotional. To identify a fallacy of relevance, therefore, one must be able to distinguish genuine evidence from various forms of emotional appeal.

### 1.  Appeal to Force
### (*Argumentum ad Baculum*: Appeal to the "Stick")

The fallacy of **appeal to force** occurs whenever an arguer poses a conclusion to another person and tells that person either implicitly or explicitly that some harm will come to him or her if he or she does not accept the conclusion. The fallacy always involves a threat by the arguer to the physical or psychological well-being of the listener or reader, who may be either an individual or a group of people. Obviously, such a threat is logically irrelevant to the subject matter of the conclusion, so any argument based on such a procedure is fallacious. The *ad baculum* fallacy often occurs when children argue with one another:

> *Child to playmate: Sesame Street* is the best show on TV; and if you don't believe it, I'm going to call my big brother over here and he's going to beat you up.

But it occurs among adults as well:

> *Secretary to boss:* I deserve a raise in salary for the coming year. After all, you know how friendly I am with your wife, and I'm sure you wouldn't want her to find out what's been going on between you and that sexpot client of yours.

The first example involves a physical threat, the second a psychological one. While neither threat provides any genuine evidence that the conclusion is true, both provide evidence that someone might be injured. If the two types of evidence are confused with each other, both arguer and listener may be deluded into thinking that the conclusion is supported by evidence, when in fact it is not.

The appeal to force fallacy usually accomplishes its purpose by psychologically impeding the reader or listener from acknowledging a missing premise that, if acknowl-

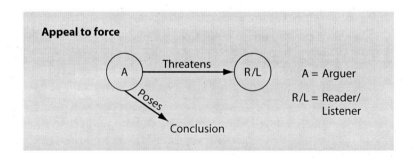

edged, would be seen to be false or at least questionable. The two examples just given can be interpreted as concealing the following premises, both of which are most likely false:

> If my brother forces you to admit that *Sesame Street* is the best show on TV, then *Sesame Street* is in fact the best show.

> If I succeed in threatening you, then I deserve a raise in salary.

The conclusion of the first argument is that *Sesame Street* is the best show on TV. But just because someone is forced into saying that it is does not mean that such is the case. Similarly, the conclusion of the second argument is that the secretary deserves a raise in salary. But if the boss is threatened into raising the secretary's salary, this does not mean that the secretary deserves a raise. Many of the other informal fallacies can be interpreted as accomplishing their purpose in this way.

## 2. Appeal to Pity (*Argumentum ad Misericordiam*)

The **appeal to pity** fallacy occurs when an arguer attempts to support a conclusion by merely evoking pity from the reader or listener. This pity may be directed toward the arguer or toward some third party. Example:

> *Taxpayer to judge:* Your Honor, I admit that I declared thirteen children as dependents on my tax return, even though I have only two. But if you find me guilty of tax evasion, my reputation will be ruined. I'll probably lose my job, my poor wife will not be able to have the operation that she desperately needs, and my kids will starve. Surely I am not guilty.

The conclusion of this argument is "Surely I am not guilty." Obviously, the conclusion is not *logically* relevant to the arguer's set of pathetic circumstances, although it is *psychologically* relevant. If the arguer succeeds in evoking pity from the listener or reader, the latter is likely to exercise his or her desire to help the arguer by accepting the argument. In this way the reader or listener may be fooled into accepting a conclusion that is not supported by any evidence. The appeal to pity is quite common and is often used by students on their instructors at exam time and by lawyers on behalf of their clients before judges and juries.

Of course, some arguments that attempt to evoke sympathetic feelings from the reader or listener are not fallacious. We might call them *arguments from compassion*. Such arguments differ from the fallacious appeal to pity in that, in addition to evoking

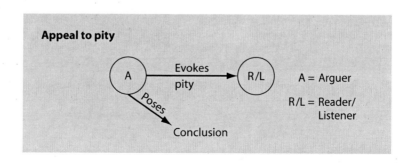

compassion on behalf of some person, they supply information about why that person is genuinely deserving of help or special consideration. Whenever possible these nonfallacious arguments should show that the person in question is a victim of circumstances and not responsible for the dire straits he finds himself in, that the recommended help or special consideration is not illegal or inappropriate, and that it will genuinely help the person in question. In contrast to such arguments, the appeal to pity proceeds by ignoring all of these considerations and attempts to support a conclusion by merely evoking pity from the reader or listener.

## 3. Appeal to the People (*Argumentum ad Populum*)

Nearly everyone wants to be loved, esteemed, admired, valued, recognized, and accepted by others. The **appeal to the people** uses these desires to get the reader or listener to accept a conclusion. Two approaches are involved: one of them direct, the other indirect.

The *direct approach* occurs when an arguer, addressing a large group of people, excites the emotions and enthusiasm of the crowd to win acceptance for his or her conclusion. The objective is to arouse a kind of mob mentality. This is the strategy used by nearly every propagandist and demagogue. Adolf Hitler was a master of the technique, but speech makers at Democratic and Republican national conventions also use it with some measure of success. Waving flags and blaring music add to the overall effect. Because the individuals in the audience want to share in the camaraderie, the euphoria, and the excitement, they find themselves accepting a variety of conclusions with ever-increasing fervor.

An appeal to negative emotions, such as suspicion and fear, can also generate a mob mentality. These emotions have produced many lynchings, and they led to the internment of Japanese Americans during World War II. Also, the direct approach is not limited to oral discourse. The same effect can be accomplished in writing. By using such emotionally charged phrasing as "fighter of communism," "champion of the free enterprise system," and "defender of the working man," polemicists can awaken the same kind of mob mentality as they would if they were speaking.

In the *indirect approach* the arguer aims his or her appeal not at the crowd as a whole but at one or more individuals separately, focusing on some aspect of their relationship to the crowd. The indirect approach includes such specific forms as the bandwagon argument, the appeal to vanity, and the appeal to snobbery. All are standard techniques of the advertising industry.

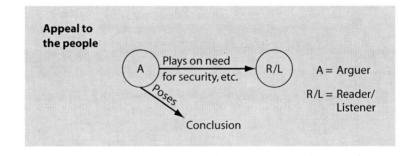

Here is an example of the **bandwagon argument:**

> Of course you want to buy Zing toothpaste. Why, 90 percent of America brushes with Zing.

The idea is that you will be left behind or left out of the group if you do not use the product.

The **appeal to vanity** often associates the product with someone who is admired, pursued, or imitated, the idea being that you, too, will be admired and pursued if you use it. The recent television and billboard ads for the U.S. Marine Corps provide an example. The ads show a strong, handsome man in uniform holding a gleaming sword, and the caption reads:

> The Few, the Proud, the Marines.

The message is that if you join the Marines, then you, too, will be admired and respected, just like the handsome man in the uniform.

The **appeal to snobbery** depends on a similar kind of association.

> A Rolls-Royce is not for everyone. If you qualify as one of the select few, this distinguished classic may be seen and driven at British Motor Cars, Ltd.
> (By appointment only, please.)

Needless to say, the indirect approach is used not only by advertisers:

> *Mother to child:* You want to grow up and be just like Wonder Woman, don't you? Then eat your liver and carrots.

These examples illustrate how the indirect version of the appeal to the people can overlap the false cause fallacy, which is presented in Section 3.3. Thus, the previous example might be interpreted to suggest that eating liver and carrots will *cause* one to become just like Wonder Woman. If so, the fallacy could be identified as false cause.

Both the direct and indirect approaches of the *ad populum* fallacy have the same basic structure:

> You want to be accepted/included in the group/loved/esteemed....Therefore, you should accept XYZ as true.

In the direct approach the arousal of a mob mentality produces an immediate feeling of belonging. Each person feels united with the crowd, and this feeling evokes a sense of strength and security. When the crowd roars its approval of the conclusions that are then offered, anyone who does not accept them automatically cuts himself or herself off from the crowd and risks the loss of his or her security, strength, and acceptance. The same thing happens in the indirect approach, but the context and technique are somewhat subtler.

## 4. Argument Against the Person (*Argumentum ad Hominem*)

This fallacy always involves two arguers. One of them advances (either directly or implicitly) a certain argument, and the other then responds by directing his or her attention not to the first person's argument but to the first person *himself*. When this occurs, the second person is said to commit an **argument against the person.**

The argument against the person occurs in three forms: the *ad hominem* abusive, the *ad hominem* circumstantial, and the *tu quoque*. In the **ad hominem abusive,** the second person responds to the first person's argument by verbally abusing the first person. Example:

> Before he died, poet Allen Ginsberg argued in favor of legalizing pornography. But Ginsberg's arguments are nothing but trash. Ginsberg was a marijuana-smoking homosexual and a thoroughgoing advocate of the drug culture.

Because Ginsberg's being a marijuana-smoking homosexual and advocate of the drug culture is irrelevant to whether the premises of this argument support the conclusion, the argument is fallacious.

Not all cases of the *ad hominem* abusive are so blunt, but they are just as fallacious. Example:

> William Buckley has argued in favor of legalizing drugs such as cocaine and heroin. But Buckley is just another one of those upper-crust intellectuals who is out of touch with real America. No sensible person should listen to his pseudosolutions.

Again, whether Buckley is an upper-crust intellectual has nothing to do with whether his premises support his conclusion.

The **ad hominem circumstantial** begins the same way as the *ad hominem* abusive, but instead of heaping verbal abuse on his or her opponent, the respondent attempts to discredit the opponent's argument by alluding to certain circumstances that affect the opponent. By doing so the respondent hopes to show that the opponent is predisposed to argue the way he or she does and should therefore not be taken seriously. Here is an example:

> The Dalai Lama argues that China has no business in Tibet and that the West should do something about it. But the Dalai Lama just wants the Chinese to leave so he can return as leader. Naturally he argues this way. Therefore, we should reject his arguments.

The author of this argument ignores the substance of the Dalai Lama's argument and attempts to discredit it by calling attention to certain circumstances that affect the Dalai Lama—namely, that he wants to return to Tibet as its leader. But the fact that the Dalai Lama happens to be affected by these circumstances is irrelevant to whether

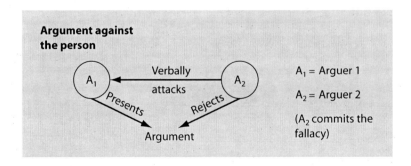

his premises support a conclusion. The *ad hominem* circumstantial is easy to recognize because it always takes this form: "Of course Mr. X argues this way; just look at the circumstances that affect him."

The **tu quoque** ("you too") fallacy begins the same way as the other two varieties of the *ad hominem* argument, except that the second arguer attempts to make the first appear to be hypocritical or arguing in bad faith. The second arguer usually accomplishes this by citing features in the life or behavior of the first arguer that conflict with the latter's conclusion. In effect, the second arguer says, "How dare you argue that I should stop doing *X*; why, you do (or have done) *X* yourself." Example:

> *Child to parent:* Your argument that I should stop stealing candy from the corner store is no good. You told me yourself just a week ago that you, too, stole candy when you were a kid.

Obviously, whether the parent stole candy is irrelevant to whether the parent's premises support the conclusion that the child should not steal candy.

Keep in mind that the purpose of an *ad hominem* argument is to discredit another person's argument by placing its author in a bad light. Thus, for the fallacy to be committed, there must always be two arguers (at least implicitly). If it should turn out that the person being attacked is not an arguer, then the personal comments made by the attacker may well be relevant to the conclusion that is drawn. In general, personal observations are relevant to conclusions about what kind of person someone is (good, bad, stingy, trustworthy, and so forth) and whether a person has done something. Example:

> International terrorist Osama bin Laden planned the destruction of the World Trade Center, killing thousands of innocent people, and he supports terrorist causes all over the world. Bin Laden is therefore a wicked and irresponsible person.

The conclusion is not that Bin Laden's argument is bad but that Bin Laden himself is bad. Because the premises give relevant support to this conclusion, the argument commits no fallacy. Another example:

> Shakespeare cannot possibly have written the thirty-six plays attributed to him, because the real Shakespeare was a two-bit country businessman who barely finished the fourth grade in school and who never left the confines of his native England.

The conclusion is not that some argument of Shakespeare's is bad but that Shakespeare did not write certain plays. Again, since the premises are relevant to this conclusion, the argument commits no *ad hominem* fallacy.

Determining what kind of person someone is includes determining whether that person is trustworthy. Thus, personal comments are often relevant in evaluating whether a person's proclamations or statements, unsupported by evidence, warrant our belief. Examples of such statements include promises to do something, testimony given by a witness, and testimonials in support of a product or service. Here is an example of an argument that discredits a witness:

> Mickey has testified that he saw Freddy set fire to the building. But Mickey was recently convicted on ten counts of perjury, and he hates Freddy with a passion and would love to see him sent to jail. Therefore, you should not believe Mickey's testimony.

This argument commits no fallacy. The conclusion is not that you should reject Mickey's argument but rather that you should reject his testimony. Testimony is not argument, and the fact that the witness is a known liar and has a motive to lie now is relevant to whether we should believe him. Furthermore, note that the conclusion is not that Mickey's statement is literally false but rather that we should not *believe* the statement. It is quite possible that Mickey really did see Freddy set fire to the building and that Mickey's statement to that effect is true. But if our only reason for believing this statement is the mere fact that Mickey has made it, then given the circumstances, we are not justified in that belief. Personal factors are never relevant to truth and falsity as such, but they are relevant to believability.

Yet there is often a close connection between truth and believability, and this provides one of the reasons why *ad hominem* arguments are often effective. In evaluating any argument there are always two issues to be considered: the quality of the reasoning and the truth of the premises. As noted, both are irrelevant to the personal characteristics of the arguer. But whether we *accept* the premises as true may depend on the credibility of the arguer. Knowing that the arguer is biased or has a motive to lie may provide good grounds for distrusting the premises. Another reason why *ad hominem* arguments are effective is that they engage the emotions of readers and listeners and thereby motivate them to transfer their negative feelings about the arguer onto the argument.

## 5. Accident

The fallacy of **accident** is committed when a general rule is applied to a specific case it was not intended to cover. Typically, the general rule is cited (either directly or implicitly) in the premises and then wrongly applied to the specific case mentioned in the conclusion. Two examples:

> Freedom of speech is a constitutionally guaranteed right. Therefore, John Q. Radical should not be arrested for his speech that incited the riot last week.

> Property should be returned to its rightful owner. That drunken sailor who is starting a fight with his opponents at the pool table lent you his .45-caliber pistol, and now he wants it back. Therefore, you should return it to him now.

In the first example, the general rule is that freedom of speech is normally guaranteed, and the specific case is the speech made by John Q. Radical. Because the speech incited

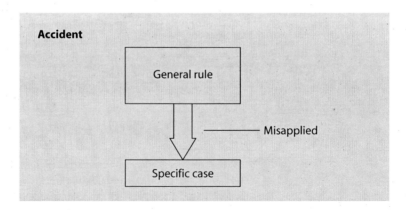

a riot, the rule does not apply. In the second example, the general rule is that property should be returned to its rightful owner, and the specific case is the sailor who wants his gun returned. The rule does not apply, because the return of the property might result in serious injury or death.

The fallacy of accident gets its name from the fact that one or more accidental features of the specific case make it an exception to the rule. In the first example the accidental feature is that the speech incited a riot; in the second example the accidental features are that the sailor is drunk, that he is starting a fight, and that the property in question is dangerous.

## 6. Straw Man

The **straw man** fallacy is committed when an arguer distorts an opponent's argument for the purpose of more easily attacking it, demolishes the distorted argument, and then concludes that the opponent's real argument has been demolished. By so doing, the arguer is said to have set up a straw man and knocked it down, only to conclude that the real man (opposing argument) has been knocked down as well. Example:

> Mr. Goldberg has argued against prayer in the public schools. Obviously Mr. Goldberg advocates atheism. But atheism is what they used to have in Russia. Atheism leads to the suppression of all religions and the replacement of God by an omnipotent state. Is that what we want for this country? I hardly think so. Clearly Mr. Goldberg's argument is nonsense.

Like the argument against the person fallacy, the straw man fallacy involves two arguers. Mr. Goldberg, who is the first arguer, has presented an argument against prayer in the public schools. The second arguer then attacks Goldberg's argument by equating it with an argument for atheism. He then attacks atheism and concludes that Goldberg's argument is nonsense. Since Goldberg's argument had nothing to do with atheism, the second argument commits the straw man fallacy.

As this example illustrates, the kind of distortion the second arguer resorts to is often an attempt to exaggerate the first person's argument or make it look more extreme than it really is. Here are two more examples:

> The garment workers have signed a petition arguing for better ventilation on the work premises. Unfortunately, air-conditioning is expensive. Air ducts would have to be run throughout the factory, and a massive heat exchange unit installed on the roof. Also, the cost of operating such a system during the summer would be astronomical. In view of these considerations the petition must be rejected.

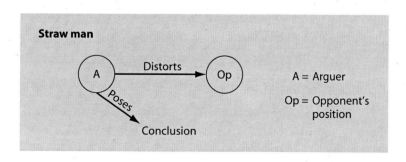

Straw man

A → Distorts → Op

A Poses → Conclusion

A = Arguer

Op = Opponent's position

> The student status committee has presented us with an argument favoring alcohol privileges on campus. What do the students want? Is it their intention to stay boozed up from the day they enter as freshmen until the day they graduate? Do they expect us to open a bar for them? Or maybe a chain of bars all over campus? Such a proposal is ridiculous!

In the first argument, the petition is merely for better ventilation in the factory—maybe a fan in the window during the summer. The arguer exaggerates this request to mean an elaborate air-conditioning system installed throughout the building. He then points out that this is too expensive and concludes by rejecting the petition. A similar strategy is used in the second argument. The arguer distorts the request for alcohol privileges to mean a chain of bars all over campus. Such an idea is so patently outlandish that no further argument is necessary.

## 7. Missing the Point (*Ignoratio Elenchi*)

All the fallacies we have discussed thus far have been instances of cases where the premises of an argument are irrelevant to the conclusion. **Missing the point** illustrates a special form of irrelevance. This fallacy occurs when the premises of an argument support one particular conclusion, but then a different conclusion, often vaguely related to the correct conclusion, is drawn. Whenever one suspects that such a fallacy is being committed, he or she should be able to identify the *correct* conclusion, the conclusion that the premises *logically* imply. This conclusion must be significantly different from the conclusion that is actually drawn. Examples:

> Crimes of theft and robbery have been increasing at an alarming rate lately. The conclusion is obvious: We must reinstate the death penalty immediately.

> Abuse of the welfare system is rampant nowadays. Our only alternative is to abolish the system altogether.

At least two correct conclusions are implied by the premise of the first argument: either "We should provide increased police protection in vulnerable neighborhoods" or "We should initiate programs to eliminate the causes of the crimes." Reinstating the death

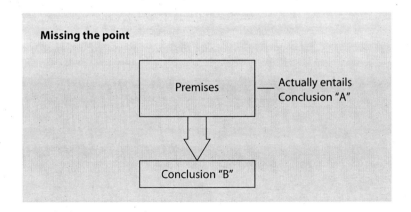

**Missing the point**

Premises —— Actually entails Conclusion "A"

Conclusion "B"

penalty is not a logical conclusion at all. Among other things, theft and robbery are not capital crimes. In the second argument the premises logically suggest some systematic effort to eliminate the cheaters rather than eliminating the system altogether.

*Ignoratio elenchi* means "ignorance of the proof." The arguer is ignorant of the logical implications of his or her own premises and, as a result, draws a conclusion that misses the point entirely. The fallacy has a distinct structure all its own, but in some ways it serves as a catchall for arguments that are not clear instances of one or more of the other fallacies. An argument should not be identified as a case of missing the point, however, if one of the other fallacies fits.

## 8. Red Herring

This fallacy is closely associated with missing the point (*ignoratio elenchi*). The **red herring** fallacy is committed when the arguer diverts the attention of the reader or listener by changing the subject to a different but sometimes subtly related one. He or she then finishes by either drawing a conclusion about this different issue or by merely presuming that some conclusion has been established. By so doing, the arguer purports to have won the argument. The fallacy gets its name from a procedure used to train hunting dogs to follow a scent. A red herring (or bag of them) is dragged across the trail with the aim of leading the dogs astray. Since red herrings have an especially potent scent (caused in part by the smoking process used to preserve them), only the best dogs will follow the original scent.

To use the red herring fallacy effectively, the arguer must change the original subject of the argument without the reader or listener noticing it. One way of doing this is to change the subject to one that is subtly related to the original subject. Here are two examples of this technique:

> Environmentalists are continually harping about the dangers of nuclear power. Unfortunately, electricity is dangerous no matter where it comes from. Every year hundreds of people are electrocuted by accident. Since most of these accidents are caused by carelessness, they could be avoided if people would just exercise greater caution.

> There is a good deal of talk these days about the need to eliminate pesticides from our fruits and vegetables. But many of these foods are essential to our health. Carrots are an excellent source of vitamin A, broccoli is rich in iron, and oranges and grapefruit have lots of vitamin C.

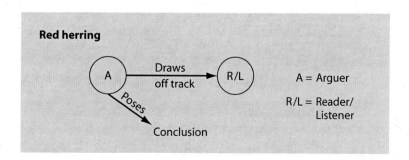

Both arguments commit the red herring fallacy. In the first, the original issue is whether nuclear power is dangerous. The arguer changes this subject to the danger of electrocution and proceeds to draw a conclusion about that. The new subject is clearly different from the possibility of nuclear explosion or meltdown, but the fact that both are related to electricity facilitates the arguer's goal of leading someone off the track. In the second argument, the original issue is pesticides, and the arguer changes it to the value of fruits and vegetables in one's diet. Again, the fact that the second topic is related to the first assists the arguer in committing the fallacy. In neither case does the arguer draw a conclusion about the original topic, but by merely diverting the attention of the reader or listener, the arguer creates the presumption of having won the argument.

A second way of using the red herring effectively is to change the subject to some flashy, eye-catching topic that is virtually guaranteed to distract the listener's attention. Topics of this sort include sex, crime, scandal, immorality, death, and any other topic that might serve as the subject of gossip. Here is an example of this technique:

> Professor Conway complains of inadequate parking on our campus. But did you know that last year Conway carried on a torrid love affair with a member of the English Department? The two used to meet every day for clandestine sex in the copier room. Apparently they didn't realize how much you can see through that fogged glass window. Even the students got an eyeful. Enough said about Conway.

The red herring fallacy can be confused with the straw man fallacy because both have the effect of drawing the reader/listener off the track. This confusion can usually be avoided by remembering the unique ways in which they accomplish this purpose. In the straw man, the arguer begins by distorting an opponent's argument and concludes by knocking down the distorted argument. In the red herring, the arguer ignores the opponent's argument (if there is one) and subtly changes the subject. Thus, to distinguish the two fallacies, one should attempt to determine whether the arguer has knocked down a distorted argument or simply changed the subject. Also keep in mind that straw man always involves two arguers, at least implicitly, whereas a red herring often does not.

Both the red herring and straw man fallacies are susceptible of being confused with missing the point, because all three involve a similar kind of irrelevancy. To avoid this confusion, one should note that both red herring and straw man proceed by generating a new set of premises, whereas missing the point does not. Straw man draws a conclusion from new premises that are obtained by distorting an earlier argument, and red herring, if it draws any conclusion at all, draws one from new premises obtained by changing the subject. Missing the point, however, draws a conclusion from the original premises. Also, in the red herring and straw man, the conclusion, if there is one, is *relevant* to the premises from which it is drawn; but in missing the point, the conclusion is *irrelevant* to the premises from which it is drawn. Finally, remember that missing the point serves in part as a kind of catchall fallacy, and a fallacious argument should not be identified as a case of missing the point if one of the other fallacies clearly fits.

## EXERCISE 3.2

I. Identify the fallacies of relevance committed by the following arguments, giving a brief explanation for your answer. If no fallacy is committed, write "no fallacy."

★1. The position open in the accounting department should be given to Frank Thompson. Frank has six hungry children to feed, and his wife desperately needs an operation to save her eyesight.

2. Erica Evans, who takes orders at the local Taco Bell, argues persuasively in favor of increasing the minimum wage. But this is exactly what you would expect. Erica is paid the minimum wage, and if the minimum wage is increased, then her own salary will go up. Obviously Erica's arguments are worthless.

3. The school board argues that our schools are in desperate need of repair. But the real reason our students are falling behind is that they spend too much time with their computers. Becoming educated means a lot more than learning how to point and click. The school board should send a letter to the parents urging them to monitor their kids' computer time.

★4. Whoever thrusts a knife into another person should be arrested. But surgeons do precisely this when operating. Therefore, surgeons should be arrested.

5. You should read Irving Stone's latest novel right away. It's sold over a million copies, and practically everyone in the Manhattan cocktail circuit is talking about it.

6. Friedrich Nietzsche's philosophy is not worth the paper it's printed on. Nietzsche was an immoral reprobate who went completely insane from syphilis before he died.

★7. Surely you welcome the opportunity to join our protective organization. Think of all the money you will lose from broken windows, overturned trucks, and damaged merchandise in the event of your not joining.

8. Senator Barrow advocates increased Social Security benefits for the poor. It is regrettable that the senator finds it necessary to advocate socialism. Socialism defeats initiative, takes away promised rewards, and leads directly to inefficiency and big government. It was tried for years in Eastern Europe, and it failed miserably. Clearly, socialism is no good.

9. Something is seriously wrong with high school education these days. After ten years of decline, SAT scores are still extremely low, and high school graduates are practically incapable of reading and writing. The obvious conclusion is that we should close the schools.

★10. The editors of the *Daily Register* have accused our company of being one of the city's worst water polluters. But the *Daily Register* is responsible for much more pollution than we are. After all, they own the Western Paper Company, and that company discharges tons of chemical residue into the city's river every day.

11. If 20 percent of adult Americans are functionally illiterate, then it's no wonder that morons get elected to public office. In fact, 20 percent of adult Americans *are* functionally illiterate. Therefore, it's no wonder that morons get elected to public office.

12. Ladies and gentlemen, today the lines of battle have been drawn. When the din of clashing armor has finally died away, the Republican party will emerge

victorious! We are the true party of the American people! We embody the values that all real Americans hold sacred! We cherish and protect our founding fathers' vision that gave birth to the Constitution! We stand for decency and righteousness; for self-determination and the liberty to conduct our affairs as each of us freely chooses! In the coming election, victory will be ours, so help us God!

★13. We've all heard the argument that too much television is the reason our students can't read and write. Yet many of today's TV shows are excellent. *Grey's Anatomy* unveils the personal lives of interns at an urban hospital, *Law and Order* explores ethical issues in our criminal justice system, and *American Idol* uncovers hidden musical talent. Today's TV is just great!

14. Surely architect Norris is not responsible for the collapse of the Central Bank Tower. Norris has had nothing but trouble lately. His daughter eloped with a child molester, his son committed suicide, and his alcoholic wife recently left for Las Vegas with his retirement savings.

15. The First Amendment to the Constitution prevents the government from interfering with the free exercise of religion. The liturgical practice of the Religion of Internal Enlightenment involves human sacrifice. Therefore, it would be wrong for the government to interfere with this religious practice.

★16. Former antiterrorism czar Richard Clark argues in his book that the Iraq war was a terrible mistake and that it undermines the war on terrorism. But it's clear that Clark makes these outlandish claims merely to drum up sales for his book. Thus, we really shouldn't take his arguments seriously.

17. Professor Pearson's arguments in favor of the theory of evolution should be discounted. Pearson is a cocaine-snorting sex pervert and, according to some reports, a member of the Communist party.

18. Rudolf Höss, commandant of the Auschwitz concentration camp, confessed to having exterminated one million people, most of whom were Jews, in the Auschwitz gas chamber. We can only conclude that Höss was either insane or an extremely evil person.

★19. TV commentator Larry Kudlow argues that government should get off the back of the American businessman. Obviously, Kudlow wants to abolish government altogether. Yet without government there would be no defense, no judicial system, no Social Security, and no health and safety regulations. None of us wants to forgo these benefits. Thus, we can see that Kudlow's argument is absurd.

20. I know that some of you oppose the appointment of David Cole as the new sales manager. On further consideration, however, I am confident you will find him well qualified for the job. If Cole is not appointed, it may become necessary to make severe personnel cutbacks in your department.

21. Animal rights activists say that animals are abused in biomedical research labs. But consider this: Pets are abused by their owners every day. Probably 25 percent of pet owners should never get near animals. Some cases of abuse are enough to make you sick.

★22. Of course you want to buy a pair of Slinky fashion jeans. Slinky jeans really show off your figure, and all the Hollywood starlets down on the Strip can be seen wearing them these days.

23. Actress Andie MacDowell says that it's healthy to drink milk. But the dairy industry pays MacDowell thousands of dollars to make these ads. Therefore, we should not take her testimonials too seriously.

24. Dr. Morrison has argued that smoking is responsible for the majority of health problems in this country and that every smoker who has even the slightest concern for his or her health should quit. Unfortunately, however, we must consign Dr. Morrison's argument to the trash bin. Only yesterday I saw none other than Dr. Morrison himself smoking a cigar.

★25. Mr. Rhodes is suffering from amnesia and has no recollection whatever of the events of the past two weeks. We can only conclude that he did not commit the crime of murdering his wife a week ago, as he has been accused of doing.

II. Answer "true" or "false" to the following statements:

1. In the appeal to force, the arguer physically attacks the listener.

2. In the direct variety of the appeal to the people, the arguer attempts to create a kind of mob mentality.

3. If an arguer attempts to discredit court room testimony or a promise by pointing out that the witness or the person making the promise is a liar, then the arguer commits an *argumentum ad hominem* (argument against the person) fallacy.

4. The *argumentum ad hominem* always involves two arguers.

5. In the *argumentum ad hominem* circumstantial, the circumstances cited by the second arguer are intended precisely to malign the character of the first arguer.

6. In the *tu quoque* fallacy, the arguer threatens the reader or listener.

7. In the fallacy of accident, a general rule is applied to a specific case where it does not fit.

8. In the straw man fallacy, an arguer often distorts another person's argument by making it look more extreme than it really is.

9. Whenever one suspects that a missing the point fallacy is being committed, one should be able to state the conclusion that is logically implied by the premises.

10. In the red herring fallacy, the arguer attempts to lead the reader or listener off the track.

III. Identify the arguments in the following dialogue, then discuss each of them in terms of the fallacies presented in this section. You should be able to find at least one case of each fallacy.

"Thanks for saving us a seat," Jodie says to her friend Frank, as she and Liz sit down with coffee cups in hand in the crowded cafeteria.
"No problem," Frank says.

"We were late getting out of Professor Conklin's social problems class," Jodie says disgustedly. "He's such a jerk! He always keeps us late, and he's the most arrogant snob I've ever met."

"I've heard that," Frank says. "What's he covering in class now?"

"Sexual harassment in the workplace," Jodie replies. "But that *is* a real problem these days."

"How so?"

"Well, my friend Amelia is a dispatcher for a trucking company, and she's told me about dozens of times she's been a victim of sexual harassment. The truckers have *Playboy* centerfolds tacked up all over the place, they constantly leer at her, they're always asking her for dates. One of them even pats her rear when she leans over at the drinking fountain."

Frank laughs. "Well, there is such a thing as the First Amendment, which supposedly guarantees freedom of expression. You wouldn't want to deny these guys their freedom of expression, would you?"

"Freedom of expression, my eye!" explodes Jodie, looking incredulously at Frank. "Patting someone's rear isn't freedom of expression, it's abusive physical contact. So it's not protected by the First Amendment. Men! The trouble with you, Frank, is you're a typical man. If you were a woman, you'd see these things for what they are," she says, looking at Liz for support.

Liz nods her head in strong agreement.

"Well," says Frank, "I think your friend is lucky to have a job, what with all the people out of work these days. I've got a friend who's spent half his retirement savings just putting food on the table for his family, after losing his job. He was in the construction business, which is dead right now. And in other parts of the country it's even worse. You should tell Amelia to quit complaining."

"Stop giving me the runaround," demands Jodie, offended. "The trouble with you men is, you always look at women as sex objects. That makes sexual harassment inevitable."

"What do you mean?" protests Frank. "It's you women who treat us men like sex objects. What about all your makeup and perfume? And the tight pants and all the see-through stuff you wear? You think men are just a pack of animals—nothing but instinct—and you think that will make us fall for you. Isn't that how you see us?"

"I won't dignify that with a reply," fumes Jodie. "Anyone who isn't blind can see that Amelia's being victimized by those truckers. If you can't see it, maybe pouring this hot coffee over your thick head will wake you up!" she threatens.

"Calm down," says Frank with a startled look. "Everyone is beginning to stare at us. Okay, suppose I agree that Amelia is a victim. The question is, what do we do about it?"

"To begin with," says Jodie firmly, "the trucking company should transfer Amelia out of dispatch and give her a better job, like executive secretary in the regional office. Her husband ran out on her recently, leaving her with all five kids—and little Tommy needs braces. She could really use the extra money."

"You're joking!" Frank laughs sarcastically. "Didn't you tell me once that Amelia never finished high school and is functionally illiterate? She could never handle a job like that."

Thinking for a moment, Jodie then replies, "Well, maybe you're right. But at least the company should adopt a policy forbidding all forms of sexual harassment. Maybe that would make the truckers see how abusive they are, and then they might stop acting that way. Practically every company in the country has such a policy, but Amelia's bosses are dragging their feet."

"Okay. But then how do you define sexual harassment?" Frank asks. "'Cause if you can't define it, any policy is useless."

"Well, I don't exactly know," Jodie hesitates. "I'll have to think about that."

"Aha! I knew it!" exclaims Frank, triumphantly. "You can't define it, which means you don't even know if it exists! If you weren't such a radical feminist, you would see that all these claims of sexual harassment are hooey."

"Me, radical?" Jodie explodes. "The truth is you're a radical sexist. What you're saying is, women are only chattel, like they were 200 years ago, and men can use or abuse them any way they please. Liz, that's what he's saying, isn't it?"

"Absolutely," Liz affirms.

"What a crazy argument," says Frank scornfully. "What you're saying is, we should abolish all distinctions between men and women and create a unisex society in which everyone acts like a bunch of robots. Isn't that right, Liz?"

"No, not at all," insists Liz. "She's trying to—"

"You're completely insane, Frank," Jodie interrupts, rising determinedly from her chair, "and your arguments are wacko!" She then throws the remains of her coffee at Frank. The other students who have been listening to the heated argument rise up shouting, "Right on, Jodie!" Some begin chanting, "End sex harassment! End sex harassment!" As more students join the demonstration, they surround Frank, gesturing crudely.

Angry and humiliated, he breaks away and dashes out the door.

## 3.3    Fallacies of Weak Induction

The **fallacies of weak induction** occur not because the premises are logically irrelevant to the conclusion, as is the case with the eight fallacies of relevance, but because the connection between premises and conclusion is not strong enough to support the conclusion. In each of the following fallacies, the premises provide at least a shred of evidence in support of the conclusion, but the evidence is not nearly good enough to cause a reasonable person to believe the conclusion. Like the fallacies of relevance, however, the fallacies of weak induction often involve emotional grounds for believing the conclusion.

### 9. Appeal to Unqualified Authority (*Argumentum ad Verecundiam*)

We saw in Chapter 1 that an argument from authority is an inductive argument in which an arguer cites the authority or testimony of another person in support of some conclusion. The **appeal to unqualified authority** fallacy is a variety of the argument from authority and occurs when the cited authority or witness lacks credibility. There are several reasons why an authority or witness might lack credibility. The person might lack the requisite expertise, might be biased or prejudiced, might have a motive

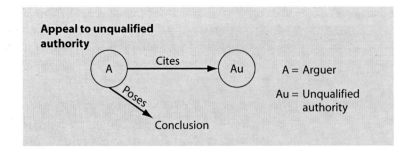

to lie or disseminate "misinformation," or might lack the requisite ability to perceive or recall. The following examples illustrate these reasons:

> Dr. Bradshaw, our family physician, has stated that the creation of muonic atoms of deuterium and tritium hold the key to producing a sustained nuclear fusion reaction at room temperature. In view of Dr. Bradshaw's expertise as a physician, we must conclude that this is indeed true.

This conclusion deals with nuclear physics, and the authority is a family physician. Because it is unlikely that a physician would be an expert in nuclear physics, the argument commits an appeal to unqualified authority.

> David Duke, former Grand Wizard of the Ku Klux Klan, has stated, "Jews are not good Americans. They have no understanding of what America is." On the basis of Duke's authority, we must therefore conclude that the Jews in this country are un-American.

As an authority, David Duke is clearly biased, so his statements cannot be trusted.

> James W. Johnston, Chairman of R. J. Reynolds Tobacco Company, testified before Congress that tobacco is not an addictive substance and that smoking cigarettes does not produce any addiction. Therefore, we should believe him and conclude that smoking does not in fact lead to any addiction.

If Mr. Johnston had admitted that tobacco is addictive, it would have opened the door to government regulation, which could put his company out of business. Thus, because Johnston had a clear motive to lie, we should not believe his statements.

> Old Mrs. Furguson (who is practically blind) has testified that she saw the defendant stab the victim with a bayonet while she was standing in the twilight shadows 100 yards from the incident. Therefore, members of the jury, you must find the defendant guilty.

Here the witness lacks the ability to perceive what she has testified to, so her testimony is untrustworthy.

Of course if an authority is credible, the resulting argument will contain no fallacy. Example:

> The county tax collector issued a press release stating that property tax revenues are higher this year than last. Therefore, we conclude that these revenues are indeed higher this year.

Normally a county tax collector would be considered a qualified expert in the area of tax revenues, so assuming the tax collector has no reason to lie, this argument is inductively strong.

In deciding whether a person is a qualified authority, one should keep two important points in mind. First, the person might be an authority in more than one field. For example, a chemist might also be an authority in biology, or an economist might also be an authority in law. The second point is that there are some areas in which practically no one can be considered an authority. Such areas include politics, morals, and religion. For example, if someone were to argue that abortion is immoral because a certain philosopher or religious leader has said so, the argument would be weak regardless of the authority's qualifications. Many questions in these areas are so hotly contested that there is no conventional wisdom an authority can depend on.

## 10.  Appeal to Ignorance (*Argumentum ad Ignorantiam*)

When the premises of an argument state that nothing has been proved one way or the other about something, and the conclusion then makes a definite assertion about that thing, the argument commits an **appeal to ignorance.** The issue usually involves something that is incapable of being proved or something that has not yet been proved. Example:

> People have been trying for centuries to provide conclusive evidence for the claims of astrology, and no one has ever succeeded. Therefore, we must conclude that astrology is a lot of nonsense.

Conversely, the following argument commits the same fallacy.

> People have been trying for centuries to disprove the claims of astrology, and no one has ever succeeded. Therefore, we must conclude that the claims of astrology are true.

The premises of an argument are supposed to provide positive evidence for the conclusion. The premises of these arguments, however, tell us nothing about astrology; rather, they tell us about what certain unnamed and unidentified people have tried unsuccessfully to do. This evidence may provide some slight reason for believing the conclusion, but certainly not sufficient reason.

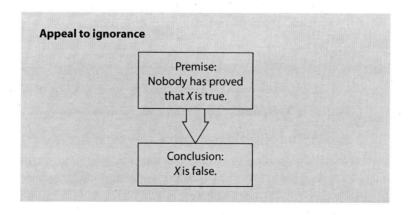

**Appeal to ignorance**

Premise:
Nobody has proved
that *X* is true.

Conclusion:
*X* is false.

These examples do, however, lead us to the first of two important exceptions to the appeal to ignorance. The first stems from the fact that if qualified researchers investigate a certain phenomenon within their range of expertise and fail to turn up any evidence that the phenomenon exists, this fruitless search by itself constitutes positive evidence about the question. Consider, for example, the following argument:

> Teams of scientists attempted over several decades to detect the existence of the luminiferous aether, and all failed to do so. Therefore, the luminiferous aether does not exist.

The premises of this argument are true. Given the circumstances, it is likely that the scientists in question would have detected the aether if in fact it did exist. Since they did not detect it, it probably does not exist. Thus, we can say that the given argument is inductively strong (but not deductively valid).

As for the two arguments about astrology, if the attempts to prove or disprove the astrological claims had been done in a systematic way by qualified experts, the arguments would more likely be good. Exactly what is required to qualify someone to investigate astrological claims is, of course, difficult to say. But as these arguments stand, the premises state nothing about the qualifications of the investigators, and so the arguments remain fallacious.

It is not always necessary, however, that the investigators have *special* qualifications. The kinds of qualifications needed depend on the situation. Sometimes the mere ability to see and report what one sees is sufficient. Example:

> No one has ever seen Mr. Andrews drink a glass of wine, beer, or any other alcoholic beverage. Probably Mr. Andrews is a nondrinker.

Because it is highly probable that if Mr. Andrews were a drinker, somebody would have seen him drinking, this argument is inductively strong. No special qualifications are needed to be able to see someone take a drink.

The second exception to the appeal to ignorance relates to courtroom procedure. In the United States and a few other countries, a person is presumed innocent until proven guilty. If the prosecutor in a criminal trial fails to prove the guilt of the defendant beyond reasonable doubt, counsel for the defense may justifiably argue that his or her client is not guilty. Example:

> Members of the jury, you have heard the prosecution present its case against the defendant. Nothing, however, has been proved beyond a reasonable doubt. Therefore, under the law, the defendant is not guilty.

This argument commits no fallacy because "not guilty" means, in the legal sense, that guilt beyond a reasonable doubt has not been proved. The defendant may indeed have committed the crime of which he or she is accused, but if the prosecutor fails to prove guilt beyond a reasonable doubt, the defendant is considered "not guilty."

## 11. Hasty Generalization (Converse Accident)

**Hasty generalization** is a fallacy that affects inductive generalizations. In Chapter 1 we saw that an inductive generalization is an argument that draws a conclusion about all members of a group from evidence that pertains to a selected sample. The fallacy oc-

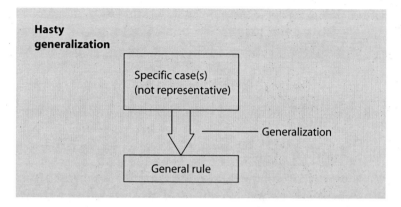

curs when there is a reasonable likelihood that the sample is not representative of the group. Such a likelihood may arise if the sample is either too small or not randomly selected. Here are two examples:

> After only one year the alternator went out in Mr. O'Grady's new Chevrolet. Mrs. Dodson's Oldsmobile developed a transmission problem after six months. The obvious conclusion is that cars made by General Motors are just a pile of junk these days.

> Ten Arab fundamentalists hijacked planes and crashed them into the World Trade Center in New York City. The message is clear: Arabs are nothing but a pack of religious fanatics prone to violence.

In these arguments a conclusion about a whole group is drawn from premises that mention only a few instances. Because such small, atypical samples are not sufficient to support a general conclusion, each argument commits a hasty generalization. The second example indicates how hasty generalization plays a role in racial and religious prejudice.

The mere fact that a sample is small, however, does not necessarily mean that it is atypical. On the other hand, the mere fact that a sample is large does not guarantee that it is typical. In the case of small samples, various factors may intervene that render such a sample typical of the larger group. Examples:

> Ten milligrams of substance Z was fed to four mice, and within two minutes all four went into shock and died. Probably substance Z, in this amount, is fatal to mice in general.

> On three separate occasions I drank a bottle of Figowitz beer and found it flat and bitter. Probably I would find every bottle of Figowitz beer flat and bitter.

Neither of these arguments commits the fallacy of hasty generalization, because in neither case is there any likelihood that the sample is atypical of the group. In the first argument the fact that the mice died in only two minutes suggests the existence of a causal connection between eating substance Z and death. If there is such a connection, it would hold for other mice as well. In the second example the fact that the taste of beer typically remains constant from bottle to bottle causes the argument to be strong, even though only three bottles were sampled.

In the case of large samples, if the sample is not random, it may not be typical of the larger group. Example:

> One hundred thousand voters from Orange County, California, were surveyed on their choice for governor, and 68 percent said they intend to vote for the Republican candidate. Clearly the Republican candidate will be elected.

Even though the sample cited in this argument is large, the argument commits a hasty generalization. The problem is that Orange County is overwhelmingly Republican, so the mere fact that 68 percent intend to vote for the Republican candidate is no indication of how others in the state intend to vote. In other words, the survey was not conducted randomly, and for this reason the argument is fatally flawed. The need for randomness in samples is discussed further in Chapter 12 of this book.

Hasty generalization is otherwise called "converse accident" because it proceeds in a direction opposite to that of accident. Whereas accident proceeds from the general to the particular, converse accident moves from the particular to the general. The premises cite some characteristic affecting one or more atypical instances of a certain class, and the conclusion then applies that characteristic to all members of the class.

## 12. False Cause

The fallacy of **false cause** occurs whenever the link between premises and conclusion depends on some imagined causal connection that probably does not exist. Whenever an argument is suspected of committing the false cause fallacy, the reader or listener should be able to say that the conclusion depends on the supposition that $X$ causes $Y$, whereas $X$ probably does not cause $Y$ at all. Examples:

> During the past two months, every time that the cheerleaders have worn blue ribbons in their hair, the basketball team has been defeated. Therefore, to prevent defeats in the future, the cheerleaders should get rid of those blue ribbons.

> Successful business executives are paid salaries in excess of $100,000. Therefore, the best way to ensure that Ferguson will become a successful executive is to raise his salary to at least $100,000.

> There are more laws on the books today than ever before, and more crimes are being committed than ever before. Therefore, to reduce crime we must eliminate the laws.

The first argument depends on the supposition that the blue ribbons caused the defeats, the second on the supposition that a high salary causes success, and the third on the supposition that laws cause crime. In no case is it likely that any causal connection exists.

The first argument illustrates a variety of the false cause fallacy called *post hoc ergo propter hoc* ("after this, therefore on account of this"). This variety of the fallacy presupposes that just because one event precedes another event, the first event causes the second. Obviously, mere temporal succession is not sufficient to establish a causal connection. Nevertheless, this kind of reasoning is quite common and lies behind most forms of superstition. (Example: "A black cat crossed my path and later I tripped and sprained my ankle. It must be that black cats really are bad luck.")

The second and third arguments illustrate a variety of the false cause fallacy called *non causa pro causa* ("not the cause for the cause"). This variety is committed when

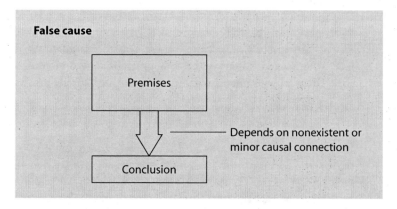

**False cause**

Premises

Conclusion

Depends on nonexistent or minor causal connection

what is taken to be the cause of something is not really the cause at all and the mistake is based on something other than mere temporal succession. In reference to the second argument, success as an executive causes increases in salary—not the other way around—so the argument mistakes the cause for the effect. In reference to the third argument, the increase in crime is, for the most part, only coincidental with the increase in the number of laws. Obviously, the mere fact that one event is coincidental with another is not sufficient reason to think that one caused the other.

A third variety of the false cause fallacy, and one that is probably committed more often than either of the others in their pure form, is *oversimplified cause.* This variety occurs when a multitude of causes is responsible for a certain effect but the arguer selects just one of these causes and represents it as if it were the sole cause. Here are some examples:

> The quality of education in our grade schools and high schools has been declining for years. Clearly, our teachers just aren't doing their job these days.

> Today, all of us can look forward to a longer life span than our parents and grandparents. Obviously we owe our thanks to the millions of dedicated doctors who expend every effort to ensure our health.

In reference to the first argument, the decline in the quality of education is caused by many factors, including lack of discipline in the home, lack of parental involvement, too much television, and drug use by students. Poor teacher performance is only one of these factors and probably a minor one at that. In the second argument, the efforts of doctors are only one among many factors responsible for our longer life span. Other, more important factors include a better diet, more exercise, reduced smoking, safer highways, and more stringent occupational safety standards.

The oversimplified cause fallacy is usually motivated by self-serving interests. Sometimes the arguer wants to take undeserved credit for himself or herself or give undeserved credit to some movement with which he or she is affiliated. At other times, the arguer wants to heap blame on an opponent or shift blame from himself or herself onto some convenient occurrence. Instances of the fallacy can resemble either the *post hoc* or the *non causa pro causa* varieties in that the alleged cause can occur either prior to or concurrently with the effect. It differs from the other varieties of false cause fallacy in that the single factor selected for credit or blame is often partly responsible for the effect, but responsible to only a minor degree.

The last variety of false cause we will consider is called the *gambler's fallacy*. This fallacy is committed whenever the conclusion of an argument depends on the supposition that independent events in a game of chance are causally related. Here is an example:

> A fair coin was flipped five times in a row, and each time it came up heads. Therefore, it is extremely likely that it will come up tails on the next flip.

In fact, it is no more likely that the coin will come up tails on the next flip than it was on the first flip. Each flip is an independent event, so earlier flips have no causal influence on later ones. Thus, the fact that the earlier flips came up heads does not increase the likelihood that the next flip will come up tails.

For the gambler's fallacy to be committed, the events must be independent or nearly independent. Such events include rolls of a pair of fair (unloaded) dice, spins of a fair roulette wheel, and selections of lottery winning numbers. Events are not completely independent whenever the skill of the gambler affects the outcome. Thus, poker, blackjack, and horse-race betting provide less-than-perfect candidates for the gambler's fallacy.

The false cause fallacy is often convincing because it is often difficult to determine whether two phenomena are causally related. A lengthy time lapse between the operation of the cause and the occurrence of the effect can exacerbate the problem. For example, the thirty-year interval between exposure to asbestos and the onset of asbestosis impeded the recognition of a causal connection. Also, when two events are causally related, determining the degree of relatedness may be hard. Thus, there may be some connection between the electromagnetic field produced by high voltage transmission lines and leukemia, but the connection may be extremely slight. Finally, when a causal connection is recognized, it may be difficult to determine which is the cause and which is the effect. For example, an allergic reaction may be connected with an episode of anxiety, but it may be hard to tell if the reaction causes the anxiety or if the anxiety causes the reaction.

The realm of human action constitutes another area in which causal connections are notoriously difficult to establish. For example, the attorneys for accused murderer Dan White argued that Twinkies, Coke, and potato chips caused him to kill San Francisco mayor George Moscone. Other attorneys have blamed their clients' crimes on PMS, rap music, childhood abuse, mental retardation, and hallucinations. The complex nature of human motivation renders all such causal claims difficult to evaluate. The situation may become even worse when a whole nation of people are involved. Thus, the recent drop in crime rates has been attributed to "three strikes" laws, but it is difficult to say whether this or some other factor is really responsible.

One point that should be kept in mind when establishing causal connections is that statistical correlations by themselves often reveal little about what is actually going on. For example, if all that we knew about smoking and lung cancer was that the two frequently occur together, we might conclude any number of things. We might conclude that both have a common cause, such as a genetic predisposition, or we might conclude that lung cancer is a disease contracted early in life and that it manifests itself in its early stages by a strong desire for tobacco. Fortunately, in this case we have more evidence than a mere statistical correlation. This additional evidence inclines us to believe that the smoking is a cause of the cancer.

## 13. Slippery Slope

The fallacy of **slippery slope** is a variety of the false cause fallacy. It occurs when the conclusion of an argument rests on an alleged chain reaction and there is not sufficient reason to think that the chain reaction will actually take place. Here is an example:

> Immediate steps should be taken to outlaw pornography once and for all. The continued manufacture and sale of pornographic material will almost certainly lead to an increase in sex-related crimes such as rape and incest. This in turn will gradually erode the moral fabric of society and result in an increase in crimes of all sorts. Eventually a complete disintegration of law and order will occur, leading in the end to the total collapse of civilization.

Because there is no good reason to think that the mere failure to outlaw pornography will result in all these dire consequences, this argument is fallacious. An equally fallacious counterargument is as follows:

> Attempts to outlaw pornography threaten basic civil rights and should be summarily abandoned. If pornography is outlawed, censorship of newspapers and news magazines is only a short step away. After that there will be censorship of textbooks, political speeches, and the content of lectures delivered by university professors. Complete mind control by the central government will be the inevitable result.

Both arguments attempt to persuade the reader or listener that the welfare of society rests on a "slippery slope" and that a single step in the wrong direction will result in an inevitable slide all the way to the bottom.

The slippery slope fallacy can involve various kinds of causality. For example, someone might argue that removing a single brick from a building would set off a chain reaction leading to the destruction of the building, or that chopping down a tall tree would set off a cascade of falling trees leading to the destruction of the forest. These arguments depend on pure physical causality. On the other hand, someone might argue that starting a rumor about the health of the economy would set off a chain reaction leading to the collapse of the stock market. Such an argument would depend on the kind of causality found in interpersonal communications. Or someone might argue that planting a seed of doubt in a person's mind about the faithfulness of his or her spouse would gnaw away at that person, leading to the breakup of the marriage. Such an argument would depend on the kind of causality that links mental states.

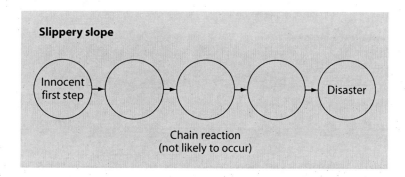

Deciding whether a slippery slope fallacy has been committed can be difficult when one is uncertain whether the alleged chain reaction will or will not occur. This question is discussed in Section 3.5. But many slippery slopes rest on a mere emotional conviction on the part of the arguer that a certain action or policy is bad, and the arguer attempts to trump up support for his or her position by citing all sorts of dire consequences that will result if the action is taken or the policy followed. In such cases there is usually little problem in identifying the argument as a slippery slope.

## 14. Weak Analogy

This fallacy affects inductive arguments from analogy. As we saw in Chapter 1, an argument from analogy is an argument in which the conclusion depends on the existence of an analogy, or similarity, between two things or situations. The fallacy of **weak analogy** is committed when the analogy is not strong enough to support the conclusion that is drawn. Example:

> Harper's new car is bright blue, has leather upholstery, and gets excellent gas mileage. Crowley's new car is also bright blue and has leather upholstery. Therefore, it probably gets excellent gas mileage, too.

Because the color of a car and the choice of upholstery have nothing to do with gasoline consumption, this argument is fallacious.

The basic structure of an argument from analogy is as follows:

> Entity A has attributes $a, b, c,$ and $z$.
> Entity B has attributes $a, b, c$.
> Therefore, entity B probably has attribute $z$ also.

Evaluating an argument having this form requires a two-step procedure: (1) Identify the attributes $a, b, c, \ldots$ that the two entities A and B share, and (2) determine how the attribute $z$, mentioned in the conclusion, relates to the attributes $a, b, c, \ldots$ If some causal or systematic relation exists between $z$ and $a, b,$ or $c$, the argument is strong; otherwise, it is weak. In the example argument, the two entities share the attributes of being cars; the attributes entailed by being a car, such as having four wheels; and the attributes of color and upholstery material. Because none of these attributes is systematically or causally related to good gas mileage, the argument is fallacious.

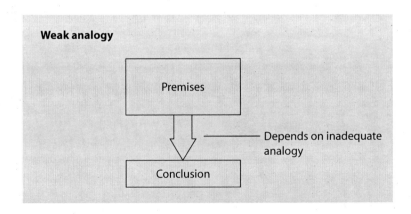

# ▪ EMINENT LOGICIANS

### *William of Ockham ca.* 1285–1347

© The Granger Collection, New York

The English philosopher and theologian, William of Ockham, was born in or near the village of Ockham not far from London. Little is known about his childhood, and his biographers are not even certain about the year of his birth, with estimates running from 1280 to 1290. However, they are certain that while Ockham was still a small boy, his parents delivered him to the nearest Franciscan monastery to be brought up in the monastic way of life. His parents' intentions were realized when he entered the Franciscan Order and was ordained in 1306.

Ockham studied theology at Oxford, possibly under Duns Scotus, and he lectured there. He also studied and taught at the University of Paris, where he wrote extensively on theology and philosophy. Ockham's theological views generated controversy among theologians of the day, some of whom vehemently opposed him. In 1324, he was called to Avignon, then the location of the papal court, to answer charges of heresy.

A panel of scholars had been appointed to review the charges made against Ockham, and he was obliged to remain at a Franciscan house in Avignon throughout the investigation, which lasted four years. During this time, the Franciscan minister general, Michael of Cesena, was called to Avignon, because he had become embroiled in a controversy with Pope John XXII over the issue of the poverty of Jesus and the apostles. Michael held that Jesus and the apostles did not own property but instead survived through goodwill offerings of people in the community. The Franciscans regarded themselves as emulating the model set by Jesus and the apostles, but the pope, who lived in luxury, obviously disagreed.

Though Ockham had more than enough problems of his own, the minister general asked him to research the issue to see which position was right—the pope's or the minister general's. Ockham ultimately came out on the side of the minister general, claiming that the pope was a heretic and had no business even being pope. This got the Avignon Franciscans into a great deal of trouble, and to extricate themselves they purloined several horses and rode out of town in the middle of the night. Ludwig of Bavaria, the Holy Roman Emperor, gave them protection, and Ockham lived out the rest of his life in Munich. While there he turned his attention to politics and political philosophy. He was a staunch advocate of the separation of church and state, claiming that the pope had no right to intervene in state affairs. The pope retaliated by excommunicating him.

Ockham is best known for endorsing a principle of parsimony that has come to be called "Ockham's razor." This principle states that, among alternative explanations, the simplest one is the best. Ockham emphasized the importance of keeping the number of entities hypothesized in an explanation to an absolute minimum. In the area of logic, he is known for his theory of truth conditions for categorical propositions, for work in the foundations of inductive reasoning, for preliminary work on a three-valued logic, and for developing a close approximation to what would later come to be known as De Morgan's rule.

As an illustration of when the requisite systematic or causal relation does and does not exist, consider the following arguments:

> The flow of electricity through a wire is similar to the flow of water through a pipe. Obviously a large-diameter pipe will carry a greater flow of water than a pipe of small diameter. Therefore, a large-diameter wire should carry a greater flow of electricity than a small-diameter wire.

> The flow of electricity through a wire is similar to the flow of water through a pipe. When water runs downhill through a pipe, the pressure at the bottom of the hill is greater than it is at the top. Thus, when electricity flows downhill through a wire, the voltage should be greater at the bottom of the hill than at the top.

The first argument is good and the second is fallacious. Both arguments depend on the similarity between water molecules flowing through a pipe and electrons flowing through a wire. In both cases there is a systematic relation between the diameter of the pipe/wire and the amount of flow. In the first argument this systematic relation provides a strong link between premises and conclusion, and so the argument is a good one. But in the second argument a causal connection exists between difference in elevation and increase in pressure that holds for water but not for electricity. Water molecules flowing through a pipe are significantly affected by gravity, but electrons flowing through a wire are not. Thus, the second argument is fallacious.

The theory and evaluation of arguments from analogy is one of the most complex and elusive subjects in all of logic. Additional material on arguments from analogy appears in Section 3.5 and Chapter 9 of this text.

## EXERCISE 3.3

I. Identify the fallacies of weak induction committed by the following arguments, giving a brief explanation for your answer. If no fallacy is committed, write "no fallacy."

★1. The *Daily News* carried an article this morning about three local teenagers who were arrested on charges of drug possession. Teenagers these days are nothing but a bunch of junkies.

2. If a car breaks down on the freeway, a passing mechanic is not obligated to render emergency road service. For similar reasons, if a person suffers a heart attack on the street, a passing physician is not obligated to render emergency medical assistance.

3. There must be something to psychical research. Three famous physicists— Oliver Lodge, James Jeans, and Arthur Stanley Eddington—took it seriously.

★4. The secretaries have asked us to provide lounge areas where they can spend their coffee breaks. This request will have to be refused. If we give them lounge areas, next they'll be asking for spas and swimming pools. Then it will be racquetball courts, tennis courts, and fitness centers. Expenditures for these facilities will drive us into bankruptcy.

5. The accumulation of pressure in a society is similar to the buildup of pressure in a boiler. If the pressure in a boiler increases beyond a critical point, the

boiler will explode. Accordingly, if a government represses its people beyond a certain point, the people will rise up in revolt.

6. A few minutes after Governor Harrison finished his speech on television, a devastating earthquake struck southern Alaska. For the safety of the people up there, it is imperative that Governor Harrison make no more speeches.

★7. No one has ever been able to prove the existence of extrasensory perception. We must therefore conclude that extrasensory perception is a myth.

8. Lester Brown, universally respected author of the yearly *State of the World* report, has said that the destruction of tropical rain forests is one of the ten most serious worldwide problems. Thus, it must be the case that this is indeed a very serious problem.

9. America's business leaders are all a bunch of crooks. Just look at the facts. Dennis Kowslowski ripped off millions of dollars from Tyco Corporation, Jeffrey Skilling and Andy Fastow did the same with Enron, Bernie Ebbers defrauded the investors of WorldCom, and the Rigas family stole millions from Adelphia.

★10. Iranian President Mahmoud Ahmadinejad says that the holocaust is a fairy tale promoted for the purpose of garnering sympathy for Israel. In view of Ahmadinejad's apparent expertise in this area, we must conclude that the holocaust is indeed a fairy tale, just as he says.

11. Probably no life exists on Venus. Teams of scientists have conducted exhaustive studies of the planet's surface and atmosphere, and no living organisms have been found.

12. We don't dare let the animal rights activists get their foot in the door. If they sell us on the idea that dogs, cats, and dolphins have rights, next it will be chickens and cows. That means no more chicken Kiev or prime rib. Next it will be worms and insects. This will lead to the decimation of our agricultural industry. The starvation of the human race will follow close behind.

★13. No one would buy a pair of shoes without trying them on. Why should anyone be expected to get married without premarital sex?

14. No one has proved conclusively that America's nuclear power plants constitute a danger to people living in their immediate vicinity. Therefore, it is perfectly safe to continue to build nuclear power plants near large metropolitan centers.

15. There are more churches in New York City than in any other city in the nation, and more crimes are committed in New York City than anywhere else. So, if we are to eliminate crime, we must abolish the churches.

II. Answer "true" or "false" to the following statements:

1. If an arguer cites a statement by a recognized expert in support of a conclusion and the statement falls within the expert's range of expertise, then the arguer commits an appeal to unqualified authority.

2. If an arguer cites a statement in support of a conclusion and the statement reflects the strong bias of its author, then the arguer commits an appeal to unqualified authority.

3. In the appeal to ignorance, the arguer accuses the reader or listener of being ignorant.

4. If an attorney for the defense in an American or Canadian criminal trial argues that the prosecution has proved nothing beyond a reasonable doubt about the guilt of the defendant, then the attorney commits an appeal to ignorance.

5. Hasty generalization always proceeds from the particular to the general.

6. The *post hoc ergo propter hoc* variety of the false cause fallacy presumes that *X* causes *Y* merely because *X* happens before *Y*.

7. If an argument concludes that *X* causes *Y* simply because *X* and *Y* occur over the same time interval, then the argument commits the *non causa pro causa* variety of the false cause fallacy.

8. If the conclusion of an argument depends on the occurrence of a chain reaction of events, and there is good reason to believe that the chain reaction will actually occur, the argument commits a slippery slope fallacy.

9. The fallacy of weak analogy always depends on an alleged similarity between two things or situations.

10. If an argument from analogy depends on a causal or systematic relationship between certain attributes, and there is good reason to believe that this relationship exists, then the argument commits no fallacy.

III. Identify the fallacies of relevance and weak induction committed by the following arguments. If no fallacy is committed, write "no fallacy."

★1. On our first date, George had his hands all over me, and I found it nearly impossible to keep him in his place. A week ago Tom gave me that stupid line about how, in order to prove my love, I had to spend the night with him. Men are all alike. All any of them want is sex.

2. Tagging by graffiti artists has become a terrible problem in recent years. Obviously our schools are stifling the creative spirit of these young people.

3. North Korean dictator Kim Jong Il has promised not to let any of his nuclear weapons fall into the hands of terrorists. But Kim is erratic, dishonest, corrupt, and possibly even insane. Therefore, we should not trust his promises for a minute.

★4. House speaker Nancy Pelosi has argued strongly against oil and gas exploration in the Arctic National Wildlife Refuge. But what would you expect? She represents the city of San Francisco, which is loaded with environmentalists. If she didn't take this position, she would be run out of office. Thus, her arguments on this issue really have no merit.

5. What the farmer sows in the spring he reaps in the fall. In the spring he sows $8-per-bushel soybeans. Therefore, in the fall he will reap $8-per-bushel soybeans.

6. World-renowned physicist Stephen Hawking claims that black holes do not gobble up everything that falls into them without leaving a trace, but that something is always left behind. Given Hawking's stature as a scientist and the

many years he has worked on this problem, we should conclude that this is indeed the case.

★7. Emily has bought over 100 tickets on the weekly state lottery, and she has never won anything. Therefore, the likelihood increases every week that she will win something if she continues to buy tickets.

8. Johnny, of course I deserve the use of your bicycle for the afternoon. After all, I'm sure you wouldn't want your mother to find out that you played hooky today.

9. Practically everyone downloads music free of charge from the Internet these days. Therefore, you should have no qualms about doing this yourself.

★10. Ellen Quinn has argued that logic is not the most important thing in life. Apparently Ellen advocates irrationality. It has taken two million years for the human race to achieve the position that it has, and Ellen would throw the whole thing into the garbage. What utter nonsense!

11. When water is poured on the top of a pile of rocks, it always trickles down to the rocks on the bottom. Similarly, when rich people make lots of money, we can expect this money to trickle down to the poor.

12. Extensive laboratory tests have failed to prove any deleterious side effects of the new painkiller lexaprine. We conclude that lexaprine is safe for human consumption.

★13. Environmentalists accuse us of blocking the plan to convert Antarctica into a world park. In fact, nothing could be further from the truth. Antarctica is a huge continent teeming with life. It is the home of millions of penguins, seals, sea birds, and sea lions. Also, great schools of finfish and whales inhabit its coastal waters.

14. Media host Howard Stern claims that leaders of the religious right are nothing but a pack of racketeers bent on destroying every vestige of free speech, and he gives numerous reasons to support this claim. But Stern is just a vulgar, smut-mouthed freak who will say anything for shock value. Nobody should listen to this nonsense.

15. The operation of a camera is similar in many ways to the operation of an eye. If you are to see anything in a darkened room, the pupils of your eyes must first dilate. Accordingly, if you are to take a photograph (without flash) in a darkened room, the aperture of the camera lens must first be increased.

★16. Certainly Miss Malone will be a capable and efficient manager. She has a great figure, a gorgeous face, and tremendous poise and she dresses very fashionably.

17. James Dobson, director of Focus on the Family, says that men have the divine obligation to lead their families, and women have the divine obligation to submit to their husband's authority. Given Dobson's apparent ability to receive messages from God, we must conclude that this statement is absolutely true.

18. Dear Internal Revenue Service: I received a notice that my taxes are being audited for last year. But you have no right to do this. The deadline for filing a return was April 15, and I filed my tax return on April 12—a full three days before the deadline.

★19. To prevent dangerous weapons from being carried aboard airliners, those seeking to board must pass through a magnetometer and submit to a possible pat-down search. Therefore, to prevent alcohol and drugs from being carried into rock concerts, those entering should submit to similar search procedures.

20. Mr. Flemming's arguments against the rent control initiative on the September ballot should be taken with a grain of salt. As a landlord he would naturally be expected to oppose the initiative.

21. India is suffering a serious drought, thousands of children are dying of starvation in their mothers' arms, and homeless beggars line the streets of the major cities. Surely we must give these poor downtrodden people the chance of bettering their condition in America, the land of wealth and opportunity.

★22. Members of the jury, you have heard Shirley Gaines testify that the defendant did not offer to perform acts of prostitution for the undercover police officer. But Gaines is a known prostitute herself and a close friend of the defendant. Also, only a year ago she was convicted of twelve counts of perjury. Therefore, you should certainly discount Gaines's testimony.

23. It is ridiculous to hear that man from Peru complaining about America's poverty. Peru has twice as much poverty as America has ever had.

24. Angela complains that the problems on the algebra test were too hard. But have you ever seen the way Angela flirts with that good-looking quarterback on the football team? She's constantly batting those long, black eyelashes at him, and her tight-fitting sweaters leave nothing to the imagination. Angela should pay more attention to her studies.

★25. Nobody has ever proved that immoral behavior by elected officials erodes public morality. Therefore, we must conclude that such behavior does not erode public morality.

26. Freedom of speech is guaranteed by the First Amendment. Therefore, your friend was acting within his rights when he shouted "Fire! Fire!" in that crowded theater, even though it was only a joke.

27. No one, on encountering a watch lying on a forest trail, would expect that it had simply appeared there without having been made by someone. For the same reason, no one should expect that the universe simply appeared without having been made by some being.

★28. On Monday I drank ten rum and Cokes, and the next morning I woke up with a headache. On Wednesday I drank eight gin and Cokes, and the next morning I woke up with a headache. On Friday I drank nine bourbon and Cokes, and the next morning I woke up with a headache. Obviously, to prevent further headaches I must give up Coke.

29. Radio entertainer Rush Limbaugh claims there is not a shred of evidence to prove that nicotine is addictive or that cigarettes cause emphysema, lung cancer, or any other disease. Given Limbaugh's apparent expertise in medical science, we can only conclude that what he says about nicotine and cigarettes is true.

30. Some of the parents in our school district have asked that we provide bilingual education in Spanish. This request will have to be denied. If we provide this service, then someone will ask for bilingual education in Greek. Then it will be German, French, and Hungarian. Polish, Russian, Chinese, Japanese, and Korean will follow close behind. We certainly can't accommodate all of them.

IV. Identify the arguments in the following dialogue, then discuss each of them in terms of the fallacies presented in this section and the previous section. You should be able to find at least one case of each fallacy.

"Hi! Glad you could make it," Ralph says to his friend Claudia at a Friday night party. "Hey, you just missed a great discussion that Tom, Ruben, and I were having about abduction by extraterrestrials. Ruben just left, but he said he's been reading this book by Whitley Strieber—I think it's called *Transformation*—in which Strieber describes being kidnapped by creatures from outer space."

"Good grief! You don't actually believe that nonsense, do you?" Claudia asks incredulously.

"Well, I don't think Strieber would lie. Also, Ruben told us an amazing personal story. He was out camping a year ago, and after he'd killed off a couple of six-packs of Moosehead, he says he saw a UFO. So, I think we have to conclude there really are UFOs."

"What a joke!" Claudia laughs scornfully. "Ruben was probably hallucinating. By the way, didn't he fail most of his classes last semester? His parents are spending a fortune for his education, and all he does is party, sleep, and ignore his studies. I think that's immoral. As for Strieber, does he give any evidence?"

"As a matter of fact, he does," Ralph replies smugly. "Apparently, a few years ago, he was driving with his wife on some country road, when both of them experienced an unusual blackout. When they woke up, they were thirty-five miles further down the road, and they had no recollection of how they got there. Later, both began having dreams about extraterrestrials performing experiments on them while they were on board their spacecraft. Extraterrestrials must have abducted them, then hypnotized them so they wouldn't remember what had happened."

"Oh yeah, now I remember who Strieber is," answers Claudia, caustically. "He's that weirdo who dreams up all kinds of fantastic stories just so he can write books about them and make lots of money. If you give that sickie one minute of your time, then you're crazier than he is."

"I think you're prejudiced," Ralph says. "Why, recent surveys show that 64 percent of the American public believe in UFOs, and the number is growing every day. That alone should convince you they're real."

"You've got to be kidding," Claudia mutters, shaking her head in disbelief.

"Well then, consider this," insists Ralph. "There are hundreds of people out there who've had similar dreams and the same unaccounted-for time lapses. They can't all be fantasizing."

"I know that Strieber is a kook," Claudia persists, "so all the others must be, too."

"Now, now, aren't we jumping to conclusions?" her friend asks condescendingly.

"Not at all. First it was UFOs and little green men. Now those little creatures are abducting people and experimenting on them. Before long they'll be manipulating our genes and trying to infiltrate the human race. In the end, everyone will suspect everyone else of being an alien, mass terror will prevail, and civilization will collapse!" Claudia exclaims in mock horror.

"Don't be a fool!" Ralph barks, irritated. "The problem with you is, you're an agnostic. Obviously, you're saying we should refuse to believe in anything we can't clearly see or touch. So, logically, God doesn't exist, and there is no immortal soul. Tom, that's what she's saying, isn't it?"

"More or less," Tom agrees halfheartedly.

"Again, not at all," Claudia responds. "What I'm saying is, people have to be just a little bit critical about what they believe. Apparently you believe any cockamamie story that comes your way. You're just so gullible. If you keep it up, everyone and their dog will take you for a ride."

"Oh yeah? If I were you, I'd take a close look at my own beliefs," Ralph gibes. "Didn't I see you reading the astrology column just the other day? Nobody in their right mind believes in astrology. Maybe I should start screaming 'Claudia believes in astrology! Claudia believes in astrology!' Then everyone will gawk at you, and that sexy physics major you're dying to get a date with will think you're a nut."

"Oh, shut up!" says Claudia, blushing. "I may read the astrology column, but I certainly don't believe it. I just read it for fun. But, the fact is, during the past twenty-five years there have been thousands of alleged sightings of UFOs, and not a single one has led to any solid evidence of their existence. What do you make of that?"

"I think we should look at this situation the other way around," Ralph says. "Up until now, nobody has shown that UFOs *don't* exist, so I think we should give those people who claim they have seen them the benefit of the doubt. We should believe in UFOs and extraterrestrials until the sightings are proved false."

"Well, okay. Let's suppose, just for the sake of argument, that I admit the existence of UFOs and their little green drivers. How are we supposed to respond to them? What are we supposed to do?" Claudia asks.

"For starters, we should extend an open invitation to them," answers Ralph. "They may come from a dying planet where millions of their compatriots desperately struggle for survival. Their sun may be burning out, their water supply exhausted, and their soil poisoned with toxic chemicals. Surely they deserve a second chance on a new planet."

"Maybe so," Claudia says in a patronizing tone. "And now that you mention it, we probably have a legal obligation to let them in. Our current immigration laws say that we have to admit at least ten thousand applicants annually, from every major nation. If those aliens would just sign the right papers, we'd have to give them permanent residency. However, what worries me is, they may have the wrong intentions. After all, didn't they conduct experiments on those people they abducted?"

"Yes, but don't we experiment on animals? If the animals don't complain, why should we? Also, medical experimentation often leads to wonderful new cures. I'm certain we have nothing to worry about," says Ralph, proud of his logic.

"Humph! I hope you're right. Well, I've got to go now—and don't let any green men kidnap you," Claudia says with a barb.

"And you, either," Ralph answers.

## 3.4 Fallacies of Presumption, Ambiguity, and Grammatical Analogy

The **fallacies of presumption** include begging the question, complex question, false dichotomy, and suppressed evidence. These fallacies arise not because the premises are irrelevant to the conclusion or provide insufficient reason for believing the conclusion but because the premises presume what they purport to prove. *Begging the question* presumes that the premises provide adequate support for the conclusion when in fact they do not, and *complex question* presumes that a question can be answered by a simple "yes," "no," or other brief answer when a more sophisticated answer is needed. *False dichotomy* presumes that an "either . . . or . . ." statement presents jointly exhaustive alternatives when in fact it does not, and *suppressed evidence* presumes that no important evidence has been overlooked by the premises when in fact it has.

The **fallacies of ambiguity** include *equivocation* and *amphiboly*. These fallacies arise from the occurrence of some form of ambiguity in either the premises or the conclusion (or both). As we saw in Section 2.1, an expression is ambiguous if it is susceptible to different interpretations in a given context. The words "light" and "bank" are ambiguous, as is the statement "Tuna are biting off the Washington coast." When the conclusion of an argument depends on a shift in meaning of an ambiguous word or phrase or on the wrong interpretation of an ambiguous statement, the argument commits a fallacy of ambiguity.

The **fallacies of grammatical analogy** include *composition* and *division*. Arguments that commit these fallacies are grammatically analogous to other arguments that are good in every respect. Because of this similarity in linguistic structure, such fallacious arguments may appear good yet be bad.

## 15. Begging the Question (*Petitio Principii*)

The fallacy of **begging the question** is committed whenever the arguer creates the illusion that inadequate premises provide adequate support for the conclusion by leaving out a possibly false (shaky) key premise, by restating a possibly false premise as the conclusion, or by reasoning in a circle. The Latin name for this fallacy, *petitio principii*, means "request for the source." The actual source of support for the conclusion is not apparent, and so the argument is said to beg the question. After reading or hearing the argument, the observer is inclined to ask, "But how do you know $X$?" where $X$ is the needed support.

The first, and most common, way of committing this fallacy is by leaving a possibly false key premise out of the argument while creating the illusion that nothing more is needed to establish the conclusion. Examples:

> Murder is morally wrong. This being the case, it follows that abortion is morally wrong.

> Of course humans and apes evolved from common ancestors. Just look how similar they are.

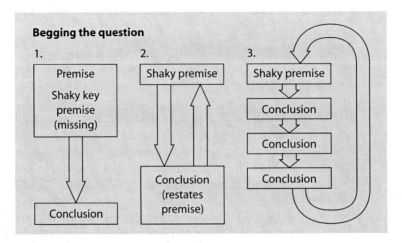

It's obvious that the poor in this country should be given handouts from the government. After all, these people earn less than the average citizen.

Clearly, terminally ill patients have a right to doctor-assisted suicide. After all, many of these people are unable to commit suicide by themselves.

The first of these arguments begs the question "How do you know that abortion is a form of murder?" The second begs the question "Does the mere fact that humans and apes look similar imply that they evolved from common ancestors?" And the third and fourth beg the questions "Just because the poor earn less than the average citizen, does this imply that the government should give them handouts?" and "Just because terminally ill patients cannot commit suicide by themselves, does it follow that they have a right to a doctor's assistance?"

These questions indicate that something has been left out of the original arguments. Thus, the first argument is missing the premise "Abortion is a form of murder"; the second is missing the premise "If humans and apes look similar, then they have common ancestors"; and so on. These premises are crucial for the soundness of the arguments. If the arguer is unable to establish the truth of these premises, then the arguments prove nothing. However, in most cases of begging the question, this is precisely the reason why such premises are left unstated. The arguer is *not* able to establish their truth, and by employing rhetorical phraseology such as "of course," "clearly," "this being the case," and "after all," the arguer hopes to create the illusion that the stated premise, by itself, provides adequate support for the conclusion when in fact it does not.

The same form of begging the question often appears in arguments concerning religious topics to justify conclusions about the existence of God, the immortality of the soul, and so on. Example:

The world in which we live displays an amazing degree of organization. Obviously this world was created by an intelligent God.

This argument begs the question "How do you know that the organization in the world could only have come from an intelligent creator?" Of course the claim that it did come from an intelligent creator may well be true, but the burden is on the arguer to prove it. Without supporting reasons or evidence, the argument proves nothing. Yet most people who are predisposed to believe the conclusion are likely to accept the argument as a good one. The same can be said of most arguments that beg the question, and this fact suggests another reason why arguers resort to this fallacy: Such arguments tend to reinforce preexisting inclinations and beliefs.

The second form of *petitio principii* occurs when the conclusion of an argument merely restates a possibly false premise in slightly different language. In such an argument, the premise supports the conclusion, and the conclusion tends to reinforce the premise. Examples:

> Capital punishment is justified for the crimes of murder and kidnapping because it is quite legitimate and appropriate that someone be put to death for having committed such hateful and inhuman acts.

> Anyone who preaches revolution has a vision of the future for the simple reason that if a person has no vision of the future he could not possibly preach revolution.

In the first argument, saying that capital punishment is "justified" means the same thing as saying that it is "legitimate and appropriate," and in the second argument the premise and the conclusion say exactly the same thing. However, by repeating the same thing in slightly different language, the arguer creates the illusion that independent evidence is being presented in support of the conclusion, when in fact it is not. Both arguments contain rhetorical phraseology ("hateful and inhuman," "*simple* reason," and "could not possibly") that help effect the illusion. The first argument begs the question "How do you know that capital punishment really is legitimate and appropriate?" and the second begs the question "How do you know that people who preach revolution really do have a vision of the future?"

The third form of *petitio principii* involves circular reasoning in a chain of inferences having a first premise that is possibly false. Example:

> Ford Motor Company clearly produces the finest cars in the United States. We know that they produce the finest cars because they have the best design engineers. This is true because they can afford to pay them more than other manufacturers. Obviously they can afford to pay them more because they produce the finest cars in the United States.

On encountering this argument, the attentive reader is inclined to ask, "Where does this reasoning begin? What is its source?" Since the argument goes in a circle, it has no beginning or source, and as a result it proves nothing. Of course, in this example the circularity is rather apparent, so the argument is not likely to convince anyone. Cases in which circular reasoning may convince involve long and complex arguments having premises that depend on one another in subtle ways and a possibly false key premise that depends on the conclusion.

In all cases of begging the question, the arguer uses some linguistic device to create the illusion that inadequate premises provide adequate support for a conclusion. Without such an illusion, the fallacy is not committed. Thus, the following arguments commit no fallacy:

> No dogs are cats.
> Therefore, no cats are dogs.
>
> London is in England and Paris is in France.
> Therefore, Paris is in France and London is in England.

In both of these examples, the premise amounts to little more than a restatement of the conclusion. Yet both arguments are sound because they are valid and have true premises. No fallacy is committed, because no illusion is created to make inadequate premises appear as adequate. We will study arguments of this sort in Chapters 4 and 7.

Here is another example:

> Rome is in Germany or Rome is in Germany.
> Therefore, Rome is in Germany.

This argument is valid, but it is unsound because it has a false premise. However, it commits no fallacy because, again, no illusion is created to cover anything up. Arguments having this form also appear in Chapter 7.

As with these examples, arguments that beg the question are normally valid. This is easy to see. Any argument that includes the conclusion as one of the premises is clearly valid, and those forms of the fallacy that leave a key premise out of the argument become valid when that key premise is introduced. The problem with arguments that beg the question is that they are usually unsound, or at least not clearly sound, because the premise needed to provide adequate support for the conclusion is, at best, of uncertain truth value. Because such arguments presume the truth of this premise, begging the question is called a fallacy of presumption.

## 16. Complex Question

The fallacy of **complex question** is committed when two (or more) questions are asked in the guise of a single question and a single answer is then given to both of them. Every complex question presumes the existence of a certain condition. When the respondent's answer is added to the complex question, an argument emerges that establishes the presumed condition. Thus, although not an argument as such, a complex question involves an implicit argument. This argument is usually intended to trap the respondent into acknowledging something that he or she might otherwise not want to acknowledge. Examples:

> Have you stopped cheating on exams?
>
> Where did you hide the marijuana you were smoking?

Let us suppose the respondent answers "yes" to the first question and "under the bed" to the second. The following arguments emerge:

> You were asked whether you have stopped cheating on exams. You answered, "Yes."
>     Therefore, it follows that you have cheated in the past.
>
> You were asked where you hid the marijuana you were smoking. You replied, "Under the bed." It follows that you were in fact smoking marijuana.

On the other hand, let us suppose that the respondent answers "no" to the first question and "nowhere" to the second. We then have the following arguments:

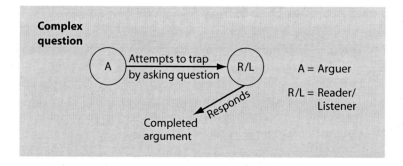

> You were asked whether you have stopped cheating on exams. You answered, "No." Therefore, you continue to cheat.

> You were asked where you hid the marijuana you were smoking. You answered, "Nowhere." It follows that you must have smoked all of it.

Obviously, each of the questions is really two questions:

> Did you cheat on exams in the past? If you did cheat in the past, have you stopped now?

> Were you smoking marijuana? If you were smoking it, where did you hide it?

If respondents are not sophisticated enough to identify a complex question when one is put to them, they may answer quite innocently and be trapped by a conclusion that is supported by no evidence at all; or, they may be tricked into providing the evidence themselves. The correct response lies in resolving the complex question into its component questions and answering each separately.

The fallacy of complex question should be distinguished from another kind of question known in law as a leading question. A *leading question* is one in which the answer is in some way suggested in the question. Whether or not a question is a leading one is important in the direct examination of a witness by counsel. Example:

> Tell us, on April 9, did you see
> the defendant shoot the
> deceased?           (leading question)
> Tell us, what did you see on
> April 9?           (straight question)

Leading questions differ from complex questions in that they involve no logical fallacies—that is, they do not attempt to trick the respondent into admitting something he or she does not want to admit. To distinguish the two, however, one sometimes needs to know whether prior questions have been asked. Here are some additional examples of complex questions:

> Are you going to be a good little boy and eat your hamburger?
> Is George Hendrix still telling lies?
> How long must I put up with your snotty behavior?
> When are you going to stop talking nonsense?

## 17.  False Dichotomy

The fallacy of **false dichotomy** is committed when a disjunctive ("either . . . or . . .") premise presents two unlikely alternatives as if they were the only ones available, and the arguer then eliminates the undesirable alternative, leaving the desirable one as the conclusion. Such an argument is clearly valid, but since the disjunctive premise is false, or at least probably false, the argument is typically unsound. The fallacy is often committed by children when arguing with their parents, by advertisers, and by adults generally. Here are three examples:

> Either you let me attend the Dixie Chicks concert or I'll be miserable for the rest of my life. I know you don't want me to be miserable for the rest of my life, so it follows that you'll let me attend the concert.

> Either you use Ultra Guard deodorant or you risk the chance of perspiration odor. Surely you don't want to risk the chance of perspiration odor. Therefore, you will want to use Ultra Guard deodorant.

> Either you buy only American-made products or you don't deserve to be called a loyal American. Yesterday you bought a new Toyota. It's therefore clear that you don't deserve to be called a loyal American.

In none of these arguments does the disjunctive premise present the only alternatives available, but in each case the arguer tries to convey that impression. For example, in the first argument, the arguer tries to convey the impression that he or she either goes to the concert or faces a lifetime of misery, and that no other alternatives are possible. Clearly, however, this is not the case.

The fallacious nature of false dichotomy lies in the illusion created by the arguer that the disjunctive premise presents jointly exhaustive alternatives. If it did, the premise would be true of necessity. For example, the statement "Either Reno is in Nevada, or it is not in Nevada" presents jointly exhaustive alternatives and is true of necessity. But in the fallacy of false dichotomy, not only do the two alternatives fail to be jointly exhaustive, but they are not even likely. As a result, the disjunctive premise is false, or at least probably false. Thus, the fallacy amounts to making a false or probably false premise appear true.

If one of the alternatives in the disjunctive premise is true, then the fallacy is not committed. For example, the following argument is valid and sound:

> Either Seattle is in Washington, or it is in Oregon.
> Seattle is not in Oregon.
> Therefore, Seattle is in Washington

False dichotomy is otherwise called "false bifurcation" and the "either-or fallacy." Also, in most cases the arguer expresses only the disjunctive premise and leaves it to the reader or listener to supply the missing statements:

> Either you buy me a new mink coat, or I'll freeze to death when winter comes.
> Either I continue smoking, or I'll get fat and you'll hate to be seen with me.

The missing premise and conclusion are easily introduced.

## 18. Suppressed Evidence

Chapter 1 explained that a cogent argument is an inductive argument with good reasoning and true premises. The requirement of true premises includes the proviso that the premises not ignore some important piece of evidence that outweighs the presented evidence and entails a very different conclusion. If an inductive argument does indeed ignore such evidence, then the argument commits the fallacy of **suppressed evidence.** Consider, for example, the following argument:

> Most dogs are friendly and pose no threat to people who pet them. Therefore, it would be safe to pet the little dog that is approaching us now.

If the arguer ignores the fact that the little dog is excited and foaming at the mouth (which suggests rabies), then the argument commits a suppressed evidence fallacy. This fallacy is classified as a fallacy of presumption because it works by creating the presumption that the premises are both true and complete when in fact they are not.

Perhaps the most common occurrence of the suppressed evidence fallacy appears in inferences based on advertisements. Nearly every ad neglects to mention certain negative features of the product advertised. As a result, an observer who sees or hears an advertisement and then draws a conclusion from it may commit the fallacy of suppressed evidence. Example:

> The ad for Kentucky Fried Chicken says, "Buy a bucket of chicken and have a barrel of fun!" Therefore, if we buy a bucket of that chicken, we will be guaranteed to have lots of fun.

The ad fails to state that the fun does not come packaged with the chicken but must be supplied by the buyer. Also, of course, the ad fails to state that the chicken is loaded with fat and that the buyer's resultant weight gain may not amount to a barrel of fun. By ignoring these facts, the argument based on the ad is fallacious.

Another way that an arguer can commit the suppressed evidence fallacy is by ignoring important events that have occurred with the passage of time that render an inductive conclusion improbable. Here is an example:

> During the past sixty years, Poland has enjoyed a rather low standard of living. Therefore, Poland will probably have a low standard of living for the next sixty years.

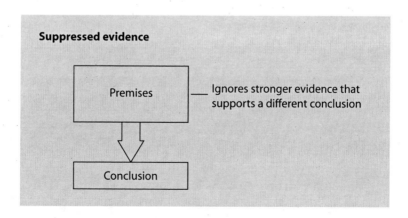

Suppressed evidence

Premises —— Ignores stronger evidence that supports a different conclusion

Conclusion

This argument ignores the fact that Poland was part of the Soviet bloc during most of the past sixty years, and this fact accounts for its rather low standard of living. However, following the collapse of the Soviet Union, Poland became an independent nation, and its economy is expected to improve steadily during the next sixty years.

Yet another form of suppressed evidence is committed by arguers who quote passages out of context from sources such as the Bible, the Constitution, and the Bill of Rights to support a conclusion that the passage was not intended to support. Consider, for example, the following argument against gun control:

> The Second Amendment to the Constitution states that the right of the people to keep and bear arms shall not be infringed. But a law controlling handguns would infringe the right to keep and bear arms. Therefore, a law controlling handguns would be unconstitutional.

In fact, the Second Amendment reads, "A well regulated militia being necessary to the security of a free state, the right of the people to keep and bear arms shall not be infringed." In other words, the amendment states that the right to bear arms shall not be infringed when the arms are necessary for the preservation of a well-regulated militia. Because a law controlling handguns (pistols) would have little effect on the preservation of a well-regulated militia, it is unlikely that such a law would be unconstitutional.

The suppressed evidence fallacy is similar to the form of begging the question in which the arguer leaves a key premise out of the argument. The difference is that suppressed evidence leaves out a premise that requires a *different* conclusion, while that form of begging the question leaves out a premise that is needed to support the *stated* conclusion. However, because both fallacies proceed by leaving a premise out of the argument, there are cases where the two fallacies overlap.

## 19. Equivocation

The fallacy of **equivocation** occurs when the conclusion of an argument depends on the fact that a word or phrase is used, either explicitly or implicitly, in two different senses in the argument. Such arguments are either invalid or have a false premise, and in either case they are unsound. Examples:

> Some triangles are obtuse. Whatever is obtuse is ignorant. Therefore, some triangles are ignorant.

> Any law can be repealed by the legislative authority. But the law of gravity is a law. Therefore, the law of gravity can be repealed by the legislative authority.

> We have a duty to do what is right. We have a right to speak out in defense of the innocent. Therefore, we have a duty to speak out in defense of the innocent.

> A mouse is an animal. Therefore, a large mouse is a large animal.

In the first argument "obtuse" is used in two different senses. In the first premise it describes a certain kind of angle, while in the second it means dull or stupid. The second argument equivocates on the word "law." In the first premise it means statutory law, and in the second it means law of nature. The third argument uses "right" in two senses. In the first premise "right" means morally correct, but in the second it means a

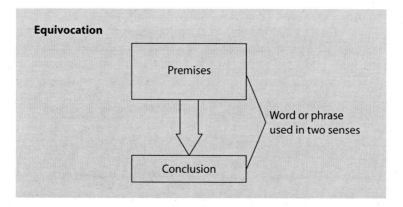

just claim or power. The fourth argument illustrates the ambiguous use of a relative word. The word "large" means different things depending on the context. Other relative words that are susceptible to this same kind of ambiguity include "small," "good," "bad," "light," "heavy," "difficult," "easy," "tall," and "short."

To be convincing, an argument that commits an equivocation must use the equivocal word in ways that are subtly related. Of the examples just given, only the third might fulfill this requirement. Since both uses of the word "right" are related to ethics, the unalert observer may not notice the shift in meaning. Another technique is to spread the shift in meaning out over the course of a lengthy argument. Political speech makers often use phrases such as "equal opportunity," "gun control," "national security," and "environmental protection" in one way at the beginning of a speech and in quite another way at the end. A third technique consists in using such phrases one way in a speech to one group and in a different way in a speech to an opposing group. If the same people are not present at both speeches, the equivocation is not detected.

## 20. Amphiboly

The fallacy of **amphiboly** occurs when the arguer misinterprets an ambiguous statement and then draws a conclusion based on this faulty interpretation. The original statement is usually asserted by someone other than the arguer, and the ambiguity usually arises from a mistake in grammar or punctuation—a missing comma, a dangling modifier, an ambiguous antecedent of a pronoun, or some other careless arrangement of words. Because of this ambiguity, the statement may be understood in two clearly distinguishable ways. The arguer typically selects the unintended interpretation and proceeds to draw a conclusion based on it. Here are some examples:

> The tour guide said that standing in Greenwich Village, the Empire State Building could easily be seen. It follows that the Empire State Building is in Greenwich Village.

> John told Henry that he had made a mistake. It follows that John has at least the courage to admit his own mistakes.

> Professor Johnson said that he will give a lecture about heart failure in the biology lecture hall. It must be the case that a number of heart failures have occurred there recently.

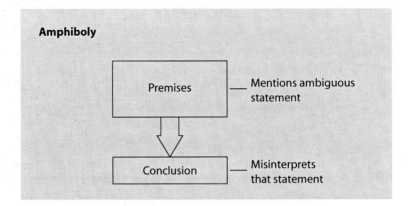

The premise of the first argument contains a dangling modifier. Is it the observer or the Empire State Building that is supposed to be standing in Greenwich Village? The factually correct interpretation is the former. In the second argument the pronoun "he" has an ambiguous antecedent; it can refer either to John or to Henry. Perhaps John told Henry that *Henry* had made a mistake. In the third argument the ambiguity concerns what takes place in the biology lecture hall; is it the lecture or the heart failures? The correct interpretation is probably the former. The ambiguity can be eliminated by inserting commas ("Professor Johnson said that he will give a lecture, about heart failure, in the biology lecture hall") or by moving the ambiguous modifier ("Professor Johnson said that he will give a lecture in the biology lecture hall about heart failure"). Ambiguities of this sort are called *syntactical ambiguities*.

Two areas where cases of amphiboly cause serious problems involve contracts and wills. The drafters of these documents often express their intentions in terms of ambiguous statements, and alternate interpretations of these statements then lead to different conclusions. Examples:

> Mrs. Hart stated in her will, "I leave my 500-carat diamond necklace and my pet chinchilla to Alice and Theresa." Therefore, we conclude that Alice gets the necklace and Theresa gets the chinchilla.

> Mr. James signed a contract that reads, "In exchange for painting my house, I promise to pay David $5,000 and give him my new Cadillac only if he finishes the job by May 1." Therefore, since David did not finish until May 10, it follows that he gets neither the $5,000 nor the Cadillac.

In the first example the conclusion obviously favors Alice. Theresa is almost certain to argue that the gift of the necklace and chinchilla should be shared equally by her and Alice. Mrs. Hart could have avoided the dispute by adding either "respectively" or "collectively" to the end of the sentence. In the second example, the conclusion favors Mr. James. David will argue that the condition that he finish by May 1 affected only the Cadillac and that he therefore is entitled to the $5,000. The dispute could have been avoided by properly inserting a comma in the language of the promise.

Amphiboly differs from equivocation in two important ways. First, equivocation is always traced to an ambiguity in the meaning of a *word* or *phrase*, whereas amphiboly involves a syntactical ambiguity in a *statement*. The second difference is that amphiboly usually involves a mistake made by the arguer in interpreting an ambiguous statement made by someone else, whereas the ambiguity in equivocation is typically the arguer's own creation. If these distinctions are kept in mind, it is usually easy to distinguish amphiboly from equivocation. Occasionally, however, the two fallacies occur together, as the following example illustrates:

> The *Great Western Cookbook* recommends that we serve the oysters when thoroughly stewed. Apparently the delicate flavor is enhanced by the intoxicated condition of the diners.

First, it is unclear whether "stewed" refers to the oysters or to the diners, and so the argument commits an amphiboly. But if "stewed" refers to the oysters it means "cooked," and if it refers to the diners it means "intoxicated." Thus, the argument also involves an equivocation.

## 21. Composition

The fallacy of **composition** is committed when the conclusion of an argument depends on the erroneous transference of an attribute from the parts of something onto the whole. In other words, the fallacy occurs when it is argued that because the parts have a certain attribute, it follows that the whole has that attribute, too, and the situation is such that the attribute in question cannot be legitimately transferred from parts to whole. Examples:

> Maria likes anchovies. She also likes chocolate ice cream. Therefore, it is certain that she would like a chocolate sundae topped with anchovies.

> Each player on this basketball team is an excellent athlete. Therefore, the team as a whole is excellent.

> Each atom in this teacup is invisible. Therefore, this teacup is invisible.

> Sodium and chlorine, the atomic components of salt, are both deadly poisons. Therefore, salt is a deadly poison.

In these arguments the attributes that are transferred from the parts onto the whole are designated by the words "Maria likes," "excellent," "invisible," and "deadly poison," respectively. In each case the transference is illegitimate, and so the argument is fallacious.

Not every such transference is illegitimate, however. Consider the following arguments:

> Every atom in this teacup has mass. Therefore, this teacup has mass.

> Every component in this picket fence is white. Therefore, the whole fence is white.

In each case an attribute (having mass, being white) is transferred from the parts onto the whole, but these transferences are quite legitimate. Indeed, the fact that the atoms have mass is the very reason *why* the teacup has mass. The same reasoning extends to the fence. Thus, the acceptability of these arguments is attributable, at least in part, to the *legitimate* transference of an attribute from parts onto the whole.

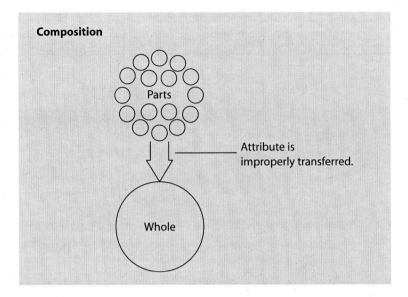

These examples illustrate the fact that the fallacy of composition is indeed an informal fallacy. It cannot be discovered by a mere inspection of the form of an argument— that is, by the mere observation that an attribute is being transferred from parts onto the whole. In addition, detecting this fallacy requires a general knowledge of the situation and of the nature of the attribute being transferred. The critic must be certain that, given the situation, the transference of this particular attribute is not allowed.

Further caution is required by the fact that composition is sometimes confused with hasty generalization. The only time this confusion is possible is when the "whole" is a class (such as the class of people in a city or the class of trees in a forest), and the "parts" are the members of the class. In such a case composition proceeds from the members of the class to the class itself. Hasty generalization, on the other hand, proceeds from the specific to the general. Because it is sometimes easy to mistake a statement about a class for a general statement, composition can be mistaken for hasty generalization. Such a mistake can be avoided if one is careful to keep in mind the distinction between these two kinds of statements. This distinction falls back on the difference between the **collective** and the **distributive** predication of an attribute. Consider the following statements:

Fleas are small.
Fleas are numerous.

The first statement is a general statement. The attribute of being small is predicated distributively; that is, it is assigned (or distributed) to each and every flea in the class. Each and every flea in the class is said to be small. The second statement, on the other hand, is a statement about a class as a whole, or what we will call a "class statement." The attribute of being numerous is predicated collectively; in other words, it is assigned not to the individual fleas but to the *class* of fleas. The meaning of the statement is not that each and every flea is numerous but that the class of fleas is large.

To distinguish composition from hasty generalization, therefore, the following procedure should be followed. Examine the conclusion of the argument. If the conclusion is a general statement—that is, a statement in which an attribute is predicated distributively to each and every member of a class—the fallacy committed is hasty generalization. But if the conclusion is a class statement—that is, a statement in which an attribute is predicated collectively to a class as a whole—the fallacy is composition. Example:

> Less gasoline is consumed by a car than by a truck. Therefore, less gasoline is consumed in the United States by cars than by trucks.

At first sight this argument might appear to proceed from the specific to the general and, consequently, to commit a hasty generalization. But in fact the conclusion is not a general statement at all but a class statement. The conclusion states that the whole class of cars uses less gas than does the whole class of trucks (which is false, because there are many more cars than trucks). Since the attribute of using less gasoline is predicated collectively, the fallacy committed is composition.

## 22. Division

The fallacy of **division** is the exact reverse of composition. As composition goes from parts to whole, division goes from whole to parts. The fallacy is committed when the conclusion of an argument depends on the erroneous transference of an attribute from a whole (or a class) onto its parts (or members). Examples:

> Salt is a nonpoisonous compound. Therefore, its component elements, sodium and chlorine, are nonpoisonous.

> This jigsaw puzzle, when assembled, is circular in shape. Therefore, each piece is circular in shape.

> The Royal Society is over 300 years old. Professor Thompson is a member of the Royal Society. Therefore, Professor Thompson is over 300 years old.

In each case the attribute, designated respectively by the terms "nonpoisonous," "circular in shape," and "over 300 years old," is illegitimately transferred from the whole or class onto the parts or members. As with the fallacy of composition, however, this kind of transference is not always illegitimate. The following arguments contain no fallacy:

> This teacup has mass. Therefore, the atoms that compose this teacup have mass.

> This field of poppies is uniformly orange. Therefore, the individual poppies are orange.

Obviously, one must be acquainted with the situation and the nature of the attribute being transferred to decide whether the fallacy of division is actually committed.

Just as composition can sometimes be confused with hasty generalization (converse accident), division can sometimes be confused with accident. As with composition, this confusion can occur only when the "whole" is a class. In such a case, division proceeds from the class to the members, whereas accident proceeds from the general to the specific. Thus, if a class statement is mistaken for a general statement, division may be mistaken for accident. To avoid such a mistake, one should analyze the premises of

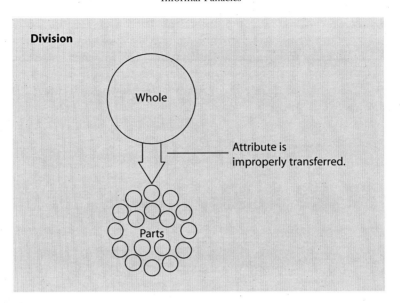

the argument. If the premises contain a general statement, the fallacy committed is accident; but if they contain a class statement, the fallacy is division. Example:

> Stanley Steamers have almost disappeared.
> This car is a Stanley Steamer.
> Therefore, this car has almost disappeared.

The first premise is not a general statement but a class statement. The attribute of having almost disappeared is predicated collectively. Accordingly, the fallacy committed is division, not accident.

This example also illustrates how cases of division that involve class statements can include a subtle form of equivocation. In the conclusion, the word "disappeared" means fading from vision, as when the lights are turned down; but in the first premise it means rarely seen. The equivocation is a kind of secondary fallacy that results from the primary fallacy, which is division.

The next example shows how division turns up in arguments dealing with averages.

> The average American family has 2.5 children.
> The Jones family is an average American family.
> Therefore, the Jones family has 2.5 children.

The statement "The average American family has 2.5 children" is not a general statement, but rather a class statement. The sense of the statement is not that each and every family has 2.5 children, but that the class of families is reducible to about 55 percent children and 45 percent adults. Thus, once again, the fallacy is division, and not accident.

In our account of composition and division, we have presented examples of arguments that commit these fallacies in conjunction with other, structurally similar arguments that do not. Because of the structural similarity between arguments that do and do not commit these fallacies, composition and division are classified as fallacies of grammatical analogy.

## SUMMARY OF INFORMAL FALLACIES

### Fallacies of Relevance

Appeal to force: Arguer threatens reader/listener.

Appeal to pity: Arguer elicits pity from reader/listener.

Appeal to the people (direct): Arguer arouses mob mentality.

Appeal to the people (indirect): Arguer appeals to reader/listener's desire for security, love, respect, etc.

Argument against the person (abusive): Arguer verbally abuses other arguer.

Argument against the person (circumstantial): Arguer presents other arguer as predisposed to argue this way.

Argument against the person (*tu quoque*): Arguer presents other arguer as hypocrite.

Accident: General rule is applied to a specific case it was not intended to cover.

Straw man: Arguer distorts opponent's argument and then attacks the distorted argument.

Missing the point: Arguer draws conclusion different from that supported by premises.

Red herring: Arguer leads reader/listener off track.

### Fallacies of Weak Induction

Appeal to unqualified authority: Arguer cites untrustworthy authority.

Appeal to ignorance: Premises report that nothing is known or proved, and then a conclusion is drawn.

Hasty generalization: Conclusion is drawn from an atypical sample.

False cause: Conclusion depends on nonexistent or minor causal connection.

Slippery slope: Conclusion depends on unlikely chain reaction.

Weak analogy: Conclusion depends on defective analogy.

### Fallacies of Presumption

Begging the question: Arguer creates the illusion that inadequate premises are adequate by leaving out a key premise, by restating the conclusion as a premise, or by reasoning in a circle.

Complex question: Multiple questions are concealed in a single question.

False dichotomy: "Either … or …" statement hides additional alternatives.

Suppressed evidence: Arguer ignores important evidence that requires a different conclusion.

### Fallacies of Ambiguity
Equivocation: Conclusion depends on a shift in meaning of a word or phrase.

Amphiboly: Conclusion depends on the wrong interpretation of a syntactically ambiguous statement.

### Fallacies of Grammatical Analogy
Composition: Attribute is wrongly transferred from parts to whole.

Division: Attribute is wrongly transferred from whole to parts.

## EXERCISE 3.4

I. Identify the fallacies of presumption, ambiguity, and grammatical analogy committed by the following arguments, giving a brief explanation for your answer. If no fallacy is committed, write "no fallacy."

★1. Either we require forced sterilization of Third World peoples or the world population will explode and all of us will die. We certainly don't want to die, so we must require forced sterilization.

2. Every sentence in this paragraph is well written. Therefore, the paragraph is well written.

3. An athlete is a human being. Therefore, a good athlete is a good human being.

★4. James said that he saw a picture of a beautiful girl stashed in Stephen's locker. We can only conclude that Stephen has broken the rules, because girls are not allowed in the locker room.

5. Why is it so difficult for you to reach a decision?

6. Water will quench one's thirst. Water is composed of hydrogen and oxygen. Therefore, hydrogen and oxygen will quench one's thirst.

★7. People who lack humility have no sense of beauty, because everyone who has a sense of beauty also has humility.

8. Butane is combustible. Therefore, it burns.

9. Twenty years ago, Kung Fong, the great sumo wrestler, could have yanked up one of the fir trees in the new municipal arboretum with a single pull. Therefore, since Mr. Fong is as strong today as he was then, he could just as easily pull up one of those trees today.

★10. If Thomas gives Marie a ring, then Thomas and Marie will be engaged. Thomas did give Marie a ring. In fact, he phoned her just the other night. Therefore, Thomas and Marie are engaged.

11. Alex, I heard your testimony in court earlier today. Tell me, why did you lie on the witness stand?

12. Johnson is employed by the General Services Administration, and everyone knows that the GSA is the most inefficient branch of the government. Therefore, Johnson must be an inefficient worker.

★13. All men are mortal. Therefore, some day man will disappear from the earth.

14. Each and every cell in this carrot is 90 percent water. Therefore, the entire carrot is 90 percent water.

15. George said that he was interviewing for a job drilling oil wells in the supervisor's office. We can only conclude that the supervisor must have an awfully dirty office.

★16. During the fifty years that Mr. Jones worked, he contributed $90,000 to Social Security. Now that he is retired, he stands to collect $200,000 from the system. Obviously he will collect a much greater monetary value than he contributed.

17. Either you marry me right now or I'll be forced to leave you and never speak to you again. I'm sure you wouldn't want me to do that. Therefore, you'll marry me right now.

18. Either Meg Ryan or Britney Spears is a popular singer. Meg Ryan is not a popular singer. Therefore, Britney Spears is a popular singer.

★19. Switzerland is 48 percent Protestant. Heidi Gilsing is a Swiss. Therefore, Heidi Gilsing is 48 percent Protestant.

20. Picasso is the greatest artist of the twentieth century. We know that this is so because art critics have described him in these terms. These art critics are correct in their assessment because they have a more keenly developed sense of appreciation than the average person. This is true because it takes a more keenly developed sense of appreciation to realize that Picasso is the greatest artist of the twentieth century.

21. An atomic bomb causes more damage than a conventional bomb. Therefore, during World War II more damage was caused by atomic bombs than by conventional bombs.

★22. Sylvia, I saw you shopping for wine the other day. Incidentally, are you still drinking excessively?

23. The author warns about numerous computational errors in his accounting text. Therefore, he must have written it very carelessly.

24. Emeralds are seldom found in this country, so you should be careful not to misplace your emerald ring.

★25. Of course abortion is permissible. After all, a woman has a right to do as she pleases with her own body.

II. Answer "true" or "false" to the following statements:

1. Arguments that commit the fallacy of begging the question are normally valid.

2. The effect of begging the question is to hide the fact that a premise may not be true.

3. The correct way of responding to a complex question is to divide the question into its component questions and answer each separately.

4. False dichotomy always involves an "either . . . or . . ." statement, at least implicitly.

5. The fallacy of equivocation arises from a syntactical defect in a statement.

6. The fallacy of amphiboly usually involves the ambiguous use of a single word.

7. Amphiboly usually arises from the arguer's misinterpreting a statement made by someone else.

8. The fallacy of composition always proceeds from whole to parts.

9. The fallacy of division always proceeds from parts to whole.

10. A general statement makes an assertion about each and every member of a class.

11. A class statement makes an assertion about a class as a whole.

12. In the statement "Divorces are increasing," an attribute is predicated distributively.

13. In the statement "Waistlines are increasing," an attribute is predicated distributively.

14. Composition and division involve the distributive predication of an attribute.

15. Equivocation and amphiboly are classified as fallacies of ambiguity.

III. Identify the fallacies of relevance, weak induction, presumption, ambiguity, and grammatical analogy committed by the following arguments, giving a brief explanation for your answer. If no fallacy is committed, write "no fallacy."

★1. In his *History of the American Civil War*, Jeffry Noland argues that the war had little to do with slavery. However, as a historian from Alabama, Noland could not possibly present an accurate account. Therefore, his arguments should be discounted.

2. Mr. Wilson said that on July 4 he went out on the veranda and watched the fireworks go up in his pajamas. We conclude that Mr. Wilson must have had an exciting evening.

3. Televangelist Jerry Falwell said that God's anger with feminism led to the destruction of the World Trade Center. Given Falwell's closeness to God, we have no alternative than to blame the feminists for this atrocity.

★4. A crust of bread is better than nothing. Nothing is better than true love. Therefore, a crust of bread is better than true love.

5. Every member of the Delta Club is over 70 years old. Therefore, the Delta Club must be over 70 years old.

6. Of course you should eat Wheaties. Wheaties is the breakfast of champions, you know.

★7. It's obvious that animals have rights. Just look at how powerless they are in comparison with modern humans.

8. The idea that black people in this country live in poverty is ridiculous. Look at Bill Cosby. He's a millionaire. And so are Denzel Washington and Oprah Winfrey.

9. No one has ever proved that the human fetus is not a person with rights. Therefore, abortion is morally wrong.

★10. California condors are rapidly disappearing. This bird is a California condor. Therefore, this bird should disappear any minute now.

11. When a car breaks down so often that repairs become pointless, the car is thrown on the junk heap. Similarly, when a person becomes old and diseased, he or she should be mercifully put to death.

12. The twenty-story Carson Building is constructed of concrete blocks. Each and every concrete block in the structure can withstand an earthquake of 9.5 on the Richter scale. Therefore, the building can withstand an earthquake of 9.5 on the Richter scale.

★13. Terrorists from the Middle East have crossed our borders and traveled through the country at will. Obviously the Immigration Service has not been doing its job.

14. This administration is not anti-German, as it has been alleged. Germany is a great country. It has contributed immensely to the world's artistic treasury. Goethe and Schiller made magnificent contributions to literature, and Bach, Beethoven, Wagner, and Brahms did the same in music.

15. Paul, it was great to see you at the party the other night. Everyone there was doing crack. Incidentally, how long have you been dealing that stuff?

★16. Duane Richards, CEO of the Western Fuels Association, an organization that supplies coal to electric utilities, says that there is no evidence that burning fossil fuels causes global warming. In view of Mr. Richards's wealth of expertise in the area of fossil fuels, we must conclude that what he says about global warming is true.

17. Senator Kennedy's arguments in favor of health care for the poor and aged should be ignored. Kennedy is a do-gooder who supports this kind of legislation only to get his name in the newspapers.

18. Professor Andrews, surely I deserve a B in logic. I know that I have gotten Fs on all the tests, but if you give me an F for my final grade, I will lose my scholarship. That will force me to drop out of school, and my poor, aged parents, who yearn to see me graduate, will be grief stricken for the rest of their lives.

★19. Molecules are in constant random motion. The Statue of Liberty is composed of molecules. Therefore, the Statue of Liberty is in constant random motion.

20. Either we have prayer in our public schools or the moral fabric of society will disintegrate. The choice should be obvious.

21. White sheep eat more than black sheep (because there are more of them). Therefore, this white sheep eats more than that black sheep.

★22. If someone rents a piece of land and plants crops on it, the landlord is never permitted to come and take those crops for himself when harvest time arrives. Similarly, if couples enlist the services of a surrogate mother to provide them with a baby, the mother should never be allowed to welch on the deal and keep the baby for herself once it is born.

23. Motives and desires exert forces on people, causing them to choose one thing over another. But force is a physical quantity, governed by the laws of physics. Therefore, human choices are governed by the laws of physics.

24. Each and every brick in the completely brick-faced Wainright Building has a reddish brown color. Therefore, the Wainright Building has a reddish brown color.

★25. Humanitarian groups have argued in favor of housing for the poor. Apparently what they want is another high-density project. Unfortunately, these projects have been tried in the past and have failed. In no time they turn into ghettos with astronomical rates of crime and delinquency. Chicago's Cabrini-Green is a prime example. Clearly, these humanitarian arguments are not what they seem.

26. Pauline said that after she had removed her new mink coat from the shipping carton she threw it into the trash. We conclude that Pauline has no appreciation for fine furs.

27. We know that induction will provide dependable results in the future because it has always worked in the past. Whatever has consistently worked in the past will continue to work in the future, and we know that this is true because it has been established by induction.

★28. What goes up must come down. The price of housing has been going up for years. Therefore, it will surely come down soon.

29. Mr. Prime Minister, I am certain you will want to release the members of our National Liberation Group whom you currently hold in prison. After all, I'm sure you will want to avoid having car bombs go off in the centers of your most heavily populated cities.

30. San Diego has the same latitude as Yuma, Arizona, and San Diego enjoys moderate temperatures through the summer months. Therefore, probably Yuma enjoys moderate temperatures through the summer months.

★31. We're all familiar with the complaint that over 40 million Americans are without health insurance. But America's doctors, nurses, and hospitals are among the best in the world. Thousands of people come from abroad every year to be treated here. Clearly there is nothing wrong with our health care system.

32. Real estate mogul Donald Trump argues that good management is essential to any business. But who is he to talk? Trump's own mismanagement drove Trump Hotels and Casino Resorts into bankruptcy twice in twelve years.

33. The farmers of our state have asked that we introduce legislation to provide subsidies for soybeans. Unfortunately, we will have to turn down their request. If we give subsidies to the soybean farmers, then the corn and wheat growers

will ask for the same thing. Then it will be the cotton growers, citrus growers, truck farmers, and cattle raisers. In the end, the cost will be astronomical.

★34. The travel brochure states that walking up O'Connell Street, the statue of Parnell comes into view. Apparently that statue has no trouble getting around.

35. Criminals are basically stupid, because anyone who isn't basically stupid wouldn't be a criminal.

36. Professor Glazebrooks's theory about the origin of the Martian craters is undoubtedly true. Rudolph Orkin, the great concert pianist, announced his support of the theory in this morning's newspaper.

★37. Mr. Franklin has lost at the craps table for the last ten throws of the dice. Therefore, it is extremely likely that he will win on the next throw.

38. Raising a child is like growing a tree. Sometimes violent things, such as cutting off branches, have to be done to force the tree to grow straight. Similarly, corporal punishment must sometimes be inflicted on children to force them to develop properly.

39. Good steaks are rare these days, so don't order yours well done.

★40. The Book of Mormon is true because it was written by Joseph Smith. Joseph Smith wrote the truth because he was divinely inspired. We know that Joseph Smith was divinely inspired because the Book of Mormon says that he was, and the Book of Mormon is true.

41. The students attending Bradford College come from every one of the fifty states. Michelle attends Bradford College. Therefore, Michelle comes from every one of the fifty states.

42. Rhubarb pie is a dessert. Therefore, whoever eats rhubarb pie eats a dessert.

★43. The vast majority of car accidents occur within twenty miles of one's home. Apparently it is much more dangerous to drive close to home than far away from home.

44. Either you're with us or you're with the terrorists. The choice should be easy.

45. Nobody has ever proved that weapons of mass destruction do not exist in Iraq. Therefore, those weapons must be in that country somewhere.

★46. On Friday I took Virginia out to dinner. She told me that if I wasn't interested in a serious relationship, I should forget about dating her. On Saturday I took Margie to a film. When we discussed it afterward over a drink, she couldn't understand why I wasn't interested in babies. Women are all alike. All they want is a secure marriage.

47. Dozens of species of plants and animals are being wiped out every year, even though we have laws to prevent it. Clearly, we should repeal the Endangered Species Act.

48. People are driving their cars like maniacs tonight. There must be a full moon.

★49. A line is composed of points. Points have no length. Therefore, a line has no length.

50. Are you in favor of the ruinous economic policy of the Democratic Platform Committee?

IV. Identify the arguments in the following dialogue, then discuss each of them in terms of the fallacies presented in this section and the previous section. You should be able to find at least one case of each fallacy.

"Thanks for giving me a lift home," Paul says to his friend Steve, as they head toward the freeway.

"No problem; it's on my way," says Steve.

"Uh oh," warns Paul suddenly, "watch out ahead. Looks like the police have pulled somebody over."

"Thanks," Steve says. "Hope they don't beat the guy up."

"Not a chance," says Paul. "Why would you say that?"

"You're an optimist," answers Steve. "Most cops are animals; they beat up on anybody they want to. You remember Rodney King, don't you? Those cops in L.A. put King in the hospital for no reason at all. That should prove I'm right."

"I think you're overreacting," Paul says. "Daryl Gates, the L.A. police chief at the time, said the King incident was an aberration. Since he was chief, I think we should take him at his word."

"But Gates was a lunatic who refused to acknowledge even our most basic rights," Steve persists. "Also, if you recall, he was forced to resign after the King incident. I know we don't live in L.A., but our police department is just as bad as theirs. So you can bet that our friend back there is just as abusive as any of them."

"Wait a minute," Paul argues. "As far as I know, nobody has ever proved that our police force is the slightest bit violent. You've no right to draw such a conclusion."

"Well, listen to this," Steve counters, as he changes lanes and turns onto the freeway. "About a week ago, I was with my friend Casey. When I left him, he was perfectly okay, but he was picked up for going through a stop sign on the way home. I saw him a couple of days later, and he had a big bruise under his right eye. The cop who stopped Casey must have hit him with his baton."

"Hold on. Did you ask Casey what happened?"

"No. I didn't have to," says Steve, a bit righteously. "I asked Casey's wife what happened between Casey and the cop, and she said he hit him. Those were her exact words, so that was good enough for me. I bet the cop's a maniac."

"Good grief," answers his friend. "How long will it take you to get over your warped view of things?"

"My way of looking at things isn't warped," Steve insists. "The problem is, you and I are both white. If you were black, you'd see things differently. Police brutality toward African Americans is way out of hand."

"Well," counters Paul, "a study done recently by an independent agency might interest you. According to that study, for every African American whom the police use force against, there's a white person they also use force against. That proves the police treat African Americans no worse than they do whites."

"I've never heard of that study, but it seems to me there must be something wrong with it," insists Steve.

"Well, the results of that study are borne out in my experience," says Paul. "I've been pulled over three or four times in the past couple of years, and the officers have always been extremely courteous. I can only conclude that the vast majority of these allegations of police brutality are the product of fertile imaginations."

"Again, your naïveté amazes me," Steve answers, dumbfounded. "First of all, you forget that you're white and you drive a new Mercedes. Don't you think that makes a difference? In fact, that's the trouble with all these arguments that down-play police brutality. They're all concocted by white people."

"Well, the fact remains that we have a major crime problem in this country," Paul argues. "Combating crime requires a few concessions, and you do want to combat crime, don't you?"

"Sure," Steve replies grudgingly, "but at what expense? Do innocent people have to get their heads bashed in?"

"Well, I think what it comes down to is this," says Paul. "Either you allow the police to use whatever force they find necessary, or the criminals will take over this country. Now you certainly don't want that to happen, do you?"

"No, but that's the crucial question," Steve says, exiting from the freeway. "When and how much force is necessary?"

"Well, you remember when the police apprehended that serial killer a few weeks ago? When the police made the arrest, the killer attacked them. So, the police can use force when attacked."

"I agree," responds Steve thoughtfully. "But what about the way the police treated those peaceful right-to-lifers who were demonstrating in front of the abortion clinic the other day? Many of them were elderly and posed no physical threat. But the cops used those contraptions—what do you call them, nimchucks, nomchucks, I don't know—to squeeze the old folks' wrists, causing great pain and injury, and they hit the old people on the head with their batons. Do you think that was necessary?"

"Of course it was," answers Paul, agitatedly. "Those people attacked the police—they hurled epithets at them."

"Honestly, I don't know how we've managed to stay friends all these years," Steve says with some frustration. "By the way, do you know what it says on the back of all police cars? It says 'To Protect and Serve.' Now if you hired a servant to take care of you, you'd get rid of him if he disobeyed you. Right?"

"Probably."

"Well, isn't it true," Steve asks, "that whenever a police officer disobeys one of us taxpayers, that officer should be fired?"

"That may be stretching it a bit," Paul laughs.

"But seriously," continues Steve, "I think what we need is some screening device to keep violent types from ever becoming cops."

"Well, you'll be happy to know that exactly such a device has been used for the past twenty-one years," Paul states. "Before entering the police academy, every applicant goes through a battery of psychological tests that positively eliminates all the macho types and the ones prone to violence. This ensures the individual officers are nonviolent, so we know the entire police force is nonviolent."

"Hmm. Maybe your so-called solution is really the problem," Steve suggests, as he pulls up in front of Paul's house. "We've had psychological testing for twenty-one years, and all that time, police violence has been on the rise. Perhaps we should get rid of the testing program."

"Well, I don't know about the logic of that," Paul muses, stepping out of the car. "But like you said, we've been friends for a long time, so I guess we can disagree. Thanks for the ride and the discussion. See you tomorrow!"

"Sure," Steve murmurs. "Tomorrow."

---

## 3.5    Fallacies in Ordinary Language

This section addresses two topics. The first concerns the challenge of detecting the fallacies of others in ordinary language, and the second relates to the goal of avoiding fallacies in one's own arguments.

### Detecting Fallacies

Most of the informal fallacies that we have seen thus far have been clear-cut, easily recognizable instances of a specific mistake. When fallacies occur in ordinary usage, however, they are often neither clear-cut nor easily recognizable. The reason is that there are innumerable ways of making mistakes in arguing, and variations inevitably occur that may not be exact instances of any specifically named fallacy. In addition, one fallacious mode of arguing may be mixed with one or more others, and the strands of reasoning may have to be disentangled before the fallacies can be named. Yet another problem arises from the fact that arguments in ordinary language are rarely presented in complete form. A premise or conclusion often is left unexpressed, which may obscure the nature of the evidence that is presented or the strength of the link between premises and conclusion.

Consider, for example, the following letter that appeared in a newspaper:

> God, I am sick of "women's rights"! Every time one turns on the news we hear about some form of discrimination against some poor female who wants to be a fireman—or some "remark" that suggests or implies women are inferior to men.
>
> I, for one, do not want to be rescued by a "woman fireman," especially if I am a 6-foot-2 male and she is a 5-foot-6 female.
>
> Why is it that women find their "role" so degrading? What is wrong with being a wife and mother, staying home while the male goes out and "hunts for food" and brings it home to his family?
>
> I don't think women have proven themselves to be as inventive, as capable (on the average) of world leadership, as physically capable, or as "courageous" as men. They have yet to fight a war (the average American woman) and let's face it ladies, who wants to?
>
> Whether a person is female, black, white, handicapped—whatever—*ability* is what counts in the final analysis. Women cannot demand "equality"—no one can—unless it is earned.
>
> When push comes to shove and a damsel is in distress, she is hard-pressed to protect herself and usually has to be rescued by a man. Until I can move a piano, beat off a potential robber or rapist, or fight a war, I am quite content to be a woman, thank you.
>
> (Patricia Kelley)

This letter presents numerous fallacies. The phrase "poor female who wants to be a fireman" suggests a mild *ad hominem* abusive, and equating women's rights in general with the right to be a firefighter suggests a straw man. The second paragraph commits another straw man fallacy by supposing that the job of firefighter inevitably entails such activities as climbing up ladders and rescuing people. Surely there are many male firefighters who cannot do this. The same paragraph also can be interpreted as begging the question: Do women who want to be firefighters want the specific job of rescuing tall men?

The third paragraph throws out a red herring. The issue is whether women have the right to be considered for a job of their choice and whether they must be paid as much as a man in the same situation. Whether there is something wrong with being a wife and mother is quite a different issue. Also, the reference to men hunting for food suggests a possible begging of the question: Are we still locked into a "hunter-gatherer" social structure?

The paragraph about whether women have proved themselves to be as inventive, capable, and courageous as men begs yet another question: Assuming, for the sake of argument, that this is true, have women been allowed to occupy roles in society where such inventiveness, capability, and courageousness can be demonstrated? Furthermore, this paragraph commits a red herring fallacy and/or misses the point: Even if women have not proved this, what does that have to do with the issue? Most jobs do not require any high degree of inventiveness or courage or a capacity for world leadership.

The paragraph about ability begs yet another question: Is it in fact the case that women have less ability? I am not aware that anything of the sort has ever been proved. Finally, the last paragraph throws out another red herring. What does moving pianos and beating off rapists have to do with most jobs or the question of equal pay for equal work?

Probably the single most important requirement for detecting fallacies in ordinary language is alertness. The reader or listener must pay close attention to what the arguer is saying. What is the conclusion? What are the reasons given in support of the conclusion? Are the reasons relevant to the conclusion? Do the reasons support the conclusion? If the reader or listener is half asleep or lounging in that passive, drugged-out state that attends much television viewing, then none of these questions will receive answers. Under those circumstances the reader or listener will never be able to detect informal fallacies, and he or she will accept even the worst reasoning without the slightest hesitation.

## Avoiding Fallacies

Why do people commit informal fallacies? Unfortunately, this question admits of no simple, straightforward answer. The reasons underlying the commission of fallacies are complex and interconnected. However, we can identify three factors that lead to most of the informal mistakes in reasoning. The first is intent. Many fallacies are committed intentionally. The arguer may know full well that his or her reasoning is defective but goes ahead with it anyway because of some benefit for himself or herself or some other person. All of the informal fallacies we have studied can be used for that purpose, but some of them are particularly well suited to it. These include the appeal to force, appeal to pity, appeal to the people, straw man, *ad hominem*, complex question, false dichotomy, and suppressed evidence. Here is such a case of appeal to force:

> I deserve a chocolate sundae for dessert, and if you don't buy me one right now, I'll start screaming and embarrass you in front of all of the people in this restaurant.

And here is a case of false dichotomy that conveys the appearance of being intentionally committed:

> Either you take me on a Caribbean cruise, or I'll have a nervous breakdown. It's up to you.

The key to avoiding fallacies that are intentionally committed probably lies in some form of moral education. The arguer must come to realize that using intellectually dishonest means to acquire something he or she does not deserve is just another form of cheating.

The situation becomes more complicated, however, when the sought-after goal is morally justified. Arguers sometimes use fallacious reasoning intentionally to trick a person into doing something that is really for that person's own good. Here is a false dichotomy of that sort:

> Either you control your eating and get regular exercise, or you'll have a heart attack and die. The choice is yours.

Given the beneficial consequences of controlled eating and regular exercise, some moral philosophers will find nothing wrong with this argument. Others will contend that manipulating someone into doing something violates human dignity. In either case, such arguments are logically unacceptable.

The second factor that leads to the commission of informal fallacies is a careless mental posture combined with an emotional disposition favoring or opposing some person or thing. The careless mental posture opens the door, so to speak, to fallacious reasoning, and the emotional disposition pushes the arguer through it. Even people who are thoroughly versed in the informal fallacies occasionally succumb to the deadly combination of mental carelessness and emotional impetus. For example, arguments such as the following *ad hominem* abusive can sometimes be heard in the halls of university philosophy departments:

> Professor Ballard's argument in favor of restructuring our course offering isn't worth a hoot. But what would you expect from someone who publishes in such mediocre journals? And did you hear Ballard's recent lecture on Aristotle? It was total nonsense.

When people who should know better are confronted with the fact that their argument commits a common fallacy, they often admit with embarrassment that they have not been thinking and then revise their argument according to logical principles. In contrast, people who are not familiar with the distinction between good and fallacious reasoning will likely deny that there is anything wrong with their argument. Thus, the key to avoiding fallacies that arise from mental carelessness lies in developing a thorough familiarity with the informal fallacies, combined with a habitual realization of how emotions affect people's reasoning. Everyone should realize that unchecked emotions are an open invitation to illogical reasoning, and they can lead a person to commit quite blindly every one of the fallacies we have studied thus far.

The third factor that leads to the commission of informal fallacies is far more difficult to contend with than the first two. It consists in the influence of what we might call the "worldview" of the arguer. By worldview we mean a cognitive network of beliefs, attitudes, habits, memories, values, and other elements that conditions and renders meaningful the world in which we live. Beginning in infancy, our worldview emerges quietly and unconsciously from enveloping influences—culture, language, gender, religion, politics, and social and economic status. As we grow older, it continues to develop through the shaping forces of education and experience. Once it has taken root, our worldview determines how each of us sizes up the world in which we live. Given a set of circumstances, it indicates what is reasonable to believe and what is unreasonable.

In connection with the construction and evaluation of arguments, an arguer's worldview determines the answer to questions about importance, relevance, causal connections, the qualifications of authorities, whether a sample is typical or atypical of a group, what can and cannot be taken for granted, and other factors. However, because these determinations inevitably involve unexamined presuppositions, the arguer's worldview can lead to the commission of informal fallacies. All of the fallacies we have studied so far are likely candidates, but the ones especially susceptible are appeal to pity, straw man, missing the point, appeal to unqualified authority, hasty generalization, false cause, slippery slope, weak analogy, begging the question, false dichotomy, and suppressed evidence.

Thus, a person with a victim mentality may think that his pathetic circumstances really justify some favorable treatment; an uncritical conservative may cite with complete confidence the authority of Rush Limbaugh; a person with a racist worldview may conclude that the errant behavior of a handful of Asians, African Americans, or Hispanics really is typical of the larger class; a person with a liberal worldview may quite innocently distort an opponent's argument by equating it with fascism; a pro-life arguer may consider it obvious that the fetus is a person with rights, while a pro-choice arguer may take it for granted that the fetus is not a person with rights, and so on. Consider, for example, the following argument from analogy:

> A court trial is like a professional football game. In a professional football game, the most important thing is winning. Similarly, in a trial, the most important thing is winning.

This argument is consistent with the worldview of many, if not most, lawyers. Lawyers are trained as advocates, and when they enter a courtroom they see themselves going into battle for their clients. In any battle, winning is the most important objective. But this viewpoint presupposes that truth and justice are either unattainable in the courtroom or of secondary importance. Thus, while many lawyers would evaluate this argument as nonfallacious, many nonlawyers would reject it as a weak analogy.

For another example, consider the following causal inference:

> After enslaving most of Eastern Europe for nearly fifty years, the evil Soviet empire finally collapsed. Obviously God listened to our prayers.

This argument reflects the worldview of many theists. It presupposes that there is a God, that God listens to prayers, that God is affected by prayers, that God has the power to influence the course of history, and that God does influence the course of history. While the theist is likely to consider this argument a good one, the atheist will reject it as a blatant case of false cause.

To avoid fallacies that arise from the influence of worldviews, the arguer must acknowledge and critique his or her presuppositions. Doing so inclines the arguer to couch his or her arguments in language that takes those presuppositions into account. The result is nearly always an argument that is more intelligently crafted, and, it is hoped, more persuasive. However, the task of recognizing and critiquing one's presuppositions is not easy. Presuppositions are intrinsically linked to one's worldview, and many people are not even aware that they have a worldview. The reason is that worldviews are formed through a process that is largely unconscious. Thus, the arguer must first recognize that he or she has a worldview and must then exercise constant vigilance over the presuppositions it comprises.

Even after one's presuppositions have been exposed and thoroughly critiqued, however, there is no guarantee that one's arguments will agree with the arguments of others who have critiqued their worldviews. This is because a person's worldview reflects the unique perspective that person has on the world. No two people share exactly the same perspective. Nevertheless, disclosing and critiquing the presuppositions in one's worldview lays a foundation for meaningful communication with other reasonable arguers, and it provides a context of reasonableness for working out disagreements.

In summary, the three factors that are probably responsible for most informal fallacies are intent, mental carelessness combined with emotional dispositions, and unexamined presuppositions in the arguer's worldview. However, these factors rarely occur in isolation. In the vast majority of cases, two or all three conspire to produce fallacious reasoning. This fact exacerbates the difficulty in avoiding informal fallacies in one's own arguments and in detecting fallacies in the arguments of others.

Now let us consider some cases of real-life arguments in light of the factors we have just discussed. All are taken from letters to the editors of newspapers and magazines. The first relates to affirmative action programs:

> I'm a nonracist, nonsexist, white male born in 1969, who has never owned a slave, treated anyone as inferior because of his or her race, or sexually harassed a female co-worker. In other words, I don't owe women or minorities a thing. Since when are people required to pay for the sins of their predecessors simply because they belong to the same race or gender?
>
> (Ben Gibbons)

The author of this argument presupposes that racist and sexist patterns in society have not benefited him in any way. Among other things, he presupposes that his white ancestors in no way benefited from their being white and that none of these benefits passed down to him. On the other hand, given that he has received such benefits, he may presuppose that he is not obligated to pay any of them back. Of course, none of these things may have occurred, but the author should at least address these issues. Because he does not address them, the argument begs the question.

The next argument relates to second-hand smoke from cigarettes:

> Now, besides lung cancer and other nasty business, second-hand smoke causes deafness and impotence. Was second-hand smoke a problem when people heated their homes solely by fireplaces? How about those romantic teepees with the smoke hole at the top? And what about fireplaces in new homes? Let's have some research

about the problems caused by these as well as barbecues. A little cancer with your
hot dog, anyone?

(Pat Sharp)

This argument seems to commit the fallacy of equivocation. The arguer begins by
using "second-hand smoke" to refer to the smoke from burning tobacco, and then
uses the term to refer to the smoke from fireplaces, teepee fires, and barbecues. Smoke
from burning tobacco is clearly not the same thing as smoke from burning wood or
charcoal. Alternately, the argument might be seen to beg the question: "But do people
burn tobacco in their fireplaces and barbecues?" These fallacies probably arise either
from the intentions of the author or from carelessness in failing to distinguish the two
kinds of second-hand smoke. In either event, the author is probably hostile to government efforts to control second-hand tobacco smoke in confined areas.

The next argument deals with gun control:

> Detroit, the seventh largest city and one with strict gun laws, had 596 homicides last
> year. In the same year Phoenix, the ninth largest city and one that at the time did
> not require gun owners to be licensed, had 136 homicides. Criminals don't fear the
> toothless criminal-justice system, but they do fear armed citizens.

(Paul M. Berardi)

This argument commits a false cause fallacy. The author presupposes that the availability of guns caused Phoenix to have a lower homicide rate than Detroit. The arguer
also presupposes that Detroit and Phoenix are comparable as to homicide rate merely
because they are roughly the same size. As a result, the argument involves a weak analogy and also begs the question. The additional factors of emotion and intent may also
be present. The arguer probably hates the prospect of gun control, and he may be fully
aware of the fact that Phoenix and Detroit are not comparable for his purpose, but he
went ahead with the comparison anyway.

The next argument deals with religious fundamentalism:

> If we compromise God's word, we compromise the truth. To say that the fundamen-
> talist is a loud shrill voice drowning out religious moderation implies that diluted
> truth is better than absolute truth.

(Gerald Gleason)

This argument begs the question. The arguer presupposes that there is a God, that
God has spoken, that God has revealed his intentions to fundamentalist preachers,
and that those preachers accurately report the word of God. The argument also seems
to reflect an emotional disposition in favor of religious fundamentalism.

The last argument we will consider relates to English as the official U.S. language:

> This great country has been held together for more than 200 years because of one
> simple thing: the English language.
>    There are two things we must do: Make English the official language of the
> United States and do away with bilingual education.

(David Moisan)

This argument misses the point. The arguer presupposes that making English the official
language would guarantee that all citizens speak it and that doing away with bilingual

education would accelerate the learning process of immigrant children. The argument may also reflect the fear that many feel in connection with the changes U.S. society is experiencing as a result of recent immigration.

## EXERCISE 3.5

I. Most of the following selections were taken from letters to the editors of newspapers and magazines. Identify any fallacies that may be committed, giving a brief explanation for your answer. Then, if a fallacy is identified, discuss the possible factors that led the arguer to commit the fallacy.

★1. Exporting cigarettes [to Asia] is good business for America; there is no reason we should be prohibited from doing so. Asians have been smoking for decades; we are only offering variety in their habit. If the Asians made tobacco smoking illegal, that would be a different situation. But as long as it is legal, the decision is up to the smokers. The Asians are just afraid of American supremacy in the tobacco industries.

(Pat Monohan)

2. When will these upper-crust intellectuals realize that the masses of working people are not in cozy, cushy, interesting, challenging, well-paying jobs, professions and businesses? My husband is now 51; for most of the last 33 years he has worked in the same factory job, and only the thought of retiring at 62 has sustained him. When he reaches that age in 11 years, who will tell him that his aging and physically wracked body must keep going another two years? My heart cries out for all the poor souls who man the assembly lines, ride the trucks or work in the fields or mines, or in the poorly ventilated, hot-in-summer, cold-in-winter factories and garages. Many cannot afford to retire at 62, 65, or even later. Never, never let them extend the retirement age. It's a matter of survival to so many.

(Isabel Fierman)

3. Women in military combat is insane. No society in its right mind would have such a policy. The military needs only young people and that means the only women who go are those in their child-bearing years. Kill them off and society will not be able to perpetuate itself.

(Jack Carman)

★4. Dear Ann: I've read that one aspirin taken every other day will reduce the risk of heart attack. Why not take two and double the protection?

(Boston)

5. The American Civil Liberties Union did a study that found that in the last 80 years it believes twenty-five innocent people have been executed in the United States. This is unfortunate. But, there are innocent people who die each year in highway accidents. Out of 40,000 deaths, how many deaths are related to driving while intoxicated? How many more thousands are injured and incur financial ruin or are invalids and handicapped for the remainder of their lives?

(Mahlon R. Braden)

6. Mexico's president expresses legitimate concern when he questions supplying oil to Americans who are unwilling to apply "discipline" in oil consumption. In view of the fact that his country's population is expected to double in only twenty-two years, isn't it legitimate for us to ask when Mexicans will apply the discipline necessary to control population growth and quit dumping their excess millions over our borders?

(Wayne R. Bartz)

★7. A parent would never give a ten-year-old the car keys, fix him or her a martini, or let him or her wander at night through a dangerous part of town. The same holds true of the Internet. Watch what children access, but leave the Net alone. Regulation is no substitute for responsibility.

(Bobby Dunning)

8. How would you feel to see your children starving and have all doors slammed in your face? Isn't it time that all of us who believe in freedom and human rights stop thinking in terms of color and national boundaries? We should open our arms and hearts to those less fortunate and remember that a time could come when we might be in a similar situation.

(Lorna Doyle)

9. A capital gains tax [reduction] benefits everyone, not just the "rich," because everyone will have more money to invest or spend in the private economy, resulting in more jobs and increasing prosperity for all. This is certainly better than paying high taxes to a corrupt, self-serving and incompetent government that squanders our earnings on wasteful and useless programs.

(David Miller)

★10. After reading "Homosexuals in the Churches," I'd like to point out that I don't know any serious, capable exegetes who stumble over Saint Paul's denunciation of homosexuality. Only a fool (and there seem to be more and more these days) can fail to understand the plain words of Romans, Chapter one. God did not make anyone "gay." Paul tells us in Romans 1 that homosexuals become that way because of their own lusts.

(LeRoy J. Hopper)

11. When will they ever learn—that the Republican Party is not for the people who voted for it?

(Alton L. Stafford)

12. Before I came to the United States in July, 1922, I was in Berlin where I visited the famous zoo. In one of the large cages were a lion and a tiger. Both respected each other's strength. It occurred to me that it was a good illustration of "balance of power." Each beast followed the other and watched each other's moves. When one moved, the other did. When one stopped, the other stopped.

In today's world, big powers or groups of powers are trying to maintain the status quo, trying to be as strong as or stronger than the other. They realize a conflict may result in mutual destruction. As long as the countries believe there is a balance of power we may hope for peace.

(Emilie Lackow)

★13. Doctors say the birth of a baby is a high point of being a doctor. Yet a medical survey shows one out of every nine obstetricians in America has stopped delivering babies.

Expectant mothers have had to find new doctors. In some rural areas, women have had to travel elsewhere to give birth.

How did this happen? It's part of the price of the lawsuit crisis.

The number of lawsuits Americans file each year is on the rise. Obstetricians are among the hardest hit—almost three out of four have faced a malpractice claim. Many have decided it isn't worth the risk.

(Magazine ad by the Insurance Information Institute)

14. The conservative diatribe found in campus journalism comes from the mouths of a handful of affluent brats who were spoon-fed through the '80s. Put them on an ethnically more diverse campus, rather than a Princeton or a Dartmouth, and then let us see how long their newspapers survive.

(David Simons)

15. I see that our courts are being asked to rule on the propriety of outlawing video games as a "waste of time and money."

It seems that we may be onto something here. A favorable ruling would open the door to new laws eliminating show business, spectator sports, cocktail lounges, the state of Nevada, public education and, of course, the entire federal bureaucracy.

(A. G. Dobrin)

★16. The death penalty is the punishment for murder. Just as we have long jail terms for armed robbery, assault and battery, fraud, contempt of court, fines for speeding, reckless driving and other numerous traffic violations, so must we have a punishment for murder. Yes, the death penalty will not deter murders any more than a speeding ticket will deter violating speed laws again, but it is the punishment for such violation!

(Lawrence J. Barstow)

17. Would you rather invest in our nation's children or Pentagon waste? The choice is yours.

(Political ad)

18. My gun has protected me, and my son's gun taught him safety and responsibility long before he got hold of a far more lethal weapon—the family car. Cigarettes kill many times more people yearly than guns and, unlike guns, have absolutely no redeeming qualities. If John Lennon had died a long, painful and expensive death from lung cancer, would you have devoted a page to a harangue against the product of some of your biggest advertisers—the cigarette companies?

(Silvia A. DeFreitas)

★19. If the advocates of prayers in public schools win on this issue, just where will it end? Perhaps next they will ask for prayers on public transportation? Prayers by government workers before they start their job each day? Or maybe, mandatory prayers in public restaurants before starting each meal might be a good idea.

(Leonard Mendelson)

20. So you want to ban smoking in all eating establishments? Well, you go right ahead and do that little thing. And when the 40 percent of smokers stop eating out, the restaurants can do one of two things: close, or raise the price of a $20 dinner 40 percent to $28.

(Karen Sawyer)

21. Pigeons are forced to leave our city to battle for life. Their struggle is an endless search for food. What manner of person would watch these hungry creatures suffer from want of food and deny them their survival? These helpless birds are too often ignored by the people of our city, with not the least bit of compassion shown to them. Pigeons are God's creatures just as the so-called human race is. They need help.

(Leslie Ann Price)

★22. You take half of the American population every night and set them down in front of a box watching people getting stabbed, shot and blown away. And then you expect them to go out into the streets hugging each other?

(Mark Hustad)

23. So you think that putting the worst type of criminal out of his misery is wrong. How about the Americans who were sent to Korea, to Vietnam, to Beirut, to Central America? Thousands of good men were sacrificed supposedly for the good of our country. At the same time we were saving and protecting Charles Manson, Sirhan Sirhan [Robert Kennedy's murderer], and a whole raft of others too numerous to mention.

(George M. Purvis)

24. The fact is that the hype over "acid rain" and "global warming" is just that: hype. Take, for example, Stephen Schneider, author of *Global Warming*. In his current "study" he discusses a "greenhouse effect of catastrophic proportions," yet twenty years ago Schneider was a vocal proponent of the theory of a "new ice age."

(Urs Furrer)

★25. Just as our parents did for us, my husband and I rely solely on Christian Science for all the health needs of our four sons and find it invaluable for the quick cure of whatever ailments and contagions they are subject to. One particular healing that comes to mind happened several years ago when our youngest was a toddler. He had a flu-type illness that suddenly became quite serious. We called a Christian Science practitioner for treatment and he was completely well the next morning.

(Ellen Austin)

26. As somebody who has experienced the tragedy of miscarriage—or spontaneous abortion—at eight weeks, I greatly resent the position that a fetus is not

a baby. I went through the grief of losing a baby, and no one should tell me otherwise.

(Ann Fons)

27. How can we pledge allegiance to the flag of the United States of America and not establish laws to punish people who burn the flag to make a statement? We are a people who punish an individual who libels another person but will not seek redress from an individual who insults every citizen of this great country by desecrating the flag.

(William D. Lankford)

★28. The notion of "buying American" is as misguided as the notion of buying Wisconsin, or Oshkosh, Wisconsin, or South Oshkosh, Wisconsin. For the same reasons that Wisconsin increases its standard of living by trading with the rest of the nation, America increases its standard of living by trading with the rest of the world.

(Phillip Smith)

29. We've often heard the saying, "Far better to let 100 guilty men go free than to condemn one innocent man." What happens then if we apply the logic of this argument to the question, "Is a fetus an unborn human being?" Then is it not better to let 100 fetuses be born rather than to mistakenly kill one unborn human being? This line of reasoning is a strictly humanist argument against abortion.

(James Sebastian)

30. In our society it is generally considered improper for a man to sleep, shower, and dress amid a group of women to whom he normally would be sexually attracted. It seems to me, then, to be equally unacceptable that a gay man sleep, shower, and dress in a company of men to whom, we assume, he would be no less sexually attracted.

(Mark O. Temple)

★31. I say "bravo" and "right on!" Now we have some real-life humane heroes to look up to! These brave people [a group of animal liberators] went up against the insensitive bureaucratic technology, and won, saving former pet animals from senseless torture.

   If researchers want to experiment, let them use computers, or themselves—but not former pet animals! I know it's bad enough they use monkeys and rats, but if those animals are bred knowing nothing else but these Frankensteins abusing them it's different (but not better) than dogs or cats that have been loved and petted all their lives to suddenly be tortured and mutilated in the name of science. End all animal research! Free all research animals!

   Right on, animal liberators!

(Linda Magee)

32. Dear Ann: Recently I was shopping downtown in 20-below-zero weather. A stranger walked up to me and said, "I wonder how many beautiful rabbits died so you could have that coat?" I noticed she was wearing a down coat, so I asked

if the geese they got the down from to make her coat were still alive. She looked surprised. Obviously she had never given it a thought.

If people are so upset about cruelty to animals, why don't they go after the folks who refuse to spend the money to have their pets neutered and spayed? Thousands of dogs are put to death every year because the animal pounds can't feed and house them. Talk about cruelty to animals—that's the best example there is.

("Baby It's Cold Outside")

33. I prayed for the U.S. Senate to defeat the prayer amendment—and it did. There is a God.

(Richard Carr)

★34. People of the Philippines, I have returned! The hour of your redemption is here! Rally to me! Let the indomitable spirit of Bataan and Corregidor lead on! As the lines of battle roll forward to bring you within the zone of operations, rise and strike! For future generations of your sons and daughters, strike! Let no heart be faint! Let every arm be steeled! The guidance of divine God points the way! Follow in his name to the Holy Grail of righteous victory!

(General Douglas MacArthur)

35. As the oldest of eleven children (all married), I'd like to point out our combined family numbers more than 100 who vote only for pro-life candidates. Pro-lifers have children, pro-choicers do not.

(Mrs. Kitty Reickenback)

36. I am 12 years old. My class had a discussion on whether police used unnecessary force when arresting the people from Operation Rescue.

My teacher is an ex-cop, and he demonstrated police holds to us. They don't hurt at all unless the person is struggling or trying to pull away. If anybody was hurt when they were arrested, then they must have been struggling with the officers trying to arrest them.

(Ben Torre-Bueno)

★37. As corporate farms continue to gobble up smaller family farms, they control a larger percentage of the grain and produce raised in the United States. Some have already reached a point in size where, if they should decide to withhold their grain and produce from the marketplace, spot shortages could occur and higher prices would result. The choice is to pay us family farmers now or pay the corporations later.

(Delwin Yost)

38. If you buy our airline ticket now you can save 60 percent, and that means 60 percent more vacation for you.

(Radio ad)

39. Why all the flap about atomic bombs? The potential for death is always with us. Of course, if you just want something to worry about, go ahead. Franklin D. Roosevelt said it: "The only thing we have to fear is fear itself."

(Lee Flemming Reese)

★**40.** September 17 marked the anniversary of the signing of the U.S. Constitution. How well have we, the people, protected our rights? Consider what has happened to our private-property rights.

"Property has divine rights, and the moment the idea is admitted into society that property is not as sacred as the laws of God, anarchy and tyranny begin." John Quincy Adams, 1767–1848, Sixth President of the United States.

Taxes and regulations are the two-edged sword which gravely threatens the fabric of our capitalistic republic. The tyranny of which Adams speaks is with us today in the form of government regulators and regulations which have all but destroyed the right to own property. Can anarchy be far behind?

(Timothy R. Binder)

**41.** Evolution would have been dealt serious setbacks if environmentalists had been around over the eons trying to save endangered species.

Species are endangered because they just do not fit the bigger picture any more as the world changes. That's not bad. It's just life.

In most cases we have seen the "endangered species" argument is just a ruse; much deeper motives usually exist, and they are almost always selfish and personal.

(Tom Gable)

**42.** The problem that I have with the pro-choice supporters' argument is that they make "choice" the ultimate issue. Let's face facts. No one has absolute freedom of choice sanctioned by the law. One can choose to rob a bank, but it's not lawful. Others can choose to kill their one-year-old child, but it is not legal. Why then should a woman have the legal right to take the life of her unborn child?

(Loretta S. Horn)

★**43.** If a car or truck kills a person, do politicians call for car control or truck control? And call in all cars/trucks?

If a child burns down a house do we have match control or child control and call in all of each?

Gun control and confiscation is equally as pathetic a thought process in an age of supposed intelligence.

(Pete Hawes)

**44.** I was incensed to read in your article about the return of anti-Semitism that New York City Moral Majority Leader Rev. Dan C. Fore actually said that "Jews have a God-given ability to make money, almost a supernatural ability . . ." I find it incredibly ironic that he and other Moral Majority types conveniently overlook the fact that they, too, pack away a pretty tidy sum themselves through their fund-raising efforts. It is sad that anti-Semitism exists, but to have this prejudice voiced by leaders of religious organizations is deplorable. These people are in for quite a surprise come Judgment Day.

(John R. Murks)

**45.** Are Americans so stupid they don't realize that every time they pay thousands of dollars for one of those new "economical" Japanese cars, they are simultaneously making the U.S. bankrupt and giving the Japanese enough money to buy all of America?

(Sylvia Petersen Young)

★46. Why are people so shocked that Susan Smith apparently chose to kill her children because they had become an inconvenience? Doesn't this occur every day in abortion clinics across the country? We suspect Smith heard very clearly the message many feminists have been trying to deliver about the expendable nature of our children.

(Kevin and Diana Cogan)

47. What's wrong with kids today? Answer: nothing, for the majority of them. They are great.

Witness the action of two San Diego teenage boys recently, when the Normal Heights fire was at its worst. They took a garden hose to the roof of a threatened house—a house belonging to four elderly sisters, people they didn't even know. They saved the house, while neighboring houses burned to the ground.

In the Baldwin Hills fire, two teenage girls rescued a blind, retired Navy man from sure death when they braved the flames to find him, confused, outside his burning house. He would probably have perished if they hadn't run a distance to rescue him.

(Theodore H. Wickham)

48. Now that Big Brother has decided that I must wear a seatbelt when I ride in a car, how long will it take before I have to wear an inner tube when I swim in my pool, a safety harness when I climb a ladder, and shoes with steel-reinforced toecaps when I carry out the garbage?

(G. R. Turgeon)

★49. Dear Ann: I was disappointed in your response to the girl whose mother used the strap on her. The gym teacher noticed the bruises on her legs and backside and called it "child abuse." Why are you against strapping a child when the Bible tells us in plain language that this is what parents should do?

The Book of Proverbs mentions many times that the rod must be used. Proverbs 23:13 says: "Withhold not correction from the child for if thou beatest him with the rod he shall not die." Proverbs 23:14 says: "Thou shalt beat him with the rod and shalt deliver his soul from death."

There is no substitute for a good whipping. I have seen the results of trying to reason with kids. They are arrogant, disrespectful and mouthy. Parents may wish for a more "humane" way, but there is none. Beating children is God's way of getting parents to gain control over their children.

(Davisville, W.Va.)

50. The Fourth Amendment guarantees our right to freedom from unreasonable search and seizure. It does not prohibit *reasonable* search and seizure. The matter of sobriety roadblocks to stop drunk drivers boils down to this: Are such roadblocks reasonable or unreasonable? The majority of people answer:

"Reasonable." Therefore, sobriety roadblocks should not be considered to be unconstitutional.

(Haskell Collier)

51. The Supreme Court recently ruled that a police department in Florida did not violate any rights of privacy when a police helicopter flew over the back yard of a suspected drug dealer and noticed marijuana growing on his property. Many people, including groups like the Anti-Common Logic Union, felt that the suspect's right to privacy outweighed the police department's need to protect the public at large.

The simple idea of sacrificing a right to serve a greater good should be allowed in certain cases. In this particular case the danger to the public wasn't extremely large; marijuana is probably less dangerous than regular beer. But anything could have been in that back yard—a load of cocaine, an illegal stockpile of weapons, or other major threats to society.

(Matt Cookson)

★52. I am 79 and have been smoking for 60 years. My husband is 90 and has inhaled my smoke for some 50 years with no bad effects.

I see no reason to take further steps to isolate smokers in our restaurants and public places, other than we now observe.

Smokers have taken punishment enough from neurotic sniffers, some of whom belong in bubbles. There are plenty of injudicious fumes on our streets and freeways.

(Helen Gans)

53. The mainstream press finds itself left behind by talk radio, so they try to minimize its importance. Americans are finding the true spirit of democracy in community and national debate. Why should we be told what to believe by a news weekly or the nightly news when we can follow public debate as it unfolds on talk radio?

(Adam Abbott)

54. The issue is not whether we should subsidize the arts, but whether anyone should be able to force someone else to subsidize the arts. You and I are free to *give* any amount of our money to any artistic endeavor we wish to support. When the government gets involved, however, a group of bureaucrats is given the power to *take* our money and give it to the arts they wish to support. We are not consulted. That is not a way to promote a responsible culture. That is tyranny.

(Jerry Harben)

★55. Who are these Supreme Court justices who have the guts to OK the burning of our flag?

If the wife or daughter of these so-called justices were raped, could the rapist be exonerated because he took the First Amendment? That he was just expressing himself? How about murder in the same situation?

(Robert A. Lewis)

56. I have one question for those bleeding hearts who say we should not have used the atomic bomb: If the nation responsible for the Rape of Nanking, the Manchurian atrocities, Pearl Harbor and the Bataan Death March had invented the bomb first, don't you think they would have used it? So do I.

(Bill Blair)

57. Since when did military service become a right, for gays or anyone else? The military has always been allowed to discriminate against people who don't meet its requirements, including those who are overweight or too tall or too short. There is an adequate supply of personnel with the characteristics they need. And there is no national need for gays in the military.

(William R. Cnossen)

★58. There is something very wrong about the custom of tipping. When we go to a store, we don't decide what a product is worth and pay what we please; we pay the price or we leave. Prices in coffee bars and restaurants should be raised, waiters should be paid a decent wage, and the words "no tipping" should be clearly visible on menus and at counters.

(George Jochnowitz)

59. Most Americans do not favor gun control. They know that their well-being depends on their own ability to protect themselves. So-called "assault rifles" are used in few crimes. They are not the weapon of choice of criminals, but they are for people trying to protect themselves from government troops.

(Larry Herron)

60. Holding a gun, a thief robs John Q. Public of thousands of dollars. Holding a baby, an unmarried mother robs taxpayers of thousands of dollars. If one behavior is considered a crime, then so should the other.

(Louis R. Ward)

II. Turn to the editorial pages of a newspaper or the letters column of a magazine and find an instance of a fallacious argument in the editorials or letters to the editor. Identify the premises and conclusion of the argument and write an analysis at least one paragraph in length identifying the fallacy or fallacies committed and the factors that may have led the arguer to commit them.

## Summary

A fallacy is a mistake in an argument that arises from something other than merely false premises. Usually fallacies involve defects in reasoning or the creation of an illusion that makes a bad argument appear good. Fallacies can be either formal or informal. A formal fallacy is one that can be detected by analyzing the form of an argument; such fallacies affect only deductive arguments. An informal fallacy is one that can be identified only by analyzing the content of an argument; such fallacies can affect both deductive and inductive arguments.

The fallacies of relevance occur when the premises of an argument are not relevant to the conclusion. Cases of such irrelevance occur in premises that threaten the observer, elicit pity from the observer, create a mob mentality in a group of observers, appeal to the observer's desire for security, verbally abuse an opposing arguer, present an opposing arguer as predisposed to argue as he does, present an opposing arguer as a hypocrite, misapply a general rule, distort an opponent's argument, or lead the observer off the track. A kind of catchall fallacy, missing the point, occurs when an arguer draws a conclusion different from the one implied by the premises.

The fallacies of weak induction occur when the premises, although possibly relevant to the conclusion, provide insufficient support for the conclusion. Cases of such inadequate support occur when the arguer cites an authority who is not qualified, draws a conclusion from premises that give no positive evidence, draws a conclusion from an atypical sample, depends on a nonexistent or minor causal connection, depends on a chain reaction that is unlikely to occur, or draws a conclusion from an analogy that is not close enough to support it.

The fallacies of presumption occur when the premises presume what they purport to prove. Such presumptions occur when the arguer creates the illusion that inadequate premises are adequate, asks a question that comprises two or more questions, uses a disjunctive statement that falsely claims to exhaust the available alternatives, or ignores important evidence that requires a different conclusion.

The fallacies of ambiguity occur when the conclusion depends on some form of linguistic ambiguity. Either a word or phrase is used in more than one sense or the wrong interpretation is given to an ambiguous statement.

The fallacies of grammatical analogy occur when a defective argument appears good owing to a grammatical similarity to some argument that is not fallacious. Such grammatical similarities occur in arguments that wrongly transfer an attribute from parts to a whole or from a whole to its parts.

Fallacies that occur in real-life argumentation are harder to detect than those in manufactured examples because they may not exactly fit the structure of the named fallacies and because several fallacies can be woven together in a single passage. Three factors that underlie the commission of fallacies in real-life argumentation are the intent of the arguer, mental carelessness combined with unchecked emotions, and unexamined presuppositions in the arguer's worldview.

# Answers to Selected Exercises

## Exercise 3.1
1. Formal fallacy.
4. Informal fallacy.

7. Informal fallacy.
10. Formal fallacy.

## Exercise 3.2
I.
1. Appeal to pity.
4. Accident.
7. Appeal to force.
10. *Tu quoque* (you, too).
13. Red herring.

16. *Ad hominem* circumstantial.
19. Straw man.
22. Appeal to the people, indirect variety.
25. Missing the point.

## Exercise 3.3
I.
1. Hasty generalization (converse accident).
4. Slippery slope.
III.
1. Hasty generalization.
4. *Ad hominem* circumstantial.
7. False cause (gambler's fallacy).
10. Straw man.
13. Red herring.

7. Appeal to ignorance.
10. Appeal to unqualified authority.
13. Weak analogy.

16. Missing the point.
19. Weak analogy.
22. No fallacy.
25. Appeal to ignorance.
28. False cause.

## Exercise 3.4
I.
1. False dichotomy.
4. Amphiboly.
7. Begging the question.
10. Equivocation.
13. Composition.

16. Suppressed evidence.
19. Division.
22. Complex question.
25. Begging the question.

**III.**

1. *Ad hominem* circumstantial.
4. Equivocation.
7. Begging the question.
10. Division.
13. False cause (oversimplified cause).
16. Appeal to unqualified authority.
19. Composition.
22. Weak analogy.
25. Straw man.

28. Accident.
31. Red herring.
34. Amphiboly.
37. False cause (gambler's fallacy).
40. Begging the question.
43. Missing the point or suppressed evidence.
46. Hasty generalization.
49. Composition.

### Exercise 3.5

**I.**

1. Missing the point or begging the question.
4. Composition.
7. No fallacy? Weak analogy?
10. Appeal to unqualified authority. The statement "Only a fool . . ." involves an *ad hominem* abusive.
13. False cause, suppressed evidence, begging the question. There is little or no evidence of any causal connection between malpractice suits and the decision of some obstetricians to leave the field. An unmentioned factor is the inconvenience of being on call twenty-four hours per day waiting for patients to deliver. There is also little or no evidence of any genuine "lawsuit crisis."
16. Begging the question?                    19. Slippery slope.
    (Strange argument!)
22. False cause? No fallacy?                  25. False cause.
28. Suppressed evidence? Begging the question? No fallacy? The Commerce Clause of the U.S. Constitution and pertinent federal legislation prohibit unfair trade practices between states. No equivalent regulations exist for international trade.
31. Appeal to the people (direct variety). Also appeal to pity?
34. Appeal to the people (direct variety)?
37. False dichotomy? No fallacy?
40. Appeal to unqualified authority, slippery slope.
43. Several cases of weak analogy. Also, a possible case of *ad hominem* abusive.
46. Begging the question; straw man.
49. Appeal to unqualified authority. The last paragraph suggests a hasty generalization.
52. Hasty generalization. *Ad hominem* abusive? Also, begging the question or red herring?
55. Weak analogy.
58. Weak analogy? No fallacy?

# index